Sexual Sports Rhetoric

PETER LANG
New York • Washington, D.C./Baltimore • Bern
Frankfurt am Main • Berlin • Brussels • Vienna • Oxford

Sexual Sports Rhetoric

Historical and Media Contexts of Violence

EDITED BY
Linda K. Fuller

PETER LANG
New York • Washington, D.C./Baltimore • Bern
Frankfurt am Main • Berlin • Brussels • Vienna • Oxford

Library of Congress Cataloging-in-Publication Data

Sexual sports rhetoric: historical and media contexts of violence /
edited by Linda K. Fuller.
p. cm.
Includes bibliographical references and index.
1. Violence in sports—Sociological aspects.
2. Sports for women—Sociological aspects.
3. Gender identity. I. Fuller, Linda K.
GV706.7 .S49 306.4'83—dc22 2009034446
ISBN 978-1-4331-0507-4 (hardcover)
ISBN 978-1-4331-0508-1 (paperback)

Bibliographic information published by **Die Deutsche Nationalbibliothek**.
Die Deutsche Nationalbibliothek lists this publication in the "Deutsche Nationalbibliografie"; detailed bibliographic data is available on the Internet at http://dnb.d-nb.de/.

The paper in this book meets the guidelines for permanence and durability of the Committee on Production Guidelines for Book Longevity of the Council of Library Resources.

29 Broadway, 18th floor, New York, NY 10006
www.peterlang.com

Printed in the United States of America

Michael A. Messner (University of Southern California)'s ground-breaking work in the area of sport, gender, language, and violence has inspired many colleagues and this collection.

Contents

Part III Sports Literature

Part IV Broadcast Media Representations

Part V Visual Media Representations

Part VI Classic Case Studies

Introduction

LINDA K. FULLER

> Is violence in sport an essential ingredient that underpins its appeal to spectators? Does violence affect audience appreciation of mediated sports contests? Clearly, combative sports such as boxing and wrestling are very popular... Other sports, such as soccer, rugby, American football, ice hockey, and basketball are not intrinsically violent in the same sense as combat sports, but they do comprise certain aggressive aspects in the ways they are played. Does violence, when it occurs, enhance the entertainment value of these sports?
>
> —BARRIE GUNTER, *SPORT, VIOLENCE, AND THE MEDIA* (2006: 356)

It is not as if sport violence is a new subject; as we all know, it has been discussed ever since athletes began to be determined to win—David Trend (2007: 106) reminding us that "the public appetite for violent sports entertainment dates to the Roman era of gladiator spectacles." Still, what might be somewhat new about the topic of sport violence are the following issues:

1. As media becomes evermore global, regional concerns for actions such as hooliganism reach a wider audience (Armstrong, 1998; Brimson, 2000, 2003, 2007; Dunning, Murphy, Waddinton, and Astrinakis, 2002; Frosdick and Marsh, 2005; Giulianotti, Bonney, and Hepworth, 1994; Kerr, 1994; Murphy, Williams, and Dunning, 1990; Perryman, 2002).

2. With a number of 24-hour sports television programs on air, both to fill space and to please consumers, more attention is being devoted to the topic of sports than ever before.
3. Multimillion-dollar contracts encourage the cult of celebrity, despite (or because of?) news about the number of star athletes who have been arrested for crimes ranging from assault to sexual battery or even murder.
4. Bad-boy athletes such as Michael Vick and Adam "Packman" Jones command the most publicity. Even "goody"-packaged role models such as Kobe Bryant can bring our sarcasm when they are accused of crimes.
5. World Wrestling Entertainment (WWE) has become the most popular program on television (McQuarrie, 2006), especially for young boys, and the wild antics of NASCAR (Simkins, 2005) facilitates its becoming the fastest-growing spectator sport.
6. Even sport spectator violence makes the news—and not just on the sports pages or programs!

Against this backdrop, what we are interested in is the rhetoric—both the language that is used to report on sport violence and the words that are embedded in actual events. In the tradition of *Sport, Rhetoric, and Gender: Historical Perspectives and Media Representations* (Fuller, 2006), this volume includes chapters that cover issues ranging from hooliganism, spousal abuse, and racial and/or gender orientation to literary, televised, filmic, and photographic (pornographic?) images of sports violence. Some of the sports represented include ice hockey, stock car racing, football, body building, baseball, boxing, rugby, wrestling, and even pool.

SPORTS VIOLENCE

Brief History

Sport violence has been encouraged, even elevated, since at least the original Olympic Games. No matter how you frame it—as a mirror of society, a result of fan behavior (Lewis, 2007), economic incentives, innate aggression, "sports rage" (Jamieson and Orr, 2009), and/or a manifestation of psychological stress or social learning—the jury is still out as to how it should be handled. "Football's historical prominence in sport media and folk culture has sustained a hegemonic model of masculinity that prioritizes competitiveness, asceticism, success (winning), aggression, violence, superiority to women, and respect for and compliance with male authority," according to Sabo and Panepinto (1990: 115). Approaching football as cultural text, Michael Oriard (1993: xxii) suggests that its example "can suggest more generally how meaning is produced in a mass-mediated society. Popular spectator sports such as football differ in important ways from related cultural representations; in contrast to movies and television dramas, for example, football games are unscripted, their action real. But...whatever the violence in football means to specific spectators, the issue of violence is inescapable."

W. James Potter (1999: 11–22) outlines a number of theories on media violence, several of which might be applicable here:

1. Biological: instinct, hormones
2. Ecological: confluence, socialization, cultivation
3. Cognitive: cognitive abilities, construct accessibility
4. Interactionist: drive, excitation transfer, catharsis, social learning, priming effects, social cognition (see also Cummins, 2006).

Literature Review

Stating that "sports violence may be seen as either reflecting or shaping social norms and values, as either legally punishable 'real' violence or as ritual, symbolic play," Jeffrey Goldstein (1983: 3) outlines the role of both external and internal constraints, determining the importance of historical, social, and psychological contexts. It is a topic that has recently generated academic interest (e.g., Messner and Sabo, 1994; Welch, 1997; Benedict and Yeager, 1998; Bridges, 1999; Dunning, 1999; Leizman, 1999; Barry, 2001; Ruskin and Laemmer, 2001). The scholarship of Jeff Benedict (1997, 1998, 2000) has concentrated on violence perpetrated by athletes against women. Jib Fowles (1999: 83) makes this astute observation: "In analyses of sporting events, the word 'violence' is often reserved for aggressive actions that are illegal and reproachable, but it is clear that much of what occurs within the rules is also violent by everyday standards. This is indisputable for football, in which players are maimed on a regular basis, sometimes to a paralyzing, life-threatening extent."

Yet, there have been surprisingly few studies relative to the language of sport and its concomitant association with violence. A few terms relative to football do exist: Adler has collected *Football Coach Quotes: The Wit, Wisdom, and Winning Words of Leaders on the Gridiron* (1992), Considine (1982) includes football terms, and Bohnert (2003) has a silly one geared to women. And let me draw your attention to Mariah Burton Nelson's *The Stronger Women Get, the More Men Love Football: Sexism and the American Culture of Sports* (1994).

My own analyses of the language of sport (Fuller, 1992a and b, 1999, 2000, 2003, 2005) began with a sportscast of the Super Bowl during the Persian Gulf

War, in response to learning how instances of domestic violence in the United States escalated during celebration of the country's largest annual television event. Small wonder, when one considers the mix of militaristic and sexist terms implicit in the football commentary, such as the following:

1. *Wartalk: blitz* (from the German *blitzkrieg*, a term referring to the advance of Hitler's troops into 1939 Poland), *bombs and bomb squads, offense/defense, flanks, victories and defeats, casualties, chucking, cleating, killing, hitting, holding, hooking, ammunition, weapons, taking aim, fighting, detonating, squeezing the trigger*, and *dominating*. Other terms included phrases such as "blockading the way," "ground and air attacks," "fighting and dying on the frontlines," and "battling in the trenches." Strategies and tactics included *offenses, sticking to a game plan*, using "two-minute drills," *kamikaze squads*, or the "two-platoon system," "weaving through minefields," sometimes being reduced to employing "unnecessary roughness," even having sportscasters and newscasters use "telestrators" for charting movements. We still await allusions to "scuds."
2. *Sextalk:* think of how sexualized the vocabulary used in football is, with terms such as "going all the way," *pinching, squeezing, pumping*, "deep penetration," "grinding it out," "clutch plays," using "bump and run" stratagem, "gang-tackling," "naked reverses," and "belly-backing" techniques. Sometimes there are *fumbles, huddles, hurry-up offenses, quick hits or releases*, or even "fakes." *Kicking* is key.

Relatedly, we know how nationalism is associated with militarism—encouraging jingoistic flag-waving and hollering for our favorite sports heroes and teams. As we find ourselves currently involved in so many military messes and wars around the world, it clearly is time to question the intertwining role of sport in language, gender, and violence.

When you peruse the chapter descriptions for this volume, you will see both familiar and controversial themes, each one adding to the scholarship on the critically relevant subject of sport violence. Critical, relational studies, whether theoretical and/or empirical, of gender, language, and sport, it argues, can move us to see the wider world through another prism. Divided into six various parts—Sports Violence Per Se, Historical Perspectives, Sports Literature, Broadcast Media Representations, Visual Media Representations, and Classic Case Studies—this volume includes the following wide-ranging contributions:

In Part I, **Sports Violence Per Se**, Michael Atkinson in *It's Still Part of the Game: Dangerous Violence and Masculanization in Canadian Ice Hockey* introduces us to the world of professional ice hockey with a case study from Canada showing how a brutal event was framed as both noncriminal and essentially victimless. *Representations of Sport Violence and Spousal Abuse*, by Margery Holman, Victoria Paraschak, Patricia Weir, and Richard Moriarty, examines the exploitation of violence in sport, as projected through television, as a possible link to domestic violence—specifically, how professional hockey playoff games work as a trigger for spousal violence. To better understand the phenomenon of parental/spectator violence at minor ice-hockey games, Michael A. Robidoux and Jochen G. Bocksnick (*Playing beyond the Glass: How Parents Support Violence in Minor Hockey*) conducted a yearlong observational study at Pee-Wee (13–14) hockey games in Southern Alberta, Canada, concluding that although extreme acts of violence are somewhat rare, other more insidious forms of aggression and violence pervade minor hockey contexts.

Part II, **Historical Perspectives**, allows and encourages critical perspectives on sport, language, and violence. Ellen J. Staurowsky sat down and gave her *Reflections on Sport, Masculinity, and Nationalism in the Aftermath of 9/11,* a chapter that remains untouched since her initial reaction writing it, examining the themes of sport, masculinity, and nationalism as they emerged following September 11; analyzing *Sports Illustrated* and *ESPN* magazines, *Monday Night Football*, and selected articles from diverse publications, her emphasis is on the language of sport, the construction of masculinity, and how these concepts intersect and connect with nationalism. David "Turbo" Thompson's *Hot Wheels and High Heels: Gender Roles in Stock Car Racing* documents how stock car racing began in the American South in the 1930s, when informal speed contests were held by moonshiners (makers and transporters of illegal untaxed liquor who hopped up their cars to outrun federal alcohol tax agents), and what it has come to be today, an organized, multibillion-dollar industry with various levels of gender symbolism embedded in its culture: the frantic dash of cars as the competitive race of sperm toward an egg; the roll cage as the safety of the womb; the racing season as rutting season, when dominance is established; and the victory lane celebration has a beauty queen awarding the trophy—a symbolic "available virgin"—to the victor.

In Part III, **Sports Literature**, Dan Jenkins, author of such popular sports novels as *Semi-Tough* and *Dead Solid Perfect*, is the subject in John Mark Dempsey's *All-skates, Witch Wool, and a Blouse Full of Lungs: Dan Jenkins' Use of Masculine Sexual Language*, which he claims serves several purposes: the promotion of traditional male cultural values (i.e., hegemonic masculinity); assertions of swaggering masculinity; provisions against emotional vulnerabilities; and demonstrated defiance of convention. Based on rhetorical and literary scholarship, reviews of Jenkins' novels, and e-mail communications between himself and the author, Dempsey argues that Jenkins uses frank sexual language to portray reality and to target hypocrisy in its many forms. Anne E. Price examines *Football Hooliganism: A Rhetoric of Frustration and Honor* in the novels of John King, showing that violent football team support is a matter of personal honor, social class frustration, peer group solidarity, and recreation; using examples from *The Football Factory* (1997), *Headhunters* (1998), and *England Away* (1998), King provides fictional narratives, with brutal realism, of the subculture of English football hooligans—revealing that the reality is much more complex than the myths allow. Traditional sports literature often equates sports with masculinity; however, with the continued growth of women's athletics, sport is no longer a male domain, as Robert Sirabian points out in *Gender, Cross-Dressing, and Sport in Lewis Nordan's* The All-Girl Football Team, where the narrator reminisces about an all-girl football game in which he participated as a teen and confronted thoughts about the limits of his identity.

With the inception of cable television, sports channels such as ESPN and ESPN2 expanded their coverage to sports that had been underrepresented on broadcast television, including recreational sports, such as billiards and fishing, as well as extreme sports, such as sky surfing and snowboarding, so, in Part IV, **Broadcast Media Representations**, Gina Daddario's case study in *Media, Masculinity, and* The World's Strongest Man*: Exploring Postmodern Sports Programming* provides an important look into an alternative sport. Joy Crissey Honea's *Xclusion at the Winter X Games: The Marginalization of Women Athletes in Alternative Sport* examines the marginalization of women athletes, relegated to second-rate status and subjected to sexist language, particularly infantilizing and sexualized commentary highlighting differences between male and female athleticism and privileging male performances. The Jim Rome Show *and Negotiations of Manhood: Surviving in "The Jungle,"* by Maureen Margaret Smith, examines sport as a site of male socialization, specifically the "space" of sports talk radio; several themes were identified and explored, including how men use sport and the language of sports talk radio to define masculinity and manhood, how women are treated within the "male only" space, and how white men respond to the athletic accomplishments of black male athletes and what it means to their ever-changing definitions of masculinity.

Part V, **Visual Media Representations,** begins with Megan Chawansky's *Put Me In, Ms. Coach: Sexual Rhetoric in the Locker Room*, exploring the sexual rhetoric embedded in locker room interactions among men and examining its implications for women coaches seeking to lead men's teams; using the films *Wildcats* (1986) and *Sunset Park* (1996), it argues that the misogynist and homophobic locker room rhetoric utilized by athletes can create a hostile climate for women attempting to embark on coaching careers within men's sports.

In 1925, Harold Lloyd starred in a silent movie called *The Freshman*, an uproarious caper where he serves as "blocking dummy" on the football team; Linda K. Fuller points out in *Foul Language: A Feminist Perspective on (American) Football Film Rhetoric* that today the foul language featured in football films serves as a barometer of our relationship with the sporting world. Her content analysis of more than 100 such motion pictures, situated within various historical, political, racial, ethnic, socioeconomic, and gendered issues, provides a fascinating framework for better understanding the role that sports play in media and social violence. C. Richard King's *Hail to the Chiefs: Race, Gender, and Native American Sports Mascots* examines how race and gender intersect here, focusing specifically on the sexual rhetoric central to many arguments defending such symbols and offering a critical reading of a strand of neoconservative thought that is intent upon retaining stereotypical renderings of indigenous peoples in association with sports. *Powerful or Pornographic?: Photographs of Female Body Builders in* Muscle and Fitness, by Debra Merskin, considers portrayals of women in body building magazines as a unique opportunity to explore the relationship between pictorial presentations of women's bodies—which undermines women by portraying them as sexual objects of the male pornographic gaze—and the social construction of gender.

John P. Elia, Jon B. Martin, and Gust A. Yep's *Off His Rocker: Masculinity and the Rhetoric of Violence in America's Favorite Pastime* starts off Part VI, **Classic Case Studies**; using the case of John Rocker, a former major league baseball player for the Atlanta Braves, it focuses on the plethora of rhetorical and symbolic violence surrounding an episode as an illustration of the link of hyper-masculinity to rhetorical violence. Citing boxers Christy Martin, Mia St. John, Lucia Rijker, and Laila Ali, Shura Alexandra Gat's *Wham! Bam! Thank You, Ma'am!: The Rhetoric Surrounding Female Professional Boxers* discusses how, because boxing has long been considered a masculine sport, women who choose to box competitively, challenge popular notions about gender and femininity; examining language used to describe female boxers and how they depict themselves, she explores the ways in which femininity and sexuality are defined and negotiated for, and by, these cutting-edge athletes. Another good example comes in Jessica Hudson's *Women Playing Rugby: Rejection of "The Girly" by Girls*, which discusses the disruption of gendering cultural codes through the contradictions of women playing rugby, building muscle, becoming bruised and injured, and demonstrating hostility and aggression on and off the pitch as violent assailants and as sexual predators—thus redefining the "girly girl." We learn in Erin Reilly's *All Bust and No Balls: Gender, Language, and Pool* that sexuality and pocket billiards, commonly known as "pool," have intertwined throughout the history of the game, where the language lends itself to double entendres, such as "try my cue sweetheart, it'll guarantee you a good game," sexual puns on "kiss" and "balls," gender-marked pool argot such as the "Dolly Parton break" (all bust and no balls) and "too much testosterone" (hit too hard). Lastly, the portrait of a premiere star of elite women's freestyle wrestling in Theresa A. Walton's *Media Grappling with Female Success on the Mat: Tricia Saunders, Multiple-World Freestyle Wrestling Champion* analyzes her mediation to explicate the sexual sports rhetoric surrounding female success in a traditionally male sport by the two main wrestling periodicals: *Amateur Wrestling News* and *USA Wrestler*.

IMPLICATIONS

Whether in sport or in life, unnecessary roughness usually is penalized. Whether performed by athletes, by fans, or even by coaches or parents, unnecessary roughness needs to be examined. It behooves us to be aware of the double-edged nature of the controversy; balancing presumed consumer desires with what the market might bear, we must nevertheless be aware of what effects may accrue from sports violence.

Once we realize that most sports violence is formulaic, albeit encouraging us to think that it is spontaneous, even "fun," we begin to own the answers. Once we realize that most sports violence is merely an issue of power, albeit corporate strength so disguised that we often cannot know what corporation is actually sponsoring it, we begin to be critical media consumers. And that means all of us, regardless of educational and socioeconomic status.

And, once we understand how sports violence operates—when, where, how, and why—our next step as individuals and community members is to operationalize that knowledge. If we are teachers, we can introduce media literacy about the role(s) of entertainment in our lives; if we are policymakers, we can help influence decision-making toward inclusion of diverse, alternative ways of conceptualizing, producing, and distributing (sports) media; if we are concerned citizens, we can form coalitions of persons interested in broadening media choices. Whatever our stance(s), if we care about sports we can keep in mind its essence: Celebrating the body, enjoying the empowerment in reaching goals and the joys of teamwork, playing by the rules, and participating where possible, being spectators when not. But when all is said and done, roughness certainly should be *un*necessary.

The 20 chapters that make up this volume fall neatly into these categories: sport violence per se, historical perspectives, sports literature, broadcast media representations, visual media representations, and classic case studies. As you will note in the About the Contributors section, the authors represent a range of disciplines, institutions, and countries—all of which increases the collective value of their perspectives. I would also like to acknowledge three persons who we had hoped could contribute: Thomas Oates, School of Journalism and Mass Communication, University of Iowa; Darcy C. Plymire, Sports Management, SUNY Cortland; and Earl Smith, Sociology Department, Wake Forest University.

Contrary to the old idiom that "words will never hurt me," this volume clearly demonstrates what happens when we add violence to the equation of sport, rhetoric, and gender. Like its companion, *Sexual Sports Rhetoric: Global and Universal Contexts*, this book should sensitize you to the power of sporting language.

REFERENCES

Adler, L. (1992). *Football coach quotes: The wit, wisdom, and winning words of leaders on the gridiron.* Jefferson, NC: McFarland & Company.

Armstrong, G. (1998). *Football hooligans: Knowing the score.* Oxford, UK: Berg.

Barry, J. (2001). *Power plays: Politics, football, and other blood sports.* Jackson, MS: University Press of Mississippi.

Benedict, J. (1997). *Public heroes, private felons: Athletes and crimes against women.* Boston, MA: Northeastern University Press.

Benedict, J. (1998). *Athletes and acquaintance rape.* Thousand Oaks, CA: Sage.

Benedict, J. (2000). Out of bounds: Inside the NBA's culture of rape, violence, and crime. Boston, MA: Northeastern University Press.

Benedict, J. and Yeager, D. (1998). *Pros and cons: The criminals who play in the NFL.* New York: Warner Books.

Bohnert, S. B. (2003). *Game-day goddess: Learning football's lingo.* Glen Allen, VA: eNovel.com.

Bridges, J. (1999). *Making violence part of the game.* Commack, NY: Kroshka.

Brimson, D. (2000). *Barmy army: The changing face of football violence.* Spalding, UK: Headline Book.

Brimson, D. (2003). *Eurotrashed: The rise and rise of Europe's football hooligans.* Spalding, UK: Headline Book.

Brimson, D. (2007). *Kicking off: Why hooliganism and racism are killing football.* Spalding, UK: Headline Book.

Considine, T. (1982). *The language of sport.* New York: World Almanac.

Cummins, R. G. (2006). Sports fiction: Critical and empirical perspectives. In Raney, A. A. and Bryant, J. (Eds.), *Handbook of sports and media* (185–205). Mahwah, NJ: Lawrence Erlbaum.

Dunning, E. (1999). *Sport matters: Sociological studies of sport, violence, and civilisation.* London: Routledge.

Dunning, E., Murphy, P., Waddinton, I., and Astrinakis, A. E. (Eds.) (2002). *Fighting fans: Football hooliganism as a world phenomenon.* Dublin: University College Dublin Press.

Fowles, J. (1999). *The case for television violence.* Thousand Oaks, CA: Sage.

Frosdick, S. and Marsh, P. (2005). *Football hooliganism.* Devon, UK: Willan.

Fuller, L. K. (1992a). Reporters rights in the locker room. *Feminist Issues*, Vol. 12, No. 1 (Spring): 39–45.

Fuller, L. K. (1992b). Sportstalk/wartalk/patriotismtalk/mentalk: Super Bowl XXV. Paper presented to the International Association of Media and Communication Research, Sao Paulo, Brazil.

Fuller, L. K. (1999). Super Bowl speak: Subtexts of sex and sex talk in America's annual sports extravaganza. In Carstarphen, M. G. and Zavoina, S. C. (Eds.), *Sexual rhetoric: Media perspectives on sexuality, gender, and identity* (161–173). Westport, CT: Greenwood Press.

Fuller, L. K. (2000). The culture of violence and the rhetoric of sport violence. Paper presented to the International Association of Media and Communication Research, Singapore.

Fuller, L. K. (2003). (Un)necessary roughness: A review of sports violence. Paper presented to the Northeast Popular Culture Association, Worcester, MA.

Fuller, L. K. (2005). The warlike, violent language of sport. Paper presented to Women's Studies, Northeastern University, Boston, MA.

Fuller, L. K. (Ed.) (2006). *Sport, rhetoric, and gender: Historical perspectives and media representations.* New York: Palgrave Macmillan.

Giulianotti, R., Bonney, N., and Hepworth, M. (Eds.). (1994). *Football, violence and social identity.* London: Routledge.

Goldstein, J. H. (Ed.) (1983). *Sports violence.* New York: Springer-Verlag.

Gunter, B. (2006). Sport, violence, and the media. In Raney, A. A. and Bryant, J. (Eds.), *Handbook of sports and media* (353–364). Mahwah, NJ: Lawrence Erlbaum.

Jamieson, L. and Orr, T. (2009). *Sport and violence: A critical examination of sport violence in the world.* Burlington, MA: Butterworth-Heinemann.

Kerr, J. H. (1994). *Understanding soccer hooliganism.* Berkshire, UK: Open University Press.

Leizman, J. (1999). *Let's kill 'em: Understanding and controlling violence in sports.* Lanham, MD: University Press of America.

Lewis, J. M. (2007). *Sports fan violence in North America.* Lanham, MD: Rowman and Littlefield.

McQuarrie, F. A. E. (2006). Breaking kayfabe: The history of a history of World Wrestling Entertainment. *Management & Organizational History*, Vol. 1, No. 3: 227–250.

Messner, M. and Sabo, D. F. (1994). *Sex, violence and power in sports.* Freedom, CA: The Crossing Press.

Murphy, P. J., Williams, J., and Dunning, E. (1990). *Football on trial: Spectator violence in the football world.* Oxford, UK: Routledge.

Nelson, M. B. (1994). *The stronger women get, the more men love football: Sexism and the American culture of sports.* Orlando, FL: Harcourt Brace.

Oriard, M. (1993). *Reading football: How the popular press created an American spectacle.* Chapel Hill, NC: University of North Carolina Press.

Perryman, M. (Ed.) (2002). *Hooligan wars: Causes and effects of football violence.* Edinburgh: Mainstream.

Potter, J. W. (1999). *On media violence.* Thousand Oaks, CA: Sage.

Ruskin, H. and Laemmer, M. (Eds.) (2001). *Fair play: Violence in sport and society.* Jerusalem, Israel: Magnes Press.

Sabo, D. F. and Panepinto, J. (1990). In Messner, M. and Sabo, D. F. (Eds.), *Sport, men, and the gender order: Critical feminist perspectives* (115–126). Champaign, IL: Human Kinetics.

Simkins, C. (2005). NASCAR is America's fastest-growing spectator sport (June 1). Available: (http://www.voanews.com/english/archive/2005-06/2005-05-26-voa2.cfm).

Trend, D. (2007). *The myth of media violence: A critical introduction*. Malden, MA: Blackwell.

Welch, M. (1997). Violence against women by professional football players: A gender analysis of hypermasculinity, positional status, narcissism, and entitlement. *Journal of Sport and Social Issues* (21): 392–411.

PART I

SPORT VIOLENCE PER SE

CHAPTER ONE

It's Still Part OF THE Game: Violence AND Masculinity IN Canadian Ice Hockey

MICHAEL ATKINSON

SPORT, CRIME, AND VICTIMIZATION

Don Sanderson died on January 2, 2009, only 20 days after banging his head on the ice at the end of a hockey fight during a game that pitted his Whitby Dunlops, against rival Brantford Blast (AAA league in Canada). Three weeks later, the Whitby Dunlops hosted a tribute to the 21-year-old before a scheduled game. The pre-game ceremony climaxed on the ice when, at the end of a 35-minute video montage and public eulogizing of Sanderson's young life, his mother Dahna fell, sobbing, into her ex-husband's shoulder. As a symbolic number 40 jersey was slowly raised to the ceiling, a children's choir sang "You Raise Me Up," friends and family members remarking that Don Sanderson's fire for hockey and life led him to work harder than any of his teammates. People, including the patriarch of the Sanderson family, Mike Sanderson, suggested that his son's "fire" made him an aggressive defenseman who earned four ejections for fighting in 11 games in the 2008 season alone.

Sanderson's fateful last fight began as a mild scuffle next to the Dunlops' goal with Brantford Blast player Corey Fulton. By all accounts, it developed as a run-of-the- mill hockey fight, replete with inconsequential punches thrown by both players. Sanderson's teammates described the altercation as nothing special, adding that they thought Fulton had done nothing dirty or dangerous that may have placed Sanderson at risk of injury. Towards the end of the struggle, Sanderson's helmet slipped off and he stumbled from Fulton's grip, plummeting to the ice; then, his exposed head crashed against the ice and Sanderson then immediately slipped into unconsciousness. His tragedy almost immediately reverberated across Canada, instigating a prolonged debate about the role of fighting in the national sport. Print media, television, and the Internet were predictably abuzz. A poll reported by *Sun Media* (January 4, 2009) shortly after Sanderson's death revealed that 59 percent of respondents felt that fighting should be banned in minor and amateur hockey; yet, National Hockey League commissioner Gary Bettman routinely expressed a league reluctance to change the subcultural codes or official rules regulating fighting. Like other elite rulers in the world of hockey, he is clearly mindful of the risks involved in alienating hockey's remaining "passionate fans."

To many of the sport's devotees, hockey equals fighting, and they are unwilling to reconsider and, in some cases, even discuss the violence in their sport as uncontrolled (Atkinson and Young, 2008). That group includes iconic commentator Don Cherry (2009), who declared at Sanderson's funeral, "I can't believe that some people in the anti-fighting group would take advantage of something like this to make their point." Ross Bernstein, a pro-fighting advocate whose many books on hockey include *The Code: The Unwritten Rules of Fighting and Retaliation in the NHL* (2006), publicly commented that hockey needs fighting for two reasons: revenue and holding dirty players accountable. Still, the national hand-wringing over Sanderson's death led many Canadian hockey insiders and outsiders to lobby for change in the sport regarding what is subculturally tolerated.

Unfortunately, only a small group of sociologists of sport has offered answers as to why young men like Don Sanderson are violently victimized in the sport and why do they willfully participate, as in many cases, in their own victimization. Following Smith's (1983) ground-breaking research of sports violence, a few sociologists have critically examined the ways in which criminal activity is embedded in sports processes (Atkinson and Williams, 2001; Dunning, 1999; Reasons, 1992; Young and Wamsley, 1996; White, 1986; Young, 2002). Although sociologists and criminologists attend to a wide range of formal rule-breaking behaviors and subsequently classify such behaviors into conceptual categories such as "white collar crimes," "hate crimes," "sex crimes," and "race crimes," we have not adequately pursued, in-depth analyses of "sports crimes." Even though athletes' criminal activities away from the playing field (e.g., sexual assault, sexual deviance, gambling, battery and murder) have been well documented and meticulously analyzed in recent years (cf. Coakley, 2001), sociologists have been curiously reluctant to interrogate rule-breaking behaviors occurring on the field as crimes worthy of extra-institutional social control (Young, 1991, 2002).

Even fewer sociologists have inspected which athletes become victims of sports crimes. With the notable exception of Young (1991, 1993, 2000, 2002), most sociologists tend to dismiss the idea that hyper-violent or egregiously negligent forms of physical play may constitute criminal behaviors that produce victims. Of particular relevance here, are the common "interpretive resources" (Gubrium and Holstein, 1997) that "frame" (Goffman, 1974) how sports violence is understood by players, team members, league officials, and sports audiences. Research on player violence in sport almost uniformly illustrates how dominant understandings of masculinity, operate as the main interpretive resource for decoding both player violence and forms of victimization in sport (cf. Young, 1991, 2002). In order to fully understand the social construction of "sports crime," then, we must interrogate how (sub)culturally salient constructions of masculinity restrict players' opportunities to be protected, respected, and institutionally supported as victims.

An analysis of aspects of "criminal violence" in sport (Smith, 1983) is offered here via a case study of the social construction of player violence and victimization in professional ice hockey. Of interest are the ways in which masculine ideologies buttress discursive attempts by league owners, coaches, officials, athletes, lawyers, and court justices to depict excessively violent behavior in ice hockey as noncriminal. Through the 2000 case study of the McSorley-Brasher incident, and McSorley's criminal trial (*R v. McSorley,* 2000), it is evidenced that cultural ideologies promoting "dangerous masculinities" (White and Young, 1997, 1999) are numerous in discourses surrounding ice hockey. More specifically, using discourses strategically pointing out that players "consent" to violence in ice hockey, it underscores why social control of violence must remain within sports league, blame be shifted onto the victims of sports violence, and degree of exciting significance (Elias and Dunning, 1986) be reinforced by player violence. In brief, it shows how key agents, in and around ice hockey perpetuate the idea that there is no such thing as "sports crimes."

THE McSORLEY-BRASHEAR INCIDENT

On February 21, 2000, the Boston Bruins met with the Vancouver Canucks in British Columbia in a mid-season National Hockey League (NHL) contest. With only 2:09 minutes elapsed in the first period, long-time NHL enforcers—"policemen," in the accepted ice hockey vernacular—Marty McSorley (age 37) of the Boston Bruins and Donald Brashear (age 28) of the Vancouver Canucks clashed horns in a spirited display of on-ice pugilism. As described by broadcasters and affirmed by the Vancouver faithful in attendance, Brashear "won" the bout handily. Each player received a "fighting major" penalty of five minutes for the donnybrook. On his way to the penalty box, Brashear flexed his biceps and taunted Bruins' players. This rather typical hockey scenario raised no concern at the time, and there was no indication from anyone involved (players, referees, coaches, or fans) that a fight would be a further source of strain within the game.

But, with 7:38 seconds left in this already rough first period, Marty McSorley challenged Donald Brashear to a "rematch" by spiritedly crosschecking him. Brashear skated away indifferent to the request, and McSorley was sent to the penalty box once again, this time with a double-minor penalty for "roughing" and "crosschecking" and a ten-minute penalty for "unsportsmanlike conduct." During the ensuing power-play (only 1:35 seconds later), Brashear crashed awkwardly into Boston goaltender Byron Dafoe, who writhed on the ice and clutched at his right knee and had to be carried from the ice on a stretcher. Brad Watson assessed a two-minute penalty against Brashear for "goaltender interference."

For the rest of the evening, McSorley tried to goad Brashear into another fight—partly to seek redemption for his earlier loss to Brashear, and partly to avenge Dafoe. In the dying seconds of the game, and with the Canucks leading 5-2, Brashear and McSorley found themselves on the ice for one last shift. With under a dozen seconds remaining in the third period, McSorley skated out of his team's end of the rink and approached Brashear, who had his back turned to McSorley. He reached Brashear just inside the Canucks' blue line and, instead of dropping his gloves to fight, he clipped Brashear from behind with a two-handed stick slash to his right temple.

Immediately, Brashear went tumbling backwards to the ice in a state of unconsciousness. His head bounced off the ice, and blood started pouring from his nose. Brashear laid prone and motionless on the ice, save for the periodic twitching of his feet and rolling of his eyes. Canucks' team doctor Rui Avelar later testified that Brashear was having a seizure on the ice when he reached him, also confirming that he suffered a Grade 3 concussion from the stick's blow. Vancouver Canucks' trainers worked on Brashear for over ten minutes on the ice, and he was eventually removed on a stretcher. The hit prompted Vancouver goalie Garth Snow to physically charge at McSorley, but referee Brad Watson thwarted the assault and terminated the game forthwith. Fans pelted McSorley with various missiles as the players left the ice and returned to their respective dressing rooms. For the on-ice incident, McSorley was assessed a match penalty for "attempting to injure," and a game misconduct.

McSorley's saga only begins at this point. In response to unprecedented public outcry for stern reprimand by the league, the NHL's long arm of the law (NHL president Gary Bettman and executive vice president Colin Campbell) suspended McSorley indefinitely on March 22, 2000. One day later, the NHL further admonished McSorley by suspending him for the Bruins' remaining 23 games of the 1999–2000 season, costing him over Cdn$100,000 in lost wages. The league believed that, as the longest suspension for an on-ice incident in NHL history, the penalty would send a message that this kind of abhorrent stick-work is unacceptable. With Brashear returning to the game before the end of the 1999–2000 season, the case appeared to be closed. Feeling as if the matter had been deftly resolved through the league's private justice system, the NHL attempted to restore some semblance of normalcy to the disrupted season by engaging in a frantic public relations campaign to repolish the NHL's tarnished image.

However, a Vancouver police sergeant on duty at the February 21 contest filed a report about the on-ice incident and recommended that criminal assault charges should be laid against McSorley by the Crown prosecutor's office in Vancouver; soon, charges of assault with a weapon were filed against McSorley. The police launched their own investigation into the incident. Beginning September 25, 2000, in a sports drama that would last five days, Marty McSorley, the NHL, and violence in professional ice hockey were placed on trial—bringing to the fore issues of player violence, players' consent to sports violence, and the role of the State in governing sports violence. It also led to the revisitation of a lingering question in professional sport: Do certain acts of player violence constitute criminal behavior, and if so, who are the victims?

Marty McSorley of the Boston Bruins was found guilty of assaulting Vancouver Canucks' Donald Brashear with a weapon under section 267(2) of the *Criminal Code of Canada* (2001), sentenced to an 18-month conditional discharge (essentially probation), and ordered that he not play in any future NHL games involving Brashear. His vicious slash to Brashear's head would be a scene played, and replayed, on international sports programs for well over a year, stirring public emotion about ice hockey's place in North American culture and about the social impacts of hockey violence. Media agents, such as the Canadian news magazine *MacLean's* that used the pejorative header "Blood Sport," were widely criticized for sensationalizing the incident. When examined from every angle, debated by sports pundits, and dissected from a multitude of "theoretical" interpretations, however, the incident underlined what many hockey fans have known for quite some time: That "illegal" stick-work and other forms of player violence in the NHL are simply not under control.

Equally contested would be the social utility of the McSorley trial, and the issue of whether or not the criminal justice system has any mandate to control player violence in professional ice hockey. Amidst the video replays, talk show arguments, and torrential flood of fan responses, a recurrent discourse crystallized around the incident implying that any criminal prosecution of ice hockey players is not only ineffective and unwarranted, but in many ways also distastefully *unmasculine.* Importantly, the McSorley-Brashear incident poignantly illustrates how social constructions of masculinity are embedded in the interpretation of on-ice violence in professional ice hockey. As will be outlined here, emergent discourses about the on-ice assault, the NHL's "official" reaction, player and fan responses, and the criminal justice system's interpretation all reflect unwavering (sub)cultural tendencies to view player violence in ice hockey through the lens of dangerous masculinity. Its data, collected through a "convenience sampling" approach, cover Canadian and American media (e.g., newspaper, magazine, television, and Internet) accounts of the McSorley-Brashear event from February 21, 2000 to March 31, 2001. Including official court transcripts from *R v. McSorley* (2000), emphasis was given to media narratives featuring reactions from players, coaches, league administrators, fans, and justice system officials.

THEORETICAL UNDERPINNINGS: DANGEROUS MASCULINITY AND ICE HOCKEY VIOLENCE

For as long as sociologists of sport have inspected the cultural frameworks providing meaning to sporting practices, masculinity has been theoretically entwined with athletics (Dunning, 1986; Messner and Sabo, 1994; White and Young, 1997); in reviewing the literature, there is perhaps no other conceptual relationship as intensely scrutinized as this (Messner, Hunt, and Dunbar, 1999). From the historical analysis of "muscular Christianity" (Overman, 1997) to young men's "dominance bonding" in sport (Farr, 1988), to the examination of pain and injury processes involved in competition (Nixon, 1996; White and Young, 1997) and, more recently, to the contestation of masculine identities through sports practices (Anderson, 2000; Pronger, 1990, 1999), researchers have labored to explain the contextual contingencies underpinning how masculinity is decoded by athletes and sport audiences.

While feminist scholars (cf. Davis, 1997) and others deeply concerned with gender research feverishly theorize about the cultural and social-structural relevance of "hegemonic" masculinity, too few study masculinity "in the round" (Maguire, 1993). The hegemonic brand of masculinity establishes, enforces, and legitimates—through complex ideological and discursive frames that produce systems of socialization and matrices of institutional support—the ascribed authority of the "male" figure; as such, it is a privileging cultural status for many men. Sociological research on men in sport, highlights the constitutive social processes involved in "intextuating" (de Certeau, 1984) hegemonic masculinity into cultural practice (cf. Burstyn, 1999; Kimbrell, 1995; Kimmel and Messner, 1992; McKay, Messner, and Sabo, 2000; Trujillo, 1990). The male's corporeal power, authority, fearlessness, and ability to be violent become closely aligned with athleticism and "meaningful" competition.

Arguing that a majority of player violence and aggression in contact sports is attributable to athletes' overindulgence in hegemonic ideologies of masculinity, White and Young (1997, 1999) label it a "dangerous" cultural ideal—it places men in contexts where violent victimization, physical injury, and social marginalization are relatively guaranteed. Indeed, the correlation between dangerous masculinity and player violence is one of the strongest in sport literature. Although there are, clearly, other factors pertinent to the emergence of unsanctioned player violence, research on sports such as gridiron football, soccer, basketball, and boxing exposes how (sub)cultural constructions of masculinity are central in the etiology of player violence in sports (cf. Dunning, 1999; Young, 2000). The pursuit of dangerous masculinities, coupled with what Hughes and Coakley (1991) call the "Sport Ethic," leads athletes to treat their bodies as weapons, utilize aggressive and illegal tactics in competition, and ostracize others who fail to respect "the code" of violence/risk-taking tacitly embedded in sports cultures (Messner, 1990; Messner and Sabo, 1994).

Ice Hockey and Player Victimization

Through his groundbreaking research on violence in sports such as ice hockey, sociologist Michael Smith (1983) outlined how player violence is understood against a series of formal and informal rules structuring the games. He presents a continuum of sports violence—ranging from on one end where there is violent behavior that violates the formal rules of a sport but is informally accepted by players (e.g., *brutal body contact* and *borderline violence*), to the other end where there is violence that breaches official rules, players' norms, and the legal codes of society (*quasi-criminal* and *criminal violence*). In a similar way, victimological perspectives on sport (Faulkner, 1973; Young, 1991, 1993, 2002; Young and Reasons, 1989) indicate that, since most forms of vicious player violence tend to be subculturally accepted by players, tolerated by fans, and commercially lucrative for leagues, little concern has been afforded to athletes who are emotionally, psychologically, or physically marred by violence.

Still, research on ice hockey, both within Canada and abroad, points out that codes of dangerous masculinity influence the sport in such a way that male athletes tend not to view vicious player violence as extraordinary (cf. Young, 2000, 2002). Mark Messier, team captain of the New York Rangers and former teammate of McSorley's, responded to the incident: "It was a dangerous play. I don't know what else to say. Everybody knows it's a dangerous game and we all know injuries can happen" (Kupelian, 2000). This process of interpretive framing begins at an early age, as instruction at the "Pee Wee" or junior levels is often abound with masculinist, anti-victim discourses (Smith, 1975; Vaz, 1982; Watson and McLellan, 1986).

Key in breeding a culture of aggression or roughness in hockey, is establishing a context wherein violent behaviors become discursively normalized—so young players are taught to respect "the code" of living and dying by the proverbial sword...if you hit someone brutally, expect to be hit brutally in return (McMurtry, 1974; Pascall and White, 2000). To this end, many men involved in professional ice hockey disavow "the victim" as a potential masculine identity within the game. As Smith (1983) and Barnes (1988) note, the dangerous masculine culture of professional ice hockey flatly eschews discourses of victimization—preferring, instead, to reframe on-ice physical victimization as a process of character-building, toughening, sacrifice, or dedication. Since ice hockey players and their fans often view players as "warriors" or "ironmen," the image of the professional ice hockey player as a victim of (criminal) violence is incongruent with cultural interpretations of the game (Gruneau and Whitson, 1993).

Conforming to the codes of dangerous masculinity, even through the use of violent play, can be informally rewarded within teams through salary and contract incentives, praise, and other forms of preferential treatment (Weinstein et al., 1995). Similarly, fans and media broadcasters draw attention to the toughness and durability of the masculine/violent player and his ability to withstand ongoing victimization, often mythologizing tough players of the past as masculine legends (e.g., Gordie Howe, Bobby Orr, Maurice Richard, and Dave "Tiger" Williams).

When ice hockey players have been brought to criminal courts for excessively violent acts on the ice, Canadian courts justice have summarily rejected the validity of these cases on the grounds that players consent to victimization in the game through their acceptance of the codes of masculinity (and their violent consequences) structuring athletic competition (cf. Faulkner, 1973; Young and Wamsley, 1996); such decisions are paramount in creating cultural discourses around player violence in ice hockey as victimless (Bridges, 1999; Horrow, 1980). As evidenced by the McSorley trial, institutional discourses function in tandem to construct contemporary understandings of ice hockey, violence, and victimization.

DISCURSIVELY CONSTRUCTING VICTIMIZATION IN THE McSORLEY CASE

In the events following the McSorley-Brashear incident, standard ice hockey discourses underpinned by ideologies of dangerous masculinity were drawn upon to help interpret the violent act. While some critics called for McSorley's arrest, NHL insiders explained it as "tolerable deviance" (Stebbins, 1996).

External institutions, including the media and the legal system, produced discourses that intensified the ambiguity about the assault, proving instrumental in framing vicious forms of ice hockey violence as essentially victimless, their multi-institutional discourses structured by four major arguments: (1) Players consent to violence; (2) The control of violence must be handled within sports leagues; (3) Players are complicit in their own injury (i.e., we blame the "victim"); and, (4) Violence is an unfortunate but exciting part of ice hockey.

Player Consent

The issue of whether or not players consent to violence as part of their participation in sport—in legal terminology, the issue of *volenti non fit injuria*—is well debated within the sociology of sport literature (cf. Barnes, 1988; Young, 2002).

Nonetheless, through the promulgation of group discourses, a gray area is created between what forms of violence an ice hockey player consents to, and the forms to which one does not. For example, in the McSorley case key agents stepped forward to contend that Donald Brashear—as a player who had accumulated 1,282 minutes in penalties by this point in his career—*should have expected* to be struck by McSorley in a vicious manner given the pattern of violence created during the February 21, 2000 game.

Coupling the issue of consent with the frustration/accident defense, ice hockey insiders and supporters painted the incident as one undeserving of criminal prosecution. Portraying McSorley as a tough but fair, violent yet honorable, aggressive while proud player, individuals discounted the idea that McSorley had criminally victimized Brashear in a way *uncommon* or *unaccepted* in NHL hockey. Through the evocation of masculinist discourses of toughness, violence, and risk-taking, McSorley's actions were defended as standard practice within the game.

Control within the League

Using arguments interlaced with suggestions that McSorley's slash to Brashear did not significantly violate "the code" of violence, NHL players and executives claimed themselves to be the most appropriate judges and juries of violence within the game.

Control of player violence is held as the strict mandate of the NHL, with contestations to their authority dismissed on the grounds that outsiders cannot conceptualize the mindset (vis-à-vis the socialization) of the *men* committing violence in the game. The hegemony of the league is further rationalized on the premise that players will respect or acknowledge punishment only if administered by one familiar with the rules, codes, and ideologies of violence (*qua* masculinity) within the sport. Likened to the military and other "total institutions" (Goffman, 1961) wherein violence is tightly regulated and policed by in-house authorities, the culture of professional ice hockey is based upon a patriarchal, masculinist system of self-regulation (Horrow, 1980). Spurred on by the McSorley trial, the rhetoric of NHL players and coaches emphasized how interventions of the criminal justice system into hockey should be interpreted as an encroachment onto their institutional terrain. Questioning the "bleeding heart," "tree-hugging," or "liberalist" mentality of the criminal justice system, proponents of free-flowing ice hockey violence lambasted the intervention:

- I think this is outrageous! McSorley should not get that kind of treatment. Violence is part of hockey, hence why it is called CONTACT-hockey. Suck it up and stop whining about how terrible it is to see the sport at this level. It has always been like this and always will be. (Kim, hockey fan, posted on www.cbc.ca).
- C'mon! It's hockey! How is this any worse than any of the other countless fights/assaults on the ice? It isn't. This sets a sorry precedent. (Zach, hockey fan, posted on www.tsn.ca).
- The law should not be getting involved in sporting events. The leagues should police their own as far as what happens in the context of their sport. In the McSorley case, he did strike another player with a stick. However, this happens many times during the game, just not normally to the head. Will the police prosecute every player when they commit a slash to another player or just slashes to the head? What about one to the arm that breaks a wrist? McSorley was wrong for what he did, but in the real world, after all the judicial posturing and attorneys' fees, he would receive probation. The NHL has already punished him worse, with lost wages while being suspended. (Kevin, hockey fan, posted on www.cnnsi.com).

The McSorley-Brashear incident not only questioned the viability of the league's self-policing mentality and operational program, it also problematized the NHL's practice of selling hockey violence as a staged spectacle.

Blaming the Victim

Through an examination of how norm transgressors respond to agents of social control when accused of deviance, Sykes and Matza (1957) uncovered the discursive resources employed by people to manage negative response to their actions.

Referring to these talk strategies as "techniques of neutralization," they demonstrated how individuals expound customary ways of describing acts as socially unthreatening and undeserving of reprisal. While recognizing how victims are verbally "denied" in the process of discursively managing deviance, a technique of neutralization they overlook is that of "blaming the victim." In the world of professional ice hockey, as evident in the McSorley case, blaming the victim is a rhetorical technique used by defenders of violence in the game, neutralizing potentially negative response to player violence in a twofold manner.

First, questions about victims' credibility are generated when their status as an "innocent" is challenged. Amidst media reports of McSorley's status as the third most penalized player in NHL history (3,381 career penalty minutes), arose an emphasis on Brashear's familiarity with dangerously violent play and corrective punishment.

Second, the content of Brashear's masculine character was scrutinized in public debates about the incident. Since he exhibited reluctance to grapple with McSorley for a second time during the February 21 contest and had taunted McSorley by "dusting off" his hands and taunting the Bruins team following the first fight in the game, his status as an NHL enforcer (the pinnacle of masculinity in the hyper-masculine hockey world) seemingly conflicted with his emergent actions. Don Cherry, former Boston Bruins coach and host of the immensely popular Canadian Broadcasting Corporation's *Hockey Night in Canada* intermission segment "Coach's Corner," reflected on this matter by saying on February 26, 2000, "I'll tell you why it happened... he [Brashear] ridiculed an old warrior, an old warrior... You should never ridicule and humiliate a warrior... You play with the bull, and you're gonna get the horns." Essentially, Brashear refused to conform to a strict axiom in the enforcer's lexicon of normative behavior—to grant a vanquished opponent an opportunity for redemption.

Blaming and discrediting players such as Donald Brashear for their own injuries reinforces a dangerous masculine assumption that there are no victims of sports crimes "on the field." If defenders of hockey violence are able to neutralize the stigmatization of the game by scapegoating victims of violence, there are scant grounds for claims-making as to the need for increased criminal prosecution of players committing excessively violent acts during games. When players are castigated or blamed for their injury—in light of their apparent unwillingness to accept the codes of dangerous masculinity, in every context—player violence can be reconciled as a problem to be managed within the league or among the players themselves. Justice Kitchen's affirmation of these subcultural doctrines underscores the legally mitigating power of dangerous masculine ideologies:

> The act was unpremeditated. It was impulsive, committed when McSorley was caught in a squeeze—attempting to follow an order to fight with Brashear when there was

> too little time to do so. The rules by which he was playing I have characterized as indefinite, making compliance by the players more difficult. It is clear that an act such as this slash certainly was not permitted on any view of the rules... In assessing the seriousness of the crime, it is my conclusion that it was less serious than many assaults, but with significant consequences that cannot be ignored... *Mr. McSorley impressed us with his dedication to the game, his diligence, and his bravery*... It is clear that he regrets the incident and is remorseful. *He has not been able to admit his guilt, but that is understandable.* (*R v. McSorley*, 2000, emphasis added).

Violence and Exciting Significance

Although underplayed in many sociohistorical analyses of criminal violence in sport, the degree to which "controlled violence on the field" establishes a social outlet for experiencing collective emotional arousal cannot be discounted in research on player violence and sports crimes. As Dunning (1999) and Maguire (1999) contend, forms of violent behavior in sports elicit a level of socially acceptable (yet personally pleasurable) excitement for individuals. Elias and Dunning (1986) suggest that sport provides a context within which a moderate degree of violence is both permissible and encouraged; allowing individuals to participate (either as competitors or spectators) in that which is strictly forbidden in other social spheres. In this way, sports contests provide an interactive scenario that facilitates a "controlled decontrolling" of emotional controls among participants and spectators (Elias and Dunning, 1986). One of sport's primary roles within complex figurations is, then, to de-routinize social life. While being structured by collective understandings (via popular discourses) that the outcome of the athletic battles are (usually) not as perilous to the participants as genuine war, the emergent contests contain a tightly regulated brand of dangerous masculine display (Atkinson, 2002; Maguire, 1999).

Marty McSorley's trial highlighted the fragility of the mimetic potential of ice hockey and yet simultaneously revealed how deeply embedded ideologies of dangerous masculinity are in our collective cultural habitués. Almost immediately following the initial incident, hockey players and league officials constructed the assault as unacceptable violence, but not as a "typically" violent hockey play. Even though McSorley's actions were justified as part of a heated and emotional competition, they were configured as unrepresentative of standard, honorable ice hockey violence; in this process, potentially criminal forms of player violence are masterfully accounted for at all levels.

Since players are believed to appreciate the risks involved in practicing dangerous masculinity, popular cultural sensibilities hold that players possess relatively no legal recourse when assaulted by an opponent. In many fan mindsets there seems to be an attitude framing player violence as noncriminal. Preference is given to handling sports crimes within the league and to punishing (but not rehabilitating) problem offenders through institutional channels created therein.

DISCUSSION

Although sociologists of sport continue to inspect how violence is experienced between players in the course of competition, a concomitant goal should be to uncover how discourses about aggressive play help produce and frame cultural understandings of player violence. In the McSorley-Brashear incident, discourses of dangerous masculinity helped produce the on-ice assault and led to it becoming interpretively configured by audiences. When studied in conjunction, ideologies of dangerous masculinity and their interactive consequences shed considerable light on the form and content of such sporting practices and experiences. In particular, by recognizing how deeply codes of dangerous masculinity are engrained in sports ideologies and performances within professional ice hockey, we begin to appreciate how issues of player violence, sports crime, and victimization were constructed in the McSorley-Brashear drama.

Prevailing discourses of dangerous masculinity in the McSorley-Brashear event underscore how those involved in professional ice hockey continue to resist intervention from the State in the process of controlling player violence. Rejecting the definition of severe acts of violence on the ice as criminal, and eschewing the presence of "victims" within the game (regardless of the serious doubts raised about explicit consent in ice hockey), defenders of ice hockey violence prefer to police their territory through league or player-based forms of control. In the end, the message is perhaps most clear to ice hockey players: the philosophy of dangerous masculinity is a privileging but brutalizing code of conduct within the world of professional sport.

REFERENCES

Anderson, E. (2000). *Trailblazing: America's first openly gay track coach.* Hollywood, CA: Alyson.

Atkinson, M. (2002). Fifty million viewers can't be wrong: Professional wresting, sports-entertainment, and mimesis. *Sociology of Sport Journal* 19 (1): 47–66.

Atkinson, M. and Williams, R. (2001). Its just part of the game: Toward a new typology of sports violence. Paper presented at the American Society of Criminology, Atlanta, Georgia.

Atkinson, M. and Young, K. (2008). *Sport, deviance and social control.* Champaign, IL: Human Kinetics.

Barnes, J. (1988). *Sport and the law in Canada.* Toronto, ON: Butterworth's.

Bridges, J. (1999). *Making violence part of the game.* Commack, NY: Kroshka Books.

Burstyn, V. (1999). *The rites of men: Manhood, politics, and the culture of Sport.* Toronto, ON: University of Toronto Press.

Cherry, D. (2009). *Hockey Night in Canada*, CBC (January 3).

Coakley, J. (2001). *Sport and society: Issues and controversies*, 7th edition. New York: McGraw-Hill.

Criminal Code of Canada. (2001). Toronto, ON: Edmond Montgomery.

Davis, L. (1997). *The swimsuit issue in sport: Hegemonic masculinity in* Sports Illustrated. Albany, NY: SUNY.

de Certeau, M. (1984). *The practice of everyday life.* Berkeley, CA: University of California Press.

Dunning, E. (1986). Sport as a male preserve: Notes on the social sources of masculine identity and its transformation. *Theory, Culture and Society* (3): 79–90.

Dunning, E. (1999). *Sport matters: Sociological studies of sport, violence, and civilization.* London: Routledge.

Elias, N. and Dunning, E. (1986). *Quest for excitement: Sport and leisure in the civilizing process.* New York: Basil Blackwell.

Farr, K. (1988). Dominance bonding through the good old boys sociability group. *Sex Roles* (18): 259–277.

Faulkner, R. (1973). On respect and retribution: Toward an ethnography of violence. *Sociological Symposium* (9): 17–36.

Goffman, E. (1961). *Asylums.* Chicago, IL: Aldine.

Goffman, E. (1974). *Frame analysis.* Cambridge, MA: Harvard University Press.

Gruneau, R. and Whitson, D. (1993). *Hockey night in Canada: Sport, identities, and cultural practices.* Toronto, ON: Garamond.

Gubrium, J. and Holstein, J. (1997). *The new language of qualitative method.* New York: Oxford University Press.

Horrow, R. (1980). *Sports violence: The interaction between private law making and the criminal law.* Arlington, VA: Carrollton.

Hughes, R. and Coakley, J. (1991). Positive deviance among athletes: The implications of overconformity to the sport ethic. *Sociology of Sport Journal* 8 (4): 307–325.

Kimbrell, A. (1995). *The masculine mystique: The politics of masculinity.* New York: Ballantine.

Kimmel, M. and Messner, M. (1992). *Men's lives.* New York: Macmillan.

Kupelian, V. (2000). Players outraged by slash. *The Detroit News* (February 23).

MacLean's magazine. (2000), Blood sport (March 6.) Toronto, ON: Rogers Media.

Maguire, J. (1993). Bodies, sport cultures and societies: A critical review of some theories in the sociology of the body. *International Review for the Sociology of Sport* (28): 33–50.

Maguire, J. (1999). *Global sport: Identities, societies, civilization.* Cambridge, UK: Polity.

McKay, J., Messner, M. and Sabo, D. (2000). *Men, masculinities, and sport.* Thousand Oaks, CA: Sage.

McMurtry, W. (1974). *Investigation and inquiry into violence in amateur hockey.* Report to the Honourable Rene Brunelle, Ontario, Minister of Community and Social Services. Toronto, ON: Ontario Government Bookstore.

Messner, M. (1990). When bodies are weapons: Masculinity and violence in sport. *International Review for the Sociology of Sport* 25 (3): 203–221.

Messner, M., Hunt, D. and Dunbar, M. (1999). *Boys to men: Sports media messages about masculinity.* Oakland, CA: Children Now.

Messner, M. and Sabo, D. (1994). *Sex, violence, and power in sports: Rethinking masculinity.* Champaign, IL: Human Kinetics.

Nixon, H. (1996). Explaining pain and injury attitudes and experiences in sport in terms of gender, race, and sports status factors. *Journal of Sport and Social Issues* 20 (1): 33–44.

Overman, S. (1997). *The influence of the Protestant ethic on sport and recreation.* Brookfield, VT: Ashgate.

Pascall, B. and White, S. (2000). *Violence in hockey.* Commissioned by the Honourable Ian Waddell, Minister Responsible for Sport, British Columbia.

Pronger, B. (1990). *The arena of masculinity: Sports, homosexuality, and the meaning of sex.* New York: St. Martin's.

Pronger, B. (1999). Fear and trembling: Homophobia in men's sport. In White, P. and Young, K. (Eds.), *Sport and gender in Canada*, 182–197. Toronto, ON: Oxford University Press.

R v. McSorley (2000). B.C.J. No. 0116 (B.C.P.C).

Reasons, C. (1992). *The criminal law and sports violence: Hockey crimes.* Unpublished paper, University of British Columbia, Vancouver, BC.

Smith, M. D. (1975). The legitimation of violence: Hockey players' perceptions of their groups' sanctions for assault. *Canadian Review of Sociology and Anthropology* (12): 72–80.

Smith, M. D. (1983). *Violence and sport.* Toronto, ON: Butterworth's.

Stebbins, R. (1996). *Tolerable differences: Living with deviance.* Toronto ON: McGraw-Hill Ryerson.

Sykes, G. and Matza, D. (1957). Techniques of neutralization: A theory of delinquency. *American Sociological Review* (22): 664–670.

Trujillo, N. (1990). Hegemonic masculinity on the mound: Media representations of Nolan Ryan and American sports culture. *Critical Studies in Mass Communication* (8): 280–308.

Vaz, E. (1982). *The professionalization of young hockey players.* Lincoln, NB: University of Nebraska Press.

Watson, R. and McLellan, J. (1986). Smitting to spitting: 80 Years of ice hockey in Canadian courts. *Canadian Journal of History of Sport* 17 (2): 10–27.

Weinstein, M., Smith, M. and Wiesenthal, D. (1995). Masculinity and hockey violence. *Sex Roles* (33): 831–847.

White, D. (1986). Sports violence as criminal assault: Development of the doctrine by Canadian criminal courts. *Duke Law Journal*: 1030–1034.

White, P. and Young, K. (1997). Masculinity, sport and the injury process: A review of Canadian and international Evidence. *Avante* 3 (2): 1–30.

White, P. and Young, K. (1999). Is sport injury gendered? In White, P. and Young, K. (Eds.), *Sport and gender in Canada*, 69–84. Don Mills, ON: Oxford University Press.

Young, K. (1991). Violence in the workplace of professional sport from victimological and cultural studies perspectives. *International Review for the Sociology of Sport* 26 (1): 3–14.

Young, K. (1993). Violence, risk, and liability in male sports culture. *Sociology of Sport Journal* (10): 373–396.

Young, K. (2000). Sport and violence. In Coakley, J. J. and Dunning, E. (Eds.), *Handbook of sport and society*, 382–408. Thousand Oaks, CA: Sage.

Young, K. (2002). From sports violence to sports crime: Aspects of violence, law, and gender in the sports process. In Gatz, M., Messner, M. A., and Ball-Rokeach, S. (Eds.), *Paradoxes of youth and sport*, 207–222. Albany, NY: SUNY.

Young, K. and Reasons, C. (1989). Victimology and organizational crime: Workplace violence and the professional athlete. *Sociological Viewpoints* 5 (1): 24–34.

Young, K. and Wamsley, K. (1996). State complicity in sports assault and the gender order in 20th century Canada: Preliminary Observations. *Avante* 2 (2): 51–69.

CHAPTER TWO

Representations of Sport Violence and Spousal Abuse*

MARGERY HOLMAN, VICTORIA PARASCHAK, PATRICIA WEIR, AND RICHARD MORIARTY

"One-half of all Canadian women have experienced at least one incident of violence since the age of 16," while "one-quarter of all women have experienced violence at the hands of a current or past marital partner" and "one-in-six currently married women reported violence by their spouses" (Canadian Centre for Justice Statistics, 1993: 9). In the United States, an estimated two million women were victims of domestic violence in 1995 (Cerulo, 1998; Douglas, 1995).

The majority of individuals are not violent people, even if it is common practice that individuals will attempt to dominate others to augment their own sense of power and self-esteem. There may be a minority of individuals who resort to violence for personal control, resolutions of conflict, emotional expression, or a number of other motives. When violence is acted out towards partners and children, it can have a devastating effect on the functioning of the family unit. This study examines the relationship between media representations of sport violence and spousal abuse, focusing on the following two issues: (1) The question of whether televised professional hockey playoff games may serve as a trigger for spousal violence and (2) an assessment (by abusers, by targets of abuse, and by children whose mothers experienced abuse) of the awareness of the influence sport has in contributing to violent relationships.

Finding that statistics on domestic abuse in Canada and the United States are similar, we note that the Office of Justice Programs 2000 Annual Report, citing the National Violence Against Women Survey (NVAWS) results, mentions that "nearly 25 percent of surveyed women... said they have been raped and/or physically assaulted by a current or former spouse or partner at some time in their lives" (p. 36). Recent reports of such incidents involving professional athletes give cause for concern. Wilstein (2002: 1) noted that "every week, on average, two athletes are arrested on charges they beat up their wives or girlfriends... This month alone: Allen Iverson of the Philadelphia 76ers; race car driver Al Unser Jr.; Glenn Robinson of the Milwaukee Bucks; Scott Erickson of the Baltimore Orioles; Chris Terry of the Carolina Panthers." In Canada, there were stories about a former boxer who died in prison while serving a life sentence for the murder of his ex-girlfriend, and about many hockey-related incidents (Pappas, McKenry, and Catlett, 2004).

The questions that arise from such cases are whether or not sport, along with the mindset that begets it, is a contributing factor in spousal abuse and whether or not media depictions of competition violence that perhaps institutionalize and normalize abusive actions contribute to the perpetration of spousal violence. Our study examines the latter.

Domestic or, more recently, spousal violence research has searched extensively for causes of violence within intimate relationships. Yet, little research has been conducted on the role that *sport* may play in the creation and reinforcement of spousal/partner abuse. Thus, this research was designed to understand how viewing televised sport violence can affect violence in the home. It examines two variables—sport and the media, and the role that they may have in creating a violent society as manifested through spousal violence. Secondary data was first examined to determine the rate of spousal violence complaints filed with police departments on National Hockey League (NHL) playoff game days as compared to non-playoff game days. A second component of the study, through interviews with abusers, targets of abuse, and children within abusive relationships, examined perceptions of the relevance of media portrayals of sport violence.

Sport, we argue, is a variable worthy of study—particularly unnecessary, gratuitous violence in sport, as distinguished from the inherent aggression associated with the execution of the skills and strategies of the game. As a system of competition for the acquisition of a common goal, sport is a setting that increases the potential for aggressive behavior. In sports such as hockey, where physical contact is a natural part of the game, unnecessary violence has become a routine practice, tolerated and even valued by the sport institution, the media, and society at large.

Yet, we realize, sport is only a small piece of a large puzzle.

SPOUSAL/DOMESTIC VIOLENCE

Sport violence may serve as a risk marker of non-sport violent behavior in those individuals prone to such behavior. Relevant research and related theory with respect to spousal violence, media violence, and sport violence has revealed some pertinent factors. Shields, McCall, and Hanneke (1988: 92) suggest that "values and attitudes regarding the use of interpersonal violence are probably learned and supported by the social groups in which these men participate." Others believe that structural factors such as patriarchy, persistent sexual stereotypes, roles emphasizing gender difference, privacy of relationships, and female dependency on males can create environments supportive of or, at best, indifferent to abuse of women (Benedict, 1997; Dobash and Dobash, 1979, 1992; Messerschmidt, 1986; Messner and Solomon, 1994; Richards, Letchford, and Stratton, 2008; Sanday, 1990; Smith, 1983, 1990; Steinmetz, 1977; Yllo, 1988; Yllo and Bograd, 1988).

Sanday's (1990) studies on fraternities and Fagan's (1989) on domestic violence both agree with White et al. (1992: 158) that "participation in exclusively male subcultures and male-oriented recreational activities correlates with violence toward wives." Gelles and Cornell (1990) propose exchange/social control theory as a cause for domestic violence, based upon three premises: First, a cost-benefit balance whereby violence is more likely to be used when the abuser expects the cost of being violent to be less than the rewards; second, the absence of social controls that serve to discourage violence minimizes the cost incurred by the abuser for violent behavior, and; third, social structures combined with family structures contribute to a reduction in the cost of violence and may increase the reward for the abuser. It is this third premise that supports feminist arguments whereby inequality, patriarchy, and traditional gender roles create a structural imbalance ensuring that rewards outweigh costs.

SPORT, MEDIA, AND DOMESTIC VIOLENCE

A number of studies have looked at the effect of media violence on aggressive behavior (Bryant and Thompson, 2008; Freedman, 2002; Russell, 2008). Cannon (1995: 19) noted that, of 85 major research studies conducted, "the only one that failed to find a causal relationship between television violence and actual violence was paid for by NBC. When the study was subsequently reviewed by three independent social scientists, all three concluded that it actually did demonstrate a causal relationship."

Some researchers have examined relationships between media portrayals of violent sport and social violence. As early as 1971, Goldstein and Arms studied the effects of watching a football game on the tendency of male spectators to aggress, finding that hostility did increase after watching a football game, irrespective of the win-loss outcome of the game. White (1989) linked media of the National Football League (NFL) to incidences of homicides; later, White, Katz, and Scarborough (1992: 167) looked at professional football games and the hospital emergency room admissions of women, suggesting that "the identification with an organization that is successful or dominates through violent behavior may stimulate violence toward women in some men." A Canadian study (Moriarty, McCabe, and Prpich, 1979) took an extended approach in analyzing the effect of televised violence on aggression in the sport culture by examining both pro-social and anti-social influences; their findings suggested the presence of such influences.

Little study has been conducted linking the three variables of sport, the media, and domestic violence. Goldstein (1998: 20) addresses the allure of violent sport as a form of entertainment: "The alleged catharsis achieved by watching violent sports does not occur. The implications are rather the opposite; aggression can be learned and watching sports is one way to learn it."

THEORIES OF VIOLENCE

Theories designed to provide some understanding of male violence directed towards females have focused on the issues of social approval of violence (Kurz, 1989), economic dependency, masculinity and patriarchy (Bowker, 1998; Dobash and Dobash, 1979; Jacobson and Gottman, 1998; Lindsey, 1994) and social learning theory (Bandura, 1973). McMurtry (1974: 17) conducted an investigation into violence in amateur hockey, concurring with social scientists that "there are two main determinants for most behaviour, violent or otherwise":

1. The model or examples available, particularly if these are successful;
2. The conduct encouraged or rewarded in the immediate environment.

Two of the causes for violence in amateur hockey have particular relevance for our study: "The influence of professional hockey (particularly the NHL) with its emphasis on winning and use of violence as a tactical instrument to achieve that goal" and "a rule structure (in professional and amateur hockey) which not only tolerates violence but encourages its use by rewarding those who excel at physical intimidation" (Ibid.).

Feminist analyses suggest that the socio-structural context of sport is reflective of society's social power structure, where the male-female relationship is central to the allocation of power; scholars emphasize the need to move responsibility for wife abuse from the individual to the public domain. Components of male sport are hypermasculinity and a homophobic culture where heterosexuality and the objectification of women are traditional (Messner, 1992a; Kidd, 1987; Sabo and Panepinto, 1990). These characteristics are reflective of the patriarchal structure that, Yllo (1988) claims, encourages abuse.

By looking at social institutions and their responsibility for domestic violence, we see that the family is only one of many places where male dominance is produced and reproduced. Sport is another. When power and control form the basis upon which relationships function, the sport environment becomes a medium in which aggression is condoned and nurtured, masculinity is valued and encouraged, control and dominance are rewarded, and winning or being the best are symbols of self-worth.

METHODS, RESULTS AND DISCUSSION

The Association of NHL Playoff Games and Police Records on Domestic Violence

The first phase of this study used a quantitative approach to identify relationships between viewing televised sport and spousal violence. The rate of spousal violence in Canada as reported in police records was examined over a five-year period in cities that are home to an NHL team compared to others that are not. Analysis of the frequency of reported spousal violence within each city was completed to determine whether this increased, decreased, or remained constant on those days when NHL playoff games were televised compared to those days when there were no televised playoff games. A multivariate analysis of the violence data was performed using the following variables: (1) NHL city and non-NHL city; (2) Playoff date and non-playoff date; (3) Day of the week; (4) Home and away sites; (5) Win and loss results; (6) Alcohol and non-alcohol use of abuser; and (7) Record of abuser as a repeat- or non-repeat offender.

There were two findings of significance. Table 1 shows the results of frequency as a function of non-playoff date versus control date. City A showed a significant increase in the frequency of reported complaints of spousal violence for playoff as compared to non-playoff dates. No significant difference was found in the frequency rates when home/away site and win/loss result variables were included.

City B showed a significant increase in the frequency of reported complaints of spousal violence for non-playoff dates compared to playoff dates. Sufficient data was available to analyze only the effects of win-loss, and no significance was found related to win-loss outcomes. The remaining cities showed no significant differences. Frequency of spousal violence complaints was not significantly related to the viewing of games, home-away sites, or win-loss results.

Overall, two (NHL) of the 12 cities revealed a significant difference in the rate of reporting spousal violence as a function of non-playoff versus playoff date. Table 2 demonstrates, with a sample city, that there was no significance as a function of win-loss record. The pattern was either the same for other cities or there was insufficient data for meaningful comparisons, suggesting that outcomes may have no effect on assaultive behaviors towards female partners.

The data on alcohol also had limited value, since there was no consistency in its reportage in the police records of domestic violence complaints. Recognizing this limitation, Table 3 shows results indicating that alcohol cannot be considered a significant factor in contributing to increases in spousal violence—thus supporting caregivers who claim that alcohol is not a contributory factor to violent tendencies but an excuse used for explaining violence (Jacobson and Gottman, 1998). There is insufficient support for the hypothesis that media portrayals of

Table 1: Frequency as a function of non-playoff date versus playoff date

City	Non-playoff	Playoff	# of games
A	11.13	16.20*	12
B	38.11*	30.82	51
C	17.67	17.08	12

Table 2: Sample result of spousal violence as a function of win-loss

City B	Home	Away
Win	29.07	33.57
Loss	27.64	28.29

Table 3: Sample result of spousal violence as a function of alcohol

City B	Non-playoff	Playoff
Alcohol Absence	38.11	30.82
Alcohol Related	4.44	5.91

NHL hockey contribute to increases in complaints of spousal violence, even if there is sufficient justification for the further study of this relationship.

Perceptions on the Association between Viewing Sport Violence and Spousal Abuse

Phase II of the study examined the relationship between exposure to televised hockey, as well as sport in general, and violence on the part of the viewer from a sociological perspective. The interview was an essential research tool for the thorough investigation of the day-to-day meanings of sport and the interpretation of aggressive behaviors within the context of their lives. With the cooperation of staff at Hiatus House, a shelter for battered women and their children, where women are given an alternative to living with spousal abuse and where programs exist for male batterers, we performed in-depth interviews with 10 female and 10 male victims of abuse in intimate relationships and spoke to 20 children in the shelter.

THE WOMEN'S VOICE

The majority of the women interviewees indicated that sport was important to them, one saying, "It gives us self-confidence, it makes us stronger," another bemoaning that it is not good for boys because "it makes them more aggressive and more verbal." Another believed that it is "important for a girl to know that just because she's a girl there's not things she can't do... a girl will get low self-esteem if she is always told there are things she can't do. Tell her she can do it too and it will build up her self-esteem and maybe one day she won't be in a shelter... It's a control thing, it starts when you're young."

When asked if they considered any of the sports that they watched to be too violent, five women identified hockey, three wrestling and football, and two boxing/kickboxing. "Boxing, kick boxing... even with hockey. I have to explain to my kids that when the players get a penalty that is the same as a time out in our house. So I tell them look at that bad player—he had to have a time out because he was fighting and that's bad," one added. This mother's strategy is supported by Josephson's (1987) research, concluding that children who cannot place televised violence in its proper context are susceptible to the negative messages that it may seem to impart.

From these women, coming from violent environments, reflections on the role of televised sport violence provides us with some insights. Two of them stated outright that they felt watching hockey and other sport violence on television affected their partner's violence towards them, one adding, "Yah, I guess—it's more complicated than that...If his team doesn't win or you are interrupting him or the kids are making noise or you haven't gotten their beer, yah." Another woman shared, "Not just the violence—the sport. When they've watched a fight—one little thing happens and they're all pumped up—they want to act it out or they have an urge to act it out."

PERSPECTIVES OF MALE ABUSERS

Our male interviewees generally considered themselves to be athletic—most being hockey players, followed by baseball and football. Much research has examined the role of sport in the construction of masculinity (Gruneau and Whitson, 1993; Kidd, 1990; Messner, 1992b; Messner and Sabo, 1994; Sabo and Panepinto, 1990). Theory has evolved that contributes to an understanding of how society values those sports that differentiate males from females through the employment of power, strength, and aggression as tools to dominate an opponent. Males learn to identify with these sports, such as ice hockey and football, through their own experiences with the sport and through the vicarious pleasure of viewing others at play and media portrayals of the sports and their elite participants. For the men in this study, the role that their sport experience has had in their lives, relative to their use of violence in a domestic relationship, may provide one explanation for their decision to abuse.

One respondent indicated that, for boys, sport teaches teamwork and self-discipline—confirming research by Birrell (1988) and Coakley (2007), who argue that girls and boys are socialized differently. This attitude was reinforced more candidly by another's response that sport is "good for boys' manhood," while for girls sports such as softball and volleyball are good but "not hockey or football—too rough." "Girls are more feminine than boys—I worry about them getting physically hurt," another added. Sport, we see, is an institution legitimizing a hierarchy mirrored in the home, reflecting higher degrees of structural inequality as a contributing factor to spousal abuse.

Three men responded that televised sport is too violent to watch—notably, hockey, football, basketball, and boxing. One stated that the sport violence is "sending out messages like it is okay to hit someone." When this happens, sport permits and even encourages the use of physical violence to control the world. A common behavior that occurs when these men watch NHL games on television is yelling at the action. One of them acknowledged that he believed watching sport, particularly sport with a lot of physical contact, had triggered his violent behavior: "[It] brings out excitement [resulting in verbal abuse] due to bad refereeing calls—or bad plays." But, most of the others did not believe that viewing sport with a lot of physical contact had ever triggered their violent behaviors. This provides some preliminary information.

THE CHILDREN SPEAK OUT

The children interviewed for this study generally liked sport. Some responded enthusiastically, others with some reservations. Most associated with sport sufficiently enough to have an athlete with whom they identified, although no one named a female sport model. Sport is promoted as a healthy means of relieving the stress in their lives.

Although they did not report watching a lot of sport on television, when they did, hockey was a popular selection. One believed that "seeing some guy thrown half across the rink is really something. I know wrestling is fake but when they go flying across the rink and then get up that's really amazing..." The concern for children in the cycle of family violence is critical, providing an opportunity to use sport to replicate and reinforce the violence that they see at home as a means of control, self-gratification, and conflict resolution. Also, they have an opportunity to use sport as an environment where fair play, cooperation, and sociability can contribute to pro-social behaviors both within and outside of the sport environment.

CONCLUSIONS

This research has looked at sport and the media, and the interactions of these two powerful social institutions, in an attempt to further understand violent male behavior in the family setting. As such, it is the first to look at the relationship of media presentation of sport violence within the context of its impact on the family unit.

According to the statistical results of this study, professional hockey playoff games do not increase the frequency of spousal violence; however, the results were not conclusive. Two NHL cities showed a significant difference in the rate of spousal abuse reports—one an increase in filed reports, the other a decrease. These findings suggest that there is sufficient evidence to warrant further study of this issue.

The interview data from 40 interviews were analyzed to determine the research participants' experiences with sport and with media presentations of sport, their general attitudes toward violence in sport, whether or not they were violent as athletes or while viewing sport on television, and whether or not they possess traditional views on women in sport. Albeit based on a small sample, this study may be the only attempt made to date to gather information from batterers, their victims, and the children of battered women on how media presentations of sport are perceived to have shaped their lives. There is some evidence that sport is one method by which males are socialized, through both their participation and their identification with televised professional sport, to use violence as a form of controlling their own environment. Again, further study may provide a better understanding of this relationship.

Establishing the magnitude of the social problem of domestic abuse and its relationship to sport and the sport media was restricted by a number of factors. There was a lack of common definition of spousal violence for its reporting throughout the various correctional services, as well as an absence of accurate or standardized formats for registering and maintaining records of spousal violence complaints. For a combination of reasons, there is the ever-present risk of underreporting incidents of partner abuse, likely to occur because of the history of the legal system, the ultimate fear of reprisal, victim blaming, and victim self-blame. There are currently national attempts to standardize the reporting instruments and to centralize statistics for tracking patterns of spousal abuse.

The findings of this study provide some evidence for the cultural propagation of violence within society. Further study will provide greater enlightenment. A richer understanding of the nature of various factors can contribute to the development of policy and intervention programs. Understanding that social dominance, family dominance, and sport dominance do not function independently but intersect to reinforce each other provides a better insight into how sport functions as a contributor of risk factors in spousal violence.

RECOMMENDATIONS AND FUTURE RESEARCH

There is no one cause of spousal abuse in society and, correspondingly, no single solution. This research has attempted to examine the extent of the problem relative to sport and the media while exploring some of the social and structural causes of spousal violence. The following 14 recommendations have emerged from our research:

1. *Legal Records*: To fully understand the problem of spousal violence and its multiple sources, there is a need for correctional services and the entire legal system to respond with some degree of consistency. Definitions, documentation, responses, and records should be standardized and centralized to allow analyses of related issues and identification of risk factors.

2. *Statistics*: There is a need to determine how information on domestic violence complaints is processed, followed by recommendations to standardize.
3. *Influence of sport*: While a majority may not respond to violence in the sport media with violence, some may, either as direct or indirect effects. One of the first steps that sport organizations must take is to confront their denial of responsibility; since sport exists as a powerful social institution, the development of strategies, including internal legislation, to address the prevention of abuse may provide a positive influence.
4. *Long-term study*: To identify meaningful risk markers associated with sport, and pending the availability of relevant data, as per recommendation #1, it is proposed that a longitudinal study be conducted, in cooperation with the justice system, to determine the effect of televised sport violence on spousal abuse.
5. *Implications for research and policy*: Research on spousal violence in the past has failed to incorporate the potential influence of sport, as an institution, in (re)constructing power imbalances in society and acknowledging its role in teaching violent behavior towards women. The economic, political, social, and personal power that sport bestows on its advocates can result in resistance to change.
6. *Sport as a solution*: There is potential for sport to be developed as a tool for social intervention and rehabilitation in the lives of abusers; consider the Harassment and Abuse in Sport Initiative, a collective of National Sport Organizations (NSOs) and National Multi-sport/service Organizations (MSOs), and Canadian Hockey Association's (CHA) Speak Out! Program.
7. *Social cost-benefit*: There must be an increase in the cost and a reduction of the reward benefit attached to violent displays of behavior, both within sport and outside of sport.
8. *Structural change*: Many believe that the structures of economically driven sport and media as well as how they promote sport are unchangeable, but we must aim for gender inclusive and social equality.
9. *Past research*: Response to past research findings and their recommendations has demonstrated resistance to change; however, a review of the recommendations contained in these studies would be worthwhile.
10. *Resolution within sport*: Sport organizations who do not perceive that their structure contributes to spousal abuse in any way can, if they do not see themselves as part of the problem, become part of the solution by incorporating some of these recommendations into their organizational goals and behaviors.

11. *Sport programming*: Sport programs should be developed to provide opportunities for women, particularly those at risk, where they can develop a sense of empowerment.
12. *Media*: Media should develop strategies to target different markets—ones that appreciate skill and strategy while denouncing violence.
13. *Parental education*: Strategies should be explored for the education of parents about the potential effects of viewing sport violence on television and the important role that they can play in mediating these influences.
14. *Implementation*: It is proposed that a panel be struck to discuss the findings of this research to offer strategies for implementation.

In addition, education for prevention is critical and recommended. Replacing violence and aggression with technical skills and strategic advantages emphasizes the positive elements of sport. This study was exploratory in nature, generating a number of unanswered questions. Much more study is needed to understand the role that sport may have in spousal violence.

NOTE

*Research for this study was funded by the Department of Canadian Heritage—Canadian Identity Sector, as part of its Family Violence Initiative, but the views expressed here are those of the authors. Sincere appreciation is extended to all of those who assisted with the completion of this research, particularly the research participants.

REFERENCES

Bandura, A. (1973). *Aggression: A social learning analysis*. Stanford, CA: Stanford University Press.

Benedict, J. (1997). *Public heroes, private felons: Athletes and crimes against women*. Boston, MA: Northeastern University Press.

Birrell, S. (1988). Discourses on the gender/sport relationship: From women in sport to gender relations in sport. *Exercise and Sport Science Reviews* (16): 459–502.

Bowker, L. H. (Ed.). (1998). *Masculinities and violence: Research on men and masculinities*. Thousand Oaks, CA: Sage.

Bryant, J. and Thompson, S. (2008). *Fundamentals of media effects*. New York: McGraw-Hill.

Cannon, C. (1995). Media violence increases violence in society. In Wekesser, C. (Ed.), *Violence in the media*, 17–24. San Diego, CA: Greenhaven Press.

Cerulo, K. A. (1998). *Deciphering violence: The cognitive structure of right and wrong*. New York: Routledge.

Coakley, J. J. (2007). *Sport in society: Issues and controversies*, 9th edition. New York: McGraw-Hill.

Dobash, R. E. and Dobash, R. P. (1979). *Violence against wives: A case against the patriarchy*. New York: Free Press.

Dobash, R. E. and Dobash, R. P. (1992). *Women, violence and social change*. New York: Routledge.

Douglas, S. (1995). Violence in TV news promotes violence against women. In Wekesser, C. (Ed.). *Violence in the media*, 28–30. San Diego, CA: Greenhaven.

Fagan, J. (1989). Cessation of family violence: Deterrence + dissuasion. In Ohlin, L. and Tonry, M. (Eds.), *Family violence*, 377–426. Chicago: University of Chicago Press.

Freedman, J. L. (2002). *Media violence and its effect on aggression: Assessing the scientific evidence*. Toronto: University of Toronto Press.

Gelles, R. J. and Cornell, C. P. (1990). *Intimate violence in families*. Newbury Park, CA: Sage Publications.

Goldstein, J. (Ed.) (1998). *Why we watch: The attractions of violent entertainment*. New York: Oxford University Press.

Goldstein, J. H. and Arms, R. L. (1971). Effects of observing athletic contests on hostility. *Sociometry*, 34 (1): 83–90.

Gruneau, R. and Whitson, D. (1993). *Hockey night in Canada: Sport, identities and cultural politics*. Toronto: Garamond.

Jacobson, N. and Gottman, J. (1998). *When men batter women: New insights into ending abusive relationships*. New York: Simon & Schuster.

Josephson, W. L. (1987). Television violence and children's aggression: Testing the priming, social script, and disinhibition predictions. *Journal of Personality and Social Psychology* (53): 882–890.

Kidd, B. (1987). Sports and masculinity. In Kaufman, M. (Ed.), *Beyond patriarchy: Essays by men on pleasure, power and change*, 250–265. Toronto: Oxford.

Kidd, B. (1990). The men's cultural centre: Sports and the dynamic of women's oppression/men's repression. In Messner, M. A. and Sabo, D. F. (Eds.), *Sport, men and the gender order: Critical feminist perspectives*, 31–43. Champaign, IL: Human Kinetics.

Kurz, D. (1989). Social science perspectives on wife abuse: Current debates and future directions. *Gender & Society*, 3 (4): 489–505.

Lindsey, L. (1994). *Gender roles: A sociological perspective*. Englewood Cliffs, NJ: Prentice Hall.

McMurtry, W. R. (1974). *Investigation and inquiry into violence in amateur hockey*. Ottawa: Ministry of Community and Social Services.

Messerschmidt, J. W. (1986). *Capitalism, patriarchy, and crime: Toward a socialist feminist criminology*. Totowa, NJ: Rowman and Littlefield.

Messner, M. A. (1992a). Boyhood, organized sports, and the construction of masculinity. In Kimmel, M. S. and Messner, M. A. (Eds.), *Men's Lives*, 161–176. New York: Macmillan.

Messner, M. A. (1992b). *Power at play: Sports and the problem of masculinity*. Boston, MA: Beacon.

Messner, M. A. and Sabo, D. F. (1994). *Sex, violence and power in sports: Rethinking masculinity*. Freedom, CA: Crossing.

Messner, M. A. and Solomon, W. (1994). Sin and redemption: The Sugar Ray Leonard wife-abuse story. In Messner, M. A. and Sabo, D. F. (Eds.), *Sex, violence and power in sports: Rethinking masculinity*, 53–65. Freedom, CA: Crossing.

Moriarty, D., McCabe, A. and Prpich, M. (1979). SIR/CAR studies of television and youth sports. International Journal of Sport Psychology, 10 (2): 122–129.

Office of Justice Programs 2000 Annual Report: Combating family violence (2000). Available: (www.ojp.gov/annualreport).

Pappas, N. T., McKenry, P. C., and Catlett, B. S. (2004). Athlete aggression on the rink and off the ice. *Men and Masculinities* (6/3): 291–312.

Richards, L., Letchford, S. and Stratton, S. (2008). *Policing domestic violence*. New York: Oxford University Press.

Russell, G. W. (2008). *Aggression in the sports world: A social psychological perspective*. New York: Oxford University Press.

Sabo, D. and Panepinto, J. (1990). Football ritual and the social reproduction of masculinity. In Messner, M. A. and Sabo, D. F. (Eds.), *Sex, violence and power in sports*, 202–213. Freedom, CA: Crossing.

Sanday, P. R. (1990). *Fraternity gang rape*. New York: New York University Press.

Shields, N. M., McCall, G. J., and Hanneke, C. R. (1988). Patterns of family and non-family violence: Violent husbands and violent men. *Violence and Victims*, 3 (2): 83–97.

Smith, M. D. (1983). *Violence and sport*. Toronto: Butterworths.

Steinmetz, S. K. (1977). *The cycle of violence. Assertive, aggressive and abusive family interaction*. New York: Praeger.

White, G. F. (1989). Media and violence: The case of professional football championship games. *Aggressive Behavior*, (15): 423–433.

White, G. F., Katz, J., and Scarborough, K. E. (1992). The impact of professional football games upon violent assaults on women. *Violence and Victims*, 7 (2): 157–171.

Wilstein, S. (2002, July 30). *Batterers don't belong in sports*. Available: (www.findlaw.com).

Yllo, K. (1988). Political and methodological debates in wife abuse research. In Yllo, K. and Bograd, M. (Eds.). *Feminist perspectives on wife abuse*, 28–51. Newbury Park, CA: Sage.

Yllo, D. and Bograd, M. (Eds.). (1988). *Feminist perspectives on wife abuse*. Newbury Park, CA: Sage.

CHAPTER THREE

Playing BEYOND THE Glass: How Parents Support Violence IN Minor Hockey

MICHAEL A. ROBIDOUX AND JOCHEN G. BOCKSNICK

The game of hockey in Canada has had a long and troubling history of violence. By the turn of the twentieth century, concern was being expressed about the excessive violence surrounding the game where there was "overt brutality evident in open fighting on the ice and in mob scenes involving fans and players" (Gruneau and Whitson, 1993: 75). Significant here is that violent acts—which have on occasion led to fatalities (Gruneau and Whitson, 1993: 75–76)—are accredited to both participants and spectators and continue to haunt the game in its present form. What is surprising is that the majority of accounts of spectator violence in Canadian arenas lately are being reported at the local minor hockey league level, not the elite/professional hockey level.

Over the past ten years, there have been several incidents of parental/spectator violence at minor hockey games that have received national media attention. In February 2001, officials during a PeeWee (ages 12–13) hockey game were forced to eject all spectators from the arena because of an endless barrage of verbal abuse and physical objects directed toward the referees. The incidents have become so frequent that, Deacon, McClelland, and Smart (2001: 20) comment,

> it even has its own name—rink rage. In recent months, some B.C. [British Columbia] referees boycotted youth games to protest abuse from fans. A coach in Quebec was hospitalized after being attacked between periods by the father of one of his players. In Ontario, a coach was charged with threatening to kill a teenage referee. Last week

> in Winnipeg, a police constable—already suspended from the force for a previous assault conviction—was arrested and charged with threatening another parent during his nine-year-old son's hockey game.

Regional Hockey Associations have responded by putting into place a variety of programs that are essentially "zero-tolerance" policies to eliminate such negative behaviors. However the frequency and intensity of abusive and violent behaviors suggest that initial steps are not bringing about desired change.

For this reason, we conducted a year-long research project where we observed and interpreted interacting behaviors of parents/spectators at PeeWee hockey games in Southern Alberta, Canada, documenting how they responded to playing situations and analyzing how their behaviors impacted fellow spectators/parents and the games themselves. From this study it was evident that extreme acts of violence are somewhat rare in youth hockey; yet, other more insidious forms of aggression and violence pervade minor hockey contexts, bringing about serious consequences to the actors. We discuss what was documented over the course of the 2001–2002 hockey season in hopes of providing insight into the role parents/spectators play at youth hockey games. It is also our intention to illustrate why the various policies that have been implemented to correct problematic behaviors at youth hockey games will continue to be ineffective until behaviors currently deemed acceptable and appropriate in minor hockey arenas are properly recognized as the detrimental and damaging behaviors they are.

BACKGROUND

Incidences of misbehavior in sport arenas are not unfamiliar to the general public (Nack and Munson, 2000). With a consistent, if not necessarily frequent regularity, the media inform society of the behavioral misconduct of sport fans, such as group rioting in soccer hooliganism (Cox, 2002). Violent outbreaks of this magnitude are less common in North America. The cases that make it to the news are generally those of great severity, as was the case in the fatal assault on Michael Costin by Thomas Junta, when one hockey father killed another (Nack and Munson, 2000). It is necessary to exercise caution in assuming that these are the only behavioral misconducts that occur. On the contrary, it can be speculated that there are numerous acts of aggression and violence that go unreported by the public press and broadcast media. Whatever the case, these incidences show that sport may not always be as pristine as hoped (Donnelly, 2000).

Based on these considerations, the initial question for this investigation was to document the occurrences of behavioral misconduct in youth sporting contexts. More specifically, our objective was to observe minor hockey and hopefully gain an understanding of (1) the potential interdependence among plausible contributors to aggressive and violent actions and (2) the type of actions.

To understand the contextual setting of hockey (Ingham and Dewar, 1999), it is necessary to picture the various contributors involved in the arena. First, there are players of two teams competing against each other to win the game. In doing so, driven by heightened levels of arousal and the desire to outperform the opposing player or team, rules may be broken. This in itself may be the consequence or the cause of an aggressive act. Second, there are officials whose role is to control and enforce the rules of the game by which both sides must abide. Since officiating is often subject to interpretation, it is no surprise that rulings are often disputed by players. However, it is not only the players that may be affected by "disputed" calls but also the coaching staff and their supporters (Trudel, Côté, and Bernard, 1996). Thus, the third and fourth viable causes of behavioral misconduct can be assigned to coaches and the crowd respectively. Based on previous records, it can be argued that there is a reciprocal relationship among the game crowd and all of the previously mentioned groups, team members, coaching staffs, and game officials (Slepicka, 1995).

Our primary focus here is on the fourth and final contributor to the potentially volatile environment at minor hockey arenas: the crowd. In attempting to understand the crowd and its actions, it is favorable to distinguish between spectators and fans (Wann, Merrill, Russell, and Pease, 2001; Zillman and Paulus, 1993). Spectators are driven to watch and observe a sport because of their appreciation for a sport and the associated athleticism. Spectators show appreciation for the parties involved in the pursuit of the sport, appreciating and acknowledging athletic competencies. They see the event or performance in a relatively objective and unbiased manner; yet, "to understand spectator reactions it is necessary to realize that emotions have a multidimensional base" (Slepicka, 1995), and this is where spectators differ from sports fans.

Fans have an overtly biased approach to the event (Wann et al., 2001). The interest in the performance (i.e., winning a contest) of a specific team/athlete supersedes other interpretations of the game. It can be said that fans interpret the progress and outcome of a game in the interest of the team they support (Zillman and Paulus, 1993). Researchers have argued that fans distinguish themselves from spectators through their identification with a team. It is, however, also noteworthy that fan behaviors can range from "lowly to highly identified behaviors" (Wann et al., 2001). Importantly, individuals can move among these categories and thus display highly identified fan behaviors at one time while spectator behaviors at another time.

Overt behaviors can be used to distinguish between lowly and highly identified fans and spectators. Highly identified fans are completely immersed in the contest (Wann, Carlson, and Schrader, 1999; Wann et al., 2001). They provide vocal support of their team, including positive and encouraging comments for their own team, while discouraging and distracting comments and/or actions for the opposing team. Highly identified fans are likely to challenge calls of officials because they consider it to be in the best interest of their own team and not necessarily within the rules of the game (Zillman and Paulus, 1993).

Lowly identified fans exhibit a lesser degree of vocal and physical support (Wann et al., 2001). For example, this group may clap and use noisemakers less frequently. Although in support of a specific team, lowly identified individuals may not pay their fullest attention to the game and may engage in conversation with other individuals.

It becomes clear that distinguishing lowly from highly identified fans or spectators can be difficult because of the fluidity and magnitude of the identification process. Generally, the more fans identify with a team the greater the emphasis on that team's success (i.e., winning) and a concurrent dislike for the team's rival (Zillman and Paulus, 1993). However, belonging to any of these groups cannot be considered an irrevocable classification, as the dynamics of an event can trigger changes in affiliation. Events unfolding either in the stands or, as in the case of hockey, on the ice can affect the behaviors that classify individuals. Pavel Slepicka (1995: 282) addresses this issue of reciprocity by emphasizing the effect of observational learning, arguing, "In this connection it is important that the spectator be able to see what the player is doing or what is happening to the player."

Our main focus is trying to understand the behaviors considered less socially acceptable and inappropriate, that is, gaining an understanding that can lead to the concept of aggression. Jay Coakley (1998: 180) defines aggression as "behavior that intends to destroy property or injure another person, or is grounded in a total disregard for the well-being of self and others," and Richard Cox (2002) adds to this by stating that aggression in its more severe form is considered violence. In general, our interest has been to study the "dark side" of behavior—actions that in some way show disregard for the well-being of self and of others.

There exists a need, however, to differentiate among hostile and instrumental acts of aggression (Pargman, 1998) when trying to understand the complexity of actions that are visible and audible in hockey arenas. It is noteworthy that physical and verbal actions are considered equal as signs of aggressive behaviors; yet, both need to be understood within the situational context of an event (Ibid.) An aggressive act is considered hostile if the intent is to harm, and as instrumental if the aggressive behavior is a means to attain an end lying beyond the realm of harming. To illustrate, a slash to a player's wrist must be considered an act of hostile aggression if performed out of play (i.e., no puck within the players' proximity). It demonstrates an intentional act of harming. The same slash is an instrumental act of aggression if performed to prevent the opposing player's puck control and is still a rule-breaking action. Interestingly, of great relevance to crowd behaviors is that aggressive acts are most often verbal (Wann et al., 2001). Demeaning and condescending comments directed toward a player are considered acts of hostile aggression, while screaming at a player to distract his concentration prior to taking a penalty shot represents a behavior of instrumental aggression.

Including verbal acts as part of aggressive behaviors rather than restricting aggression to physical acts of violence (as it used to be conceptualized in dated sport psychology literature) is important for the understanding of the interaction between crowd and players (Husman and Silva, 1984; Wann et al., 1999). As long as the definition of aggressive behaviors is restricted to physical actions, there is a limited possibility to understand adverse crowd effects on players.

The etiology of aggression is manifested not only in its overt representation but also through its development (Cox, 2002). Two theoretical approaches are suggested for gaining an understanding of aggressive behaviors (Pargman, 1998): First, according to the Frustration-Aggression Hypothesis, people may act aggressively in response to frustration. Endless examples could illustrate when and how players, coaches, and the crowd feel frustrated (Rowe, 1998). And in response to this frustration, there is an increased potential for retaliatory aggression. Second, according to the Social Learning Theory, individuals can learn when and how to act by receiving vicarious reinforcement for their action and this applies equally to socially acceptable and unacceptable behaviors. This is of particular relevance when considering that members of the crowd (i.e., parents) represent significant others to those playing the game (Slepicka, 1995). These members of the crowd are reinforcing, approving, and encouraging some behaviors while undermining and devaluing others. In other words, parental behavior in the crowd is an active source of shaping behaviors on the ice.

To summarize, the background for the study was based on a contemporary definition and understanding of aggression. This included the acceptance of verbal assaults as a part of aggressive behaviors. The intention was to record aggressive and violent behaviors, primarily as exhibited by members of the crowd. To understand these actions, however, we chose to describe the interdependent relationship of those involved in minor hockey. This included the players of opposing teams, the coaching staffs, the game officials, and the crowd.

METHOD

Prior to our discussion of what was observed throughout this research period, it is important to reveal how it was conducted. We set out to follow three Lethbridge

PeeWee teams: two Double AA teams (highest division in Lethbridge), and one A team (second highest division). The teams were made up entirely of male players. We decided to follow these teams because PeeWee is where full-body contact is introduced to players and parents. One PeeWee coach told us that this was a good decision because "this is the first time parents see their little Johnny getting hit." We attended 50 games over the course of the 2001–2002 hockey season, mostly in Lethbridge and surrounding areas, as well as in Calgary during Minor Hockey week.

Data was collected by means of taking field notes and video-recording hockey games. At the beginning of the study (i.e., October and November), we took field notes throughout the games but had to change to writing summary notes during intermissions (i.e., between 1st and 2nd periods and 2nd and 3rd periods) and after the game. This change was necessitated by changes in spectator behaviors in response to our note-taking, which will be addressed below. Correspondingly, video data was collected at irregular intervals throughout the season to identify the relationship between actions on the ice and those in the stands. We detected strengths and weaknesses in each method of collecting data, but in the end we felt that what was collected was a sufficient representation of general behaviors at youth hockey games in Southern Alberta. At the conclusion of each week of attending games, we researchers and four student research assistants would meet as a group to share observations and discuss our interpretations of the field experience.

PARENTAL SPEECH

In order to discuss what was observed over the course of the year it is worth stating that, as our research team first entered the arena, there were two things that struck us as extraordinary: The first was the ferocious physical contact of the play itself, the second was the intensity of spectators' (primarily parents) verbal responses. The discourse was perturbing not only in terms of its messages, but also in the manner in which it was performed. This is not to say that what we witnessed were out-of-control parents screaming obscenities at players, coaches, and referees. This perhaps would have been easier to deal with as researchers, because this behaviour is openly acknowledged by leagues and parents as inappropriate and is understood as inexcusable in this community. Rather, what we are dealing with for the most part are vocal expressions deemed acceptable and appropriate by the spectators. These comments are understood as supportive and positive in view of attaining the athletic goal; in other words, the comments are not breaking conventions of speech within this community but instead communicate attitudes not only of the speaker but of the group as well.

It is from this collective communicative position that we began considering spectators at youth hockey games for the simple reason that we were astounded and bewildered by what we describe as esoteric communicative performances. Early in our observations it became apparent that words and the manner in which they were performed were meaningful in group-specific ways, forcing us to consider the group as a distinct "speech community."

The concept of a speech community was initially developed by Noam Chomsky (1965) to describe a community solely on the basis of language. Chomsky's speech theories, however influential, have since been contested by scholars such as Dell Hymes (1973), who has insisted that speech communities be understood as social entities and not merely as linguistic ones. For example, a group of people sharing the same language may not necessarily share the same linguistic "competence." If we stick to Chomsky, the idea of linguistic competence would follow Cartesian dualistic principles, where competence can never truly be achieved through its actual performance, since the performance of speech is merely a flawed representation of language in its mentally constructed (ideal) form (1965). Hymes would, however, argue that linguistic competence is based on one's ability to effectively communicate according to the conventions of a particular group. Thus, a group might share English as a common language, but it might be made up of different speech communities sharing distinct conventions that make English intelligible in highly specific ways. For example, this discussion of youth hockey spectatorship may not be intelligible to other English speakers, perhaps those without any formal academic training. Similarly, we as researchers encountered deficiencies in our own linguistic competence while conducting this study of the local hockey spectator community. "Grammatical knowledge of a form of speech is not a sufficient" (1973, 49) measure, then, for competence.

Competence as defined by Hymes (1973: 51) is based on one's ability to share "knowledge of rules for the conduct and interpretation of speech." Key here is that this knowledge is collective, where competence is achieved through community. This interdependence of language is emphasized in George Herbert Mead's (1974: 89) enduring work *The Problem of Society*:

> The peculiar importance of the vocal gesture is that it affects the individual who makes it just as much as it affects the individual to who it is directed...The effect of the attitude which we produce in others comes back on ourselves. It is in this way that participation arises out of communication. When we indicate something to another form, we are calling out in that other individual a certain response.

In this way language becomes both individual- and group-affirming, since language "cannot be arbitrarily spoken uncommon to the group, if one wishes to be understood" (Tyler 1978: 6). The basic acknowledgment here is that language is not merely a linguistic entity but is, rather, a "phenomenon of the social group" (Ibid.)

It can be argued that, in performing a speech act, one elicits a response from the community in which the word is spoken. This response may simply be an interpretative one, yet a response is necessary or the communicative act is impossible. For this reason, the speech act must conform to preexisting conventions of speech—what Jacques Derrida (1977: 18) describes as "an iterable model." He asks if a speech act could "succeed if its formulation did not repeat a 'coded' or iterable utterance, or in other words, if the formula I pronounce in order to open a meeting, launch a ship or a marriage were not identifiable in some way as conforming with an iterable model, if it were not then identifiable in some way as a 'citation'?"

By their very nature, then, speech acts are collective performances requiring both speaker and audience. Community members are complicit in the generation of meaning, in that words require consumption to become communicative devices. In *Philosophical Grammar*, Wittgenstein (1974: 47) surmises succinctly, "Any sentence still stands in need of an interpretation"; or better yet, "no sentence can be understood without a rider."

The speech act is, therefore, a dialogic as it requires a response—at least an interpretative one—to make the utterance intelligible. Once the initial force of a word is rendered—the interpretation—the speaker situates him/herself in relation to the group, either as a member, knowledgeable of group attitudes and laws, or as one outside of the group. For researchers, this has tremendous consequences, because language performed in an intelligible manner informs us of not only the speaker's ideologies, values, and beliefs, but the group's as well. When words are successfully communicated, displaying linguistic competence, we come to know what is acceptable within the group at hand. But perhaps even more significant to us as researchers are moments when conventions are broken and not successfully maintained, positioning speaker and group at odds—creating understandable tensions, enabling us to document what was broken and how, even providing even greater insight into the constitution of the speech group. It is here that we can begin discussing minor hockey spectators as a specific speech community and the discourse within. To begin, it is important to consider various speech acts and conventions of speech that we documented over the course of the year, which make this a distinct community of speakers. Consider the following utterances:

Nail him!
Hit him!
Take him!

Get on him!
Get him!
Smoke him!
Take the man!

These expressions were routinely documented throughout the season and, despite their heightened performance, were casually received by community members—affirming their prevalence and acceptability in the community. It is important to stress that, in the context in which these utterances are performed, this discourse is perceived as supportive commentary. They are understood as directives encouraging "suitable" playing behaviors from children/players. The utterances are rationalized as supportive because they are directing players to perform in potentially legal and appropriate manners in the context of hockey. To "hit" someone falls within the rules of the game. To "get" someone means to attack the opponent, a necessary strategy in hockey. These parental comments are technically not abusive, nor are they belligerent and so do not fall within the transgressive boundaries clearly demarcated for parents on signs in arenas throughout Alberta, such as this one displayed in a rink in Calgary:

Welcome—Cheer Loud—Have Fun
But Note
Verbal/Physical Abuse of Players, Officials, Fans
Or Staff may Result in Ejection From The Arena

The persuasive power of this discourse is evident as players carry out the instructions being yelled at them from above, and as parents/spectators applaud and cheer the desired results. These comments in turn create a dialogue of its own as players respond by intensifying their physical play, and parents intensify their vocal direction and praise. At one point in our fieldwork we responded to this verbal/behavioral reciprocity by writing:

- The game gets progressively aggressive.
- Hits are happening all over the ice
- Big #11 from the Storm nails a kid and then trash-talks him on the way down
- Mothers and fathers and kids are all cheering (screaming) when hits occur
- The bigger the hit, the bigger the cheer
- Mother in front makes almost a tribal whoop, whoop (more like yip! yip! yip!) after kid gets creamed.
- It creates a hitting frenzy.

The cheering here is collective, and parents revel in each other's enthusiasm. Moreover, their cheering is intended as positive, since applauding behavior is not generally perceived as negative or detrimental.

This is not to say that negative comments are absent from the rinks. It is important to state, however, that by using the word "negative" here, we are not assigning a qualitative value, but rather a linguistic one. We use it to refer to comments that are critical of some aspect of the game, be it refereeing, the coach, the players, or other parents. For example, yelling "bullshit" after a call made by the referee and then adding, "That's what people are like from [Town Name]." These negative comments, such as "Open your eyes Reff!" or "Call it, you idiot," do not necessarily break speech community conventions, because they are expressed and subsequently received by this speech group as supportive discourse. It is difficult for those outside of the group to see berating an 18-year-old official for a perceived bad call as supportive, but for this group it is to ensure the safety of their children—whether from physical harm or the harm of losing unfairly.

By way of example, there was one incident where parents were yelling at the referee because a player supposedly kicked another kid in the head with his skate. The parents screamed at the referee to make the call and screamed at the opposing player who supposedly made the kick. The screams and berating of officials and players are perceived as being justified under these circumstances because of perceived risks facing their children: (1) a referee who allows the illegal act of kicking to occur and (2) an opposing player who is kicking other players. Within this speech community, a speaker is able to get as close to a referee as possible and, without breaking speech community conventions, tell him that he is "pathetic" (as was witnessed during one game). In fact, gestures such as these are often applauded, as various actors within these ethnographic scenes are understood as deserving of this malicious treatment.

The acceptability of this discourse is highlighted by the fact that speakers perform in these situations fearless of being reproached by their fellow spectators. That is until someone from outside of the community is present and stands alongside the parents during the games. The parents were in almost every case suspicious of our presence at the games. Our presence often forced parents to reflect—at least, temporarily—on in-group behaviors and their communicative performances during the games. In so doing, their status as a tangible speech community became even more pronounced as their own conventions were seen as being scrutinized by outsiders.

Two occasions stand out most for us: The first was at a PeeWee A game while we were writing our field notes at the end of an eventful second period, when a father of the local team came up to us and asked what we were doing. We explained that we were with the university and that we were doing a study on minor hockey in Southern Alberta. The father asked if it was about the parents "hollering and stuff" to which we replied, "Yes." We were surprised that he immediately connected our study of minor hockey to parent behavior and responded by reemphasizing that we were studying the play as well. As if to justify the "hollering and stuff," he replied: "You know, of all the sports, hockey has to be the most intense." From this encounter, we were able to discern two important things: (1) There is a basic acknowledgment by the parents that they do get riled at games and carry on in less than appropriate ways and (2) These behaviors are legitimized by this group because of the intensity of the game that prompts spectators to act inappropriately—as if saying, "It's not us, it's the game."

The next scenario occurred while we were taking notes during an altercation at a PeeWee AA hockey tournament in Lethbridge. The altercation broke out because one group of parents took exception to the other group's cheering their team's aggressive hitting. As we were scribbling down comments, a woman from the home team, who was in the middle of the altercation, confronted us demanding to know what we were writing. We responded by saying that we were with the university, observing spectator behavior at youth hockey games. The woman again asked angrily what we were writing down, and we said we were writing down what we were hearing. It was not until a friend of this woman intervened and got her to calm down that the situation subsided and attention was returned to the action on the ice.

In both situations, parents were responding to our presence by questioning our invasive positions and were made uncomfortable by the fact that we did not belong to their community. As nonmembers we seemingly lack the competence to appreciate the ensuing discourse, and they defended their position on these grounds. Thus, what we initially interpreted as a temporary acknowledgment of wrongdoing is more likely resentment to a perception of being judged by someone who cannot understand their role and the dynamics of this specific community. This defensive position reinforces the legitimacy of vocal texts and performances that seemed inappropriate to us as non-affiliated observers. Moreover these communicative events have serious consequences for the actors within: the players, the officials, the coaches, and the parents themselves, most noticeably in the sporadic physical assault cases across North America.

IMPACT OF LANGUAGE ON YOUTH HOCKEY

In discussing the consequences of language at youth hockey events, it is important to stress that our analysis was based on speech norms and conventions, not behaviors deemed excessive in this community. The reason for this is that this normalized language possesses an unrealized effect worthy of greater consideration than the more sensational narratives of physical violence that we hear about through the media. From this first phase of our research and from the relatively limited official reports of assault charges at youth hockey games, we are able to deduce that these overt acts of violence are relatively rare and, for our purposes, less of a concern. More pertinent here is the fact that everyday discourse is filled with acts of violence that tend to go unnoticed, if not reduce its danger. In fact, the danger is only enhanced and fosters what we have observed to be highly volatile situations.

The first and most direct effect of violent speech is achieved through directives literally calling for violence from the young hockey players: "Hit him!" "Nail him!", "Take him out!", and/or "Hammer him!" As indicated earlier, players respond by hitting their opponents, which is met with cheers and generate even more physical contact. But these speech acts affect another form of violence by fellow parents. To appreciate the violence fully, one has to appreciate the emotional commitment parents have to their children. As much as the parents look objectively at the kids playing on the ice as hockey players, they do not regard their own individual child the same way; in other words, parents call for players to hit other players and feel justified in doing so because they are hockey players and that is what hockey players do. But, when the act is committed against their own child, s/he is not a hockey player—in the objective sense—but their own son or daughter. Thus, when parents call for a player to hit somebody, they are calling for someone to hit somebody else's child. The consequence of this speech act is twofold: It commits an act of aggression/violence against another child and wounds also the parent of the child who witnesses his/her son/daughter succumb to the aggressive, violent act. The wound intensifies when the hit is met with cheers and people inadvertently celebrate the "pounding" of the child. This way, perceived supportive comments (i.e., cheering for successful execution) are deleterious depending on one's phenomenological position. So, the success of one action is coupled with the defeat of another, and the dialogue around the physical contact proved to be the greatest instigator of parental anger and increased volatility in the arena.

On one such occasion, a physical fight nearly broke out as parents from one team became increasingly incensed by another team's father who repeatedly called for *his* team to hit people, each response to which he then rewarded with vociferous cheers in the form of a "Wahoo!" The first team's parents began parodying the man by screaming their own "Wahoos" when their players delivered hits, creating what can be described as a scene of duelling-Wahoos. The father did not relent and instead increased the frequency and volume of his cheering. The perturbed parents began directing their comments more specifically at the father and at one point criticized a call made by the referee through him: "That's almost as dumb as Howie over here" [in reference to the late Howie Meeker, a famous Canadian hockey broadcaster]. The situation escalated to the point that the parents from the first team confronted him. Standing less than ten feet away, one father said, "You think that's funny?!", and another father declared, "You're an idiot!" Another yelled, "You're a moron!" In response, the father of the other team cleverly retorted, "You're bitter: we're better!" Tempers remained hot, but the situation did not move beyond general name-calling and town bashing. This does not detract from the seriousness of the situation; our research team was expecting a fight to ensue anytime. It was only later that we joked with one another about our obligations as researchers in this kind of situation: Do we break up the fight, or take impeccable field notes?

Another aspect of potential violent speech in this community is a gendered violence negating women by disqualifying the female voice as a legitimate presence within this community. In making this assessment, we are not implying that women are prevented from speaking during the games; in fact, they are often more vocal than the men. But what was apparent throughout our fieldwork was that women's speech was not received seriously within the community and is pronounced as such by the men. For example, one woman was angry at a call made during one of the games and she yelled at the referee: "Awww, that was weak!" A father standing beside us negated her comment in a loud voice, saying, "Nancy, that wasn't weak." The woman accepted his correction, and, although she continued to be vocal, she did not criticize anyone for the remainder of the game. On another occasion, a group of women began screaming frantically because they saw one of their players get kicked in the head by an opposing player. A father who had been offering his own commentary throughout the game dismissed these comments and ordered the women to calm down, saying, "Easy, easy Mums! Easy, easy, easy, easy, easy!!" This particular man was one of the most vocally aggressive people at the rink, with comments performed freely without any form of rebuke. Yet, he somehow felt his reproach of the women was warranted because of his privileged male position. In other words, he enacted a discriminating behavior reflective of an intolerant community.

These condescending utterances provide insight into this community's attitudes towards women, who are generally tolerated by the men but are perceived as illegitimate in the context of hockey. Words and the manner in which they are performed here are highly reductive. They not only directly disqualify female speech but also affirm masculine norms—indirectly reducing those who do not fit within this paradigm. So we hear comments such as "Wait to be tough" or "Take no prisoners," directing the children to behave according to traditional hockey standards based in male physical aggression and dominance. When men repeat these words they become formulas that have consequence in this community, but when women express these sentiments they are generally ignored or formally dismissed.

Perhaps the most obvious realization of this occurred during a tournament we attended when a group of male parents began to shout at a referee for what was perceived as poor officiating. A player was hit, and the referee estimated that it was a clean play and did not raise his arm to call a penalty. The men, whose voices bellowed throughout the small rink, were clearly affecting the young referee to the extent that he changed the call. The male parents then began to laugh at the success of their bullying tactics and started mocking the referee for his indecisiveness. In this community, it is nearly impossible for women to bring about the same effects through speech because, as women, their competence is never secured.

CONCLUSIONS

As a result of spending a year observing parents' spectator behavior at youth hockey games in Southern Alberta, it became evident that aggression spoken by parents and enacted upon by the youth is understood in this community as natural—an inevitable consequence of the game. Spectators, players, coaches, and referees contribute to these attitudes through their words, their actions, and their complicit responses that reinforce the legitimacy of these behaviors, producing what can be understood as a culture of violence. The young players and parents come to know this violence through the communicative situations in local arenas. These sites are where membership is claimed, validating one way of existence and invalidating others. In this way, community identity is pronounced and endorsed by its members, while rejecting values and beliefs not suitable in hockey—tolerance, passivity, or compassion. Moreover, it articulates the politics of gender and informs legitimate conventions and standards of behavior predefined by traditional, antiquated masculine formulas.

Especially problematic is the fact that policies being introduced to prevent "inappropriate" behaviors in youth hockey contexts are proving to be ineffective, which is why these deleterious behaviors persist. Governing bodies, such as Provincial Hockey Associations, have put into place policies directed at behaviors that are somewhat rare in Canadian rinks, while dismissing everyday expressions of aggression that were consistently observed throughout our research. In rinks across Canada, it is openly stated that verbal and/or physical abuse is not acceptable, yet calling for and then applauding a 170-pound child's hitting a 100-pound child is not only acceptable but endorsed. As celebrating aggression continues to be a legitimate communicative practice in youth hockey, parents will continue to be unnerved in these contexts, and rink volatility will remain high. The acceptability of these dangerous attitudes and behaviors is what needs to be addressed prior to implementing strategies intended to reduce volatility in Canadian rinks. Refusing to do so might suggest that people are either unwilling to create and ensure user-friendly environments for youth to play hockey, or that aggression in youth hockey is a valued and essential characteristic of Canadian hockey. Considering the current state of youth hockey environment, both scenarios are certainly plausible.

REFERENCES

Chomsky, N. (1965). *Aspects of the theory of syntax.* Cambridge: MIT Press.

Coakley, J. J. (1998). *Sport in society: Issues and controversies* (6th ed.). St. Louis: MO: Times Mirror/ Mosby.

Cox, R. H. (2002). *Sport psychology: Concepts and applications*, 5th ed. Toronto: McGraw-Hill.

Deacon, J., McClelland, S., and Smart, D. (2001). Rink rage. *MacLean's* 114 (13): 16–21.

Derrida, J. (1977). Signature, event, context. Baltimore, MD: Johns Hopkins University Press.

Donnelly, P. (Ed.). (2000). *Taking sport seriously: Social issues in Canadian sport.* 2nd ed. Toronto: Thompson Educational.

Gruneau R. and Whitson, D. (1993). *Hockey night in Canada: Sport, identities and cultural politics.* Culture and Communication Series. Toronto: Garamond.

Husman, B. F. and Silva J. M. 111, (1984). Aggression in sport: Definitional and theoretical considerations. In Silva, J. M. and Weinberg, R. S. (Eds.), *Psychological foundations of sport*, 246–260. Champaign, IL: Human Kinetics.

Hymes, D. (1973). *Foundations in sociolinguistics: An ethnographic approach.* Philadelphia: University of Pennsylvania Press.

Ingham, A. G. and Dewar, A. (1999). Through the eyes of youth: "Deep Play" in PeeWee ice hockey. In Coakley, J. J. and Donnelly, P. (Eds.). *Inside sports*, 17–27. London: Routledge.

Mead, G. H. (1974). The problem of society: How we become selves. In Bount, G. G. (Ed.) *Language, culture, and society: A book of readings*, 2nd ed. 85–94. Illinois. Waveland.

Nack, W. and Munson, L. (2000). Out of control. *Sports Illustrated* (93): 86–95.

Pargman, D. (1998). *Understanding sport behavior.* Upper Saddle River, NJ: Prentice Hall.

Rowe, C. J. (1998). Aggression and violence in sports. *Psychiatric Annals* 28 (5): 265–269.

Slepicka, P. (1995). Psychology of the sport spectator. In Biddle, S. J. H. (Ed.). *European perspectives on exercise and sport psychology*, 270–289. Champaign, IL: Human Kinetics.

Trudel, P., Côté, J., and Bernard, D. (1996). Systematic observation of youth ice hockey coaches during games. *Journal of Sport Behavior* 19 (1): 50–65.

Tyler, S. A. (1978). *The said and the unsaid: Mind, meaning, and culture.* New York: Academic Press.

Wann, D. L., Carlson, J. D., and Schrader, M. P. (1999). The impact of team identification on the hostile and instrumental verbal aggression of sport spectators. *Journal of Social Behavior and Personality* 14 (2): 279–286.

Wann, D. L., Merrill, J. M., Russell, G. W., and Pease, D. G. (2001). *Sport fans: The psychology and social impact of spectators.* New York: Routledge.

Wittgenstein, L. (1974). *Philosophical grammar*. Trans. A. Kenny. Berkeley, CA: University of California Press.

Zillman, D. and Paulus, P. B. (1993). Spectators: Reactions to sport events and effects on athletic performance. In Singer, R. N., Murphey, M., and Tennant, L. K. (Eds.), *Handbook of research on sport psychology*, 600–619. Toronto: Macmillan.

PART II

HISTORICAL PERSPECTIVES

CHAPTER FOUR

Reflections ON Sport, Masculinity, AND Nationalism IN THE Aftermath OF 9/11

ELLEN J. STAUROWSKY

Preface

This chapter was written in the immediate aftermath of the events that occurred on September 11, 2001. As such, it has not been altered from its original form apart from a brief updating of information where absolutely necessary. The piece was designed to capture the moment and, thus, has been preserved accordingly.

INTRODUCTION

In the children's tale *Chicken Little*, the centerpiece revolves around the frightening although seemingly improbable prospect of the sky disintegrating and falling on our heads. The main character, Chicken Little, mistakenly interprets an acorn's landing on her head as a sign that the sky was falling. A female alarmist or a sweetly mistaken character, depending on one's view, she sets out on a mission to tell the king. While obsessing about the imagined threat of the sky falling, Chicken Little and her friends fail to recognize a real danger in their midst in the form of Foxy Woxy, a polite and mannerly gentleman who either succeeds in destroying the innocents or is driven off by the king—a quintessential protective father figure safeguarding the young until they can better judge the motives and character of those they meet.

The lessons from Chicken Little are profoundly complex. At one level, the story raises questions about who deserves trust, how one knows when danger really exists, how one assesses the dangerous in our midst, who is entrusted to protect us when we cannot protect ourselves, and how does one bravely proceed in the face of insecurity and the unknown. At another level, it also offers a lesson about gender. Within the character construction, innocence, naiveté, and vulnerability are encoded as feminine while destruction and protection are masculine.

In the aftermath of September 11, this story takes on a haunting poignancy. Out of the sky, hijacked planes commandeered by dark-skinned[1] male assailants brought such unimagined destruction to an American mindset and worldview that it would have been relegated to the realm of fiction or fairytale if not for the harsh realities of the thousands dead in New York, Pennsylvania, and Washington DC. Symbolically, hijackers struck at the heart of American society, strategically targeting the supposed sources of our strength as a nation: Our financial markets, the military, and the seat of government, along with the innocents who had gone to work or boarded planes that day, unsuspecting that something could go terribly and fatally awry. In their success, al Qaeda imparted a message of fear to the minds and hearts of the collective U.S. populace while inspiring a stated governmental need for retaliation, retribution, and/or vengeance (Morrow, 2001).

As the unthinkable became manifest, the sky had, indeed, fallen. And with it, American sensibilities fell as well. No longer certain of who to trust and no longer confident that we could accurately assess who could be trusted, the nation's fathers— President George W. Bush, then New York City mayor Rudolph Guliani, and New York governor George Pataki—took center stage in calming fears, offering condolences, and devising a plan of action for a "measured" response to the attacks. In short order, the military was mobilized to bomb Afghanistan and hunt for the mastermind behind al Qaeda, Osama Bin Laden, while firefighters, police, and rescue crews went about searching for bodies of the dead and cleaning up physical sites of destruction.

In suffering the loss of citizens and visitors from other countries, a trauma was visited upon the body national. And, just as the human body seeks homeostasis when injured or hurt, so too was there a call for a return to "normalcy" in the wake of 9/11. Within that context, a "return to normalcy" and an engagement in a "healing process" saw popular men's sports emerge as significant symbols that the nation had experienced an attack but had not sustained a fatal blow. This chapter examines the themes of sport, masculinity, and nationalism following the events of September 11, 2001, organized around three topical areas: sport as a vehicle for conveying messages about masculinity and nationalism, mutual connections between athletic heroes and male heroes, and the athletic hero as military hero.

SPORT AS A VEHICLE FOR CONVEYING MESSAGES ABOUT MASCULINITY AND NATIONALISM

Less than eleven days after September 11, cultural critic Edward Rothstein (2001) wrote in *The New York Times* that "cataclysms not only cast shadows over human victims but also shake the foundations of intellectual life; wars can shift the direction of scholarship; genocide can upend the presumptions of sociology." He went on to suggest that flaws inherent in the subjectivity and moral relativism embodied in the work of postmodernists and postcolonialists should be reassessed in light of the stark realities of the attacks. Emblematic of the efforts made by scholars, writers, and political commentators to come to grips with the situation, the suggested reassessment of ideological perspectives created both understanding and tension.

While some have advocated support for U.S. censorship and limitations to civil liberties on the basis of national security arguments (e.g., the passage of the USA Patriot Act), others have pointed out the long and troubled histories associated with these practices (e.g., the internment of Japanese Americans during World War II, the forced assimilation and imprisonment of Native Americans) that can undermine the very democratic ideals we seek to protect (Chomsky, 2001). Scholars offering alternative perspectives to the Bush administration have been labeled anti-American and unpatriotic. As an example, the American Council of Trustees and Alumni issued a report (Martin and Neal, 2002) noting, "College and university faculty have been the weak link in America's response to the attack. Their public messages were short on patriotism and long on self-flagellation" (Blumenstyk, 2001). Since then, blacklisting of professors perceived to be anti-Semitic has been performed by an organization known as "Campus Watch" (Gerring, 2002; Pipes and Schanzer, 2002).

Regardless of one's political perspective, an inherent "masculinism" at the core of the response to September 11 about the inevitability of war renders alternatives effeminate, triggering anti-intellectual suspicions about the professoriate being soft, perverse, and morally corrupt (Hofstadter, 1963). To favor other responses or to question where the country is headed is to risk appearing as if one does not empathize with or care about those who lost their lives. Describing the shifting ideological terrain, where neither the essentialist rhetoric of the right nor the "recitation of the accumulated evils of American hegemony" of the left has been sufficient, Michael Kimmel (2001) has written, "Yes, I am critical of my government—as I have always been. But I am also feeling fiercely patriotic." It is salient, however, that in calling for a "new" context, he references an "old" style of masculinity:

> Traditional definitions of masculinity certainly have their imperious sides, brimming with homophobia and sexism. But they also contain the capacity for quiet heroism,

> selfless sacrifice, steadfast resolve, deep wells of compassion and care, and yes, a love that made these men magnificent.

In a somewhat different fashion, Charlotte Allen (2002: 9) wrote, "In the furnaces of September 11, there was suddenly forged a new social trend: the return of the guy...Their sex is male, and they do the kind of work that calls on specifically male attributes and virtues: physical strength, tough fatherly leadership (think of Rudolph Guliani), brotherly bonding into fighting units, courage, and blunt compassion." Within weeks of the tragedy, Olivia Barker (2001: 1D) reported in *USA Today* that, "after decades of disrespect and neglect, manly men...are suddenly chic." This "return" to a distinctly masculine protector role and an accompanying male heroism were noted in the sports pages as well. On the October 1, 2001 cover of *ESPN: The Magazine,* a narrative appears, against a black background, reading,

> These were the days when heroism and villainy were redefined. This was the week when sports went dark, when its spotlight swung around to the firefighters who ran up the stairs, the police and EMS crews who braved the showers destruction, the laborers who sifted through the debris of a cataclysm to find evidence of someone's life. The clichéd descriptions we so freely bestow on our athletes—words like courageous, tireless, inspirational—have taken on deeper meanings.

Professional athletes offered similar sentiments. On September 16, 2001, Curt Schilling, Cy Young Award winner and pitcher for the 2001 World Series Championship Arizona Diamondbacks, issued an open letter to families of the victims and to the relief workers who responded, thanking them for their courage and promising to honor their fortitude in the work that he would undertake as someone hired to entertain the masses.

The subtle distinctions made by writers and commentators between the *real* heroes who emerged out of the life and death circumstances of the 9/11 attack and the *imagined* Hollywood heroes and sports celebrities had some validity and persuasive power. Manifestations of "masculine" character and behavior reflected in the heroic efforts of firefighters and police officers in the aftermath of the tragedy are not "new"; they are clearly familiar—traditional representations of a masculine ideal. To attempt to suggest that there is a "new" masculinity belies how deeply rooted hegemonic masculinity is in the largely all-male enclaves of the military, fraternal orders, and sports where hegemonic masculinity has been preserved and protected, perhaps saved for just such a horrible set of circumstances.

The distinction between male heroism as demonstrated in battle and simulated conflict settings of sport ought to be made but need not negate valid relationships between the two. To deny long-standing connections between hegemonic masculinity, militarism/nationalism, and sport would be to deny the role sport serves in helping to lay the cultural foundation for these connections to be forged (Pope, 1997; Wakefield, 1997). Despite the rhetoric of the 1990s that maleness was in decline, as Lance Morrow (1994) declared, or that a "war" had been declared on the nation's boys, as Christina Hoff Sommers (2000) alleged, traditional male institutions have remained, in their core values and physical constitution, primarily male entities—be it branches of the armed services or athletic teams (Brodie, 2001; Burstyn, 1999; Goldstein, 2001; Hall, 1996; Hargreaves, 2000; Messner, 2002; Messner and Sabo, 1994).

The seamlessness of the connections between sport, masculinity, and nationalism is revealed on the cover of *Sports Illustrated* of September 10, 2001. It featured the "Rock of Ages," a reference to fiercely competitive New York Yankee pitcher Roger Clemens, known as "The Rocket." Undaunted by competition, edgy, aggressive, confident, arrogant, confrontational, physically intimidating, and strong, Clemens was the pre-September 11 representation of what Messner, Dunbar, and Hunt (2000) refer to as the "sports manhood formula." The assumed and expected relationship of this symbol of masculinity and that of the military is writ on the next page, which pictures a soldier in army fatigues emerging from the gray mists and smoky ruins of a battle scene, reaching for and being pulled forward by a fellow soldier. An ad for the movie *Band of Brothers*, the story of the men from Easy Company, it described one of the toughest army rifle companies in World War II, the men who parachuted into France on D-Day (Ambrose, 2002). The copy reads, "Ordinary Men. Extraordinary Times." So, the "sports manhood formula" is just a flip of a page away from the "military manhood formula."

The symbolic role that men's sports plays in legitimizing and fostering an appreciation for "men in uniform" was evidenced in the first *Monday Night Football* game following September 11. Commenting on the game featuring the Green Bay Packers and the Washington football franchise, broadcaster Al Michaels offered a somber and subdued commentary, noting that "the Washington Redskins represents our nation's capitol with all of its attendant history," while Green Bay represented the "heartland," "bucolic," and "pastoral." Although as professional football players the combatants would be called upon to "bang on each other" during the game, their spirits would be united as the country was united in response to the tragedy. Michaels' final comment to the audience before going into commercial was "Sit back, relax, and enjoy a three hour diversion."

When considered in isolation, Al Michaels' comments suggest that the sport of football is a benign, apolitical distraction, designed to take our minds off the sadness and sorrow of the previous days; however, the commercial sport media complex is designed expressly to play off and to promote American nationalism. Subtly, the Green Bay-Washington game emerged as part of the fabric of the larger nationalist sport structure where the National Football League, Major League Baseball (with its American and National divisions), and the National Basketball League all sport logos mirroring a color scheme reflecting the American flag. Prior to singing the national anthem, a montage of interviews interspersed shots of the flag with images of firefighters and rescue workers. The segment began with a shot of a totally black background and a message delivered in silence—a quotation from legendary coach Vince Lombardi: "It's not whether you get knocked down, it's whether you get back up." Immediately following were firefighters in New York City raising the American flag, an image evoking comparisons to the famous flag-raising memorial at Iwo Jima, accompanied by "This Land Is Your Land" playing in the background.

It is not surprising that Michaels did not acknowledge the massive displays of nationalism infusing his broadcast. He did not refer to the ABC logo recast in red, white, and blue, nor the crowd in patriotic apparel or those whose faces had the stars and stripes painted on them. The crowd erupted in a furious uproar as a Green Bay player ran onto the field bearing an American flag—what Marvin and Ingle (1999) referred to as a "blood totem," igniting frenzy but perhaps fury as well.

This was an expression of American nationalism representing a "political doctrine that dares not speak its name," referring to a process through which "disparate, local communities and social groups imagine themselves part of a national family" (O'Leary, 1999: 4). As Marvin and Ingle (1999: 1) point out, "The sacrificial system that binds American citizens has a sacred flag at its center." Regardless of how deeply divided the nation may be by inequality and exploitation, nationalist interests are served by the "mobilization of masses of people and the imaginative process," a process of "remembrance and amnesia" that smoothes the rough edges of dissent and guarantees that the citizenry will go along with the national agenda (Ibid.) The spectacle afforded by our nation's teams, our men's teams, is built around the singing of the national anthem and the saluting of the American flag. The convergence of masculine strength and national defense in this spectacle works to reaffirm a commonly shared political agenda.

MALE ATHLETICISM AND THE PREPARATION OF HEROES

On September 11, United Flight 93, one of the four planes hijacked that day, took off from Newark, New Jersey, destined for San Francisco. Approximately one hour into the flight, passengers on board discovered that their plane had been taken over by suicide bombers who took control of the cockpit and ordered the passengers into the back of the plane. It is believed that, in a display Evan Thomas (2001: 7) would call "a victory over cowardice," four passengers devised a plan to overpower their captors to avert the successful completion of the third phase of a plan of attack that had already resulted in the destruction of the World Trade Center and damaged the Pentagon.

Sportswriter Rick Reilly (2001: 94) described the four men this way: "The huge rugby player, the former high school football star and the onetime college baseball player were in first class, the former national judo champ was in coach. On the morning of September 11, at 32,000 feet, those four men teamed up to sacrifice their lives for those of perhaps thousands of others." Although Reilly pointed out that sports are "trivial" when describing actions of this magnitude, he went on to offer his assessment that sport, as a preparation and training ground for life, may have created the common values and set of qualities that unified Todd Beamer, Mark Bingham, Tom Burnett, and Jeremy Glick in that fateful moment: "But what the best athletes can do—keep their composure amid chaos, form a plan when all seems lost and find the guts to carry it out—may be why the Capitol isn't a charcoal pit."

The now-famous command "Let's roll," spoken by Todd Beamer and witnessed by Lisa Kennedy, the GTE operator who took his call, has taken on multiple meanings. President George W. Bush inserted it into his address to the nation, partly as a homage to the victims of the September 11 attack and partly as a call to arms to the citizenry (Violanti, 2002). On February 8, 2002, at the Opening Ceremony of the Salt Lake City Winter Olympic Games, Bush reported to NBC commentator Bob Costas that those were his final words to the U.S. team in admonishing them to compete for the honor and glory of their country in memory of those who had died less than six months before.

These interrelated themes of sport, masculinity, and preparation for the male heroic role is further explored in the December 24–30, 2001 edition of *Sports Illustrated*. The "manhood formula" of blending physicality with masculinity and service to one's community and country is featured on the cover where "Everybody's All-Americans" are represented as members of the Fire Department of New York's (FDNY) football, basketball, baseball, and hockey teams. On page 106 is this tribute: "Like so many other New York City firefighters who died on September 11, Mike Carroll was a dedicated athlete and loyal teammate whose indomitable spirit led him to embrace his final, heroic mission. His young son would find comfort in the company of Mike Piazza" (Bamberger, 2001: 107). In a story about a family's and a community's grief and search for solace, the reflection on Mike Carroll's life recalls the importance of sport in his early upbringing and in his professional life. This was a bond Carroll shared with many of his fellow firefighters. As Bamberger (2001) noted, "Sport imbued the lives of fallen firemen. They'd played minor league baseball and semipro football. They were weight lifters and boxers."

Whereas one can relegate these stories to their place within the overall collection of pieces about the events following 9/11, they can also be read as stories interpreting the meaning of these events for the readership of *Sports Illustrated*—primarily male, largely of military service age. Thus, the construction of masculinity is revealed as an active process, where valor and personal sacrifice become the substance for readers to reflect on and consider as part of the expectation of what it is to be a man in America.

THE MALE ATHLETE AS MILITARY HERO: THE CASE OF PAT TILLMAN

Whereas most of the stories following September 11 focused on the heroism of firefighters, police officers, and military personnel, the starting safety for the Arizona Cardinals, Pat Tillman, became the subject of attention when he opted to abandon a reported $3–4 million-dollar contract to volunteer for the United States Army along with his brother, Kevin, a former minor league baseball player. The legend of Pat Tillman, a football player who had to fight the odds with singularity of purpose, seems to have been in the making long before he elected to serve his country. Few predicted that he would ever, as a seventh-round draft pick, start in the National Football League; yet, at the height of his playing career, he chose to leave to pursue a career in the United States Army, aspiring to become a member of the elite infantry fighting force known as the Army Rangers. Tillman served as guidon (unit flag or standard) bearer for B Company in a graduation ceremony from the Army's Infantry Training Brigade at Fort Benning, Georgia, and his story has been well documented (Jenkins, 2002; Kindred, 2002; Olson, 2002; Parrish, 2002).

Although he usually declined interviews and attempted to stay out of the media spotlight, *Monday Night Football* sideline reporter Melissa Stark presented a segment on Tillman preceding the September 9, 2001 game. Through interviews with former teammates and coaches, viewers were introduced to a phantom Tillman whose actions seemed to more than make up for his absence from the screen. Arizona Cardinals head coach Dave McGinnis explained that, in order to accurately depict Tillman, one should start not with the football player, but with the person. Lyle Sentencich, former linebacker coach at Arizona State, used the words "honest" and described him as someone possessed of deep convictions.

Interestingly, although seasoned sports writer David Kindred (2002) wrote a nuanced and thoughtful piece about Pat Tillman, it is noticeable that female journalists saw a story worth telling. Lisa Olson (2002) wrote with a degree of reverence, situating Tillman as both athletic hero and military hero within the same frame, highlighting physical and emotional preparations that athletic participation can foster and reminding her readers that, "as you sip a cold one and watch your heroes in shoulder pads do battle on the gridiron, think of Tillman. Tell his story, again and again and again. It bears repeating."

The treatment of the subject of heroism and athleticism became a bit grittier, less formulaic, and more critical in Sally Jenkins' "This Ranger Is Lone in His Ways," placing Tillman's actions within the context of *Denial of Death,* Ernest Becker's 1973 Pulitzer Prize–winning book that focuses on mortality and heroism and argues that the likelihood of death can result in greater personal awareness. Jenkins wrote, in a letter to Tillman,

> I wonder if the military will alter you, and especially your ideas about heroism. Becker says we've made "animal courage into a cult," and that heroism is "first and foremost a reflex of the terror of death." As a culture, we make heroes out of athletes simply for being athletes—in part because they aren't what Becker calls "the automatic cultural man" who imagines he has control over his life if he pays an insurance premium.

In the end, however, regardless of who the author is, the message is the same: Pat Tillman, although unseen and unheard from, is a hero to be emulated and admired by virtue of his personal sacrifice and his willingness to sacrifice for others.[2]

CONCLUSIONS

The January 2002 issue of the men's journal *Everyman* was devoted to a discussion about masculinity, author Chris O'Neil (2002) pointing out that, in the wake of September 11, he chose a reflection on heroism, "the blessing and the power to be found in the sacred masculine." The "sacredness" of masculinity has come through as a fourth theme in my investigation of this material. Michael Kimmel (2001), writing just after 9/11, observed,

> And what of those men on United Flight 93 who decided to fight back against the hijackers when it became clear that their plane was going to become a bomb? It appears the men called their wives, found out what was happening, and decided to take action so that others wouldn't be killed. Such heroic sacrifice from ordinary men speaks of a love that dares not speak its name: a deep unselfish love of one's fellow human beings.

Researcher Michele Lamont (2000), analyzing *The Dignity of Working Men* identified that for firefighters, police officers, and military personnel there comes a moral order that includes responsibility, a strong work ethic, and a well-developed sense of their role as providers for their families to shape their sense of who they are. Seen from that perspective, part of the reaction to the events of 9/11 emanates from this understanding that we are on sacred ground in an ideological sense as well as in an undeniably real one. Within this construction, men set about the task of sacrificing, perhaps being called upon to make the ultimate sacrifice of their lives in service to others while those left behind, oftentimes women and children, are given the task of suffering with them and without them.

To attempt a critique when treading on sacred ground is daunting even under the most neutral of conditions; to do so in such emotionally charged times has the potential to silence those who would attempt it. However, what of the obligation to advocate for an extension of this tightly constrained male frame distorting the picture and thus our reaction to the events we have been asked to interpret? Where is there a place to raise questions similar to those of the Women's Relief Corps of the late 1890s that reflected the "views of educators who believed that too much patriotic sentiment was associated with war"? Where is there a place to challenge the presentation of the tragedy, on the sports pages and elsewhere, as a male tragedy?

Lorraine Dowler (2002) confirmed that, "in the public record of Sept. 11, 2001, grief bears two faces. One is that of the young suburban widow, soldiering through her sorrow for the sake of her children. The other is the male firefighter weeping for fallen colleagues." Although it is the case that more men than women lost their lives at Ground Zero, the demographics do not explain the virtually exclusive coverage devoted to the male heroes. Although it is the case that the FDNY employed only 25 female firefighters out of a total of 11,500, over 6,000 women worked in New York's police force and roughly a third of the city's emergency medical technicians (EMTs) were women. In order for a story to air on a major network about the women who worked at Ground Zero, Maureen McFadden, vice president of communications at the National Organization for Women, had to put together her own video and pitch it to the networks, who had not considered that there was such a story to be told.

The danger in this uncritical form of patriotism, tied to notions of hegemonic masculinity, is the conclusion reached by Charlotte Allen (2002), who believed that the male suffering and heroism in response to the events of September 11 was proof of the wrong-headedness of women seeking to intrude in places where they had no place. She wrote, "Sometimes, perhaps most of the time, those are jobs that only a guy can do, and if we lower our standards because some women may feel bad about not living up to them, it is going to cost lives. It took an act of monstrous criminality to show us this, but we now know that the crisis of masculinity is over and some of the worst excesses of affirmative action may be over. We've come to appreciate that there's nothing like a guy" (p. 9).

As I watch with interest the U.S. Department of Education's Commission on Opportunities in Athletics conduct an inquiry into the enforcement of Title IX, which took place in the wake of September 11, I find myself wondering whether Ms. Allen's sentiments will be reflected in the deliberations of the commission as well. In early October 2001, the U.S. Department of Justice retracted its support of a four-year-old sex discrimination lawsuit filed by women who alleged that the physical fitness test to be a Philadelphia transit police officer was unfair to female applicants. Could the one firewall that has been in place to insure that women receive the kind of athletic education that presumably builds American heroes and leaders be the next to fall as we grieve as a nation and rally, unquestioning, around our flag of freedom?

As we sort through the debris of our challenged ideas, we may wish to consider who is acting more like Chicken Little. Are they perhaps those who are willing to prepare only our boys for the demands of the dirty job of combat and warfare, and to mount such an effort on the assumed expendability of our male populace and presumed weakness of our female populace? One gets the impression from reading fairytales that wise leaders who fully grasp their role as protectors could devise a response to transcend the binaries of male/female, good/evil, Christian/Muslim, industrial world/third world that have thus far failed to make the world a more peaceful place.

NOTES

1. The terrorist attacks that occurred on September 11, 2001 triggered racial and ethnic stereotypes and profiling. The language used here is reflective of the sentiment at the time. The impact of these stereotypes would be documented in the aftermath. Here are just two citations (one close to the time of the event and one that addresses the impact five years later) that chronicles the links made between "terrorists" as "dark-skinned."
2. On April 22, 2004, Pat Tillman died in Afghanistan. At the time of his death, the United States government withheld details surrounding his death, resulting in a highly publicized funeral service depicting a fallen hero cut down by enemy forces. Through the efforts of family members and investigative journalists, it would eventually be revealed that Tillman had died at the hands of fellow U.S. soldiers and that the U.S. government had sought to mislead the Tillman family and American public about the circumstances surrounding his death (see Christie, 2007; Fish, 2007; Fuller, 2007; Tillman with Zacchino, 2008).

REFERENCES

Allen, C. (2002, October 1). Return of the guy. *The Women's Quarterly* (30): 9.

Ambrose, S. (2002). *Band of brothers: E-Company, 506th Regiment, 101st Airborne from Normandy to Hitler's Eagle's Nest.* New York: Touchstone Books.

Bamberger, M. (2001, December 24–30). True heart. *Sports Illustrated*: 106–122.

Barker, O. (2001, November 26). Ground Zero's manly men are turning heads. *USA Today*. Available: http://www.usatoday.com/life/2001-11-26-manlymen.htm.

Becker, E. (1973). *The denial of death*. New York: Collier McMillan.

Blumenstyk, G. (2001, November 30). Group denounces "Blame America First" response to September 11 attack. *The Chronicle of Higher Education*, 48, (14): A.12. Available: (http://www.chronicle.com).

Brodie, L. (2001). *Breaking out: VMI and the coming of women*. New York: Vintage.

Burstyn, V. (1999). *The rites of men: Manhood, politics, and the culture of sport*. Toronto: University of Toronto Press.

Chomsky, N. (2001). On terrorism in practice and in propaganda. *Democracy Now!* Available: http://www.democracynow.org/2001/9/21/noam_chomsky_on_terrorism_in_practice.

Christie, R. (2007, November). Probing Pat Tillman's final mission. *American Journalist Review*. Available: (http://www.ajr.org/Article.asp?id=4407).

Dowler, L. (2002). Invisible mourners wonder why the widowers of 9/11 are so hard to see. *Boston Globe* (November 17): D1.

Fish, M. (2007). An un-American tradegy. *ESPN*. Available: (http://sports.espn.go.com/espn/eticket/story?page=tillmanpart1).

Fuller, L. K. (2007). *Pat Tillman: Sport hero/martyr as militaristic symbol of the Iraq/Afghanistan war*. Paper presented at the International Association for Media and Communication Research 50th Anniversary Conference, Paris, France.

Gerring, N. (2002, November 2). Blacklisted politics professor speaks out. *The Ithacan*. Available: (http://www.ithaca.edu/ithacan/articles/0211/14/news/ 2blacklisted).

Goldstein, J. (2001). *War and gender*. Cambridge: Cambridge University Press.

Hall, M. A. (1996). *Feminism and sporting bodies: Essays on theory and practice*. Champaign, IL: Human Kinetics.

Hargreaves, J. (2000). Heroines of sport: The politics of difference and identity. London: Routledge.

Hofstadter, R. (1963). *Anti-intellectualism in American Life*. New York: Alfred A. Knopf.

Jenkins, S. (2002, November 23). This Ranger is lone in his ways. *Washington Post*.

Kimmel, M. (2001, October 26). Declarations of war. *The Chronicle of Higher Education*: B18. Available: (http://chronicle.com).

Kindred, D. (2002, August 12). After 9/11, public "hero" moves on to private, true heroism. *USA Today*: 15A.

Lamont, M. (2000). *The dignity of working men: Morality and the boundaries of race, class, and immigration*. New York: Russell Sage Foundation.

Martin, J. L. and Neal, A. D. (2002). *Defending civilization: How our universities are failing America and what can be done about it*. Washington, DC: American Council of Trustees and Alumni.

Marvin, C. and Ingle, D. W. (1999). *Blood sacrifice and the nation: Totem rituals and the American flag*. Cambridge: Cambridge University Press.

Messner, M. A. (2002). *Taking the field: Women, men, and sports*. Minneapolis, MN: University of Minnesota Press.

Messner, M. A. and Sabo, D. (1994). *Sex, violence, and power in sports: Rethinking masculinity*. Freedom, CA: Crossing.

Messner, M. A., Dunbar, M., and Hunt, D. (2000). The televised sports manhood formula. *Journal of Sport and Social Issues*, 24 (4): 380–394.

Morrow, L. (1994, February 14). Men: Are they really all that bad? *Time*: 52–60.

Morrow, L. (2001, September 14). The case for rage and retribution. *Time*: 48.

O'Leary, C. E. (1999). *To die for: The paradox of American patriotism*. Princeton, NJ: Princeton University Press.

Olson, L. (2002, September 15). Tillman is army of one. *New York Daily News*: 73.

O'Neil, C. (2002, January 31). Single guy stuff: The sacred masculine. *Everyman: A Men's Journal*: 32.

Parrish, P. (2002, September 7). Home of the brave: Pat Tillman's sacrifice is an unselfish example of the price of patriotism—voluntary or otherwise—displayed by athletes. *Rocky Mountain News*: 1B.

Pipes, D. and Schanzer, J. (2002, June 26). On campus, off base. *The Jerusalem Post*: 9.

Pope, S. W. (1997). *Patriotic games: Sporting traditions in the American imagination, 1876–1926*. New York: Oxford University Press.

Reilly, R. (2001, September 24). Four of a kind. *Sports Illustrated*: 94.

Rothstein, E. (2001, September 22). Attacks on U.S. challenge postmodern true believers. *The New York Times*. Available: (http://www.nytimes.com/2001/02/22/arts).

Schilling, C. (2001, September 15). Letter to America. Published at espn.com. Available: (http://www.espn.go.com/mlb/s/2001/0915/1251689.html).

Sommers, C. H. (2000). *The war against boys: How misguided feminism is harming our young men*. New York: Simon and Schuster.

Thomas, E. (2001, September 13). A new date of infamy. *Newsweek*: 22.

Tillman, M. with Zacchino, N. (2008). *Boots on the ground by dusk: My tribute to Pat Tillman*. New York: Modern Times.

Violanti, A. (2002, September 1). Making sense of tragedy. *The Buffalo News*: F5.

Wakefield, W. E. (1997). *Playing to win: Sports and the American military, 1898–1945*. Ithaca, NY: State University of New York Press.

CHAPTER FIVE

Hot Wheels AND High Heels: Gender Roles IN Stock Car Racing

DAVID "TURBO" THOMPSON

I live with fear every day. Sometimes she lets me race.

—BUMPER STICKER

There is a lot of symbolism in stock car racing, such as the frantic dash of cars representing the competitive race of sperm toward an egg; the roll cage as the safety of the womb; the racing season as rutting season, when dominance is established; and the victory lane celebration with the awarding of trophy by a beauty queen—a symbolic "available virgin" to the victor.

Many people think of stock car drivers as tough guys. Macho redneck "gearheads"—not so well educated, always ready to fight for their honor at the track. According to Tom Wolfe's (1965) explanation of the early days of organized stock car racing, just after World War II, stock car racing "was immediately regarded as some kind of manifestation of the animal irresponsibility of the lower orders. It had a truly terrible reputation.... The drivers were country boys, and they had regular feuds out there, putting each other 'up against the wall' and 'cutting tires' and everything else."

When I started racing in the late 1980s as "Turbo," while also studying for my Ph.D., my competitors were mechanics, carpenters, welders, truck drivers, doctors, lawyers, business owners, and bank executives. They never fought after a race but usually settled their differences with nonverbal communication on the track during the race. The preferred gesture of disapproval is "he fist," but using one's racecar to ram an opponent's (known as "putting the bumper to him") or to slap an opponent's fenders (known as "rubbin'") can also send a clear message.

A BRIEF INTRODUCTION TO STOCK CAR RACING

The sport of stock car racing evolved from informal speed contests among drivers running "moonshine" (illegal liquor), particularly in the Appalachian Mountain regions of Georgia, Tennessee, North Carolina, and South Carolina (Craft 1993; Crider 1987; Gabbard 1992; Hodges 1998; Menzer 2001; Middleton 2002; Rich 2002). "Whiskey trippin" was depicted in the film *Thunder Road* (1958), starring Robert Mitchum. According to Dr. John Craft (1993: 4), "Modifications [made to] the ordinary American sedan they used to complete their nightly runs were the first steps toward the purpose-built bullets that are currently blistering NASCAR tracks on the Winston Cup circuit."

NASCAR is an acronym for the National Association for Stock Car Automobile Racing. In 2008, the corporate sponsor of NASCAR's top series was a telecommunication company, and the Winston Cup Series has become the NASCAR Sprint Cup Series.

So the sport of stock car racing is built on the spirit of the renegade, the outlaw, the rogue. Danger was simply part of life for a whisky tripper. And danger has been a part of the sport of stock car racing since its origin. Its history has been well documented (Chapin 1998; Craft 1993; Fielden 1992; Gabbard 1992; Golenbock 1993; Hagstrom 1998; Hodges 1998; Howell 1997; Kirkland and Thompson 1999; Menzer 2001; Middleton 2002; Thompson 1996).

As the sport of stock car racing developed into a business, stock cars became full-blown racecars fabricated from the ground up in speed shops (Craft 1993). Now, a scientifically engineered, carefully constructed skeleton called a "roll cage" surrounds the driver like a cocoon, providing the safety of the womb at breakneck speed.

WOMEN IN STOCK CAR RACING

Professional Drivers

Although there are other women who are or have been professional stock car drivers, this chapter introduces two: Shawna Robinson and Louise Smith.

Shawna Robinson has raced against her brother and, as she told me in a personal communication on August 12, 2002, their father and mother both drove stock cars. As can be seen on her website, Robinson (2008) is the top female driver in NASCAR, the first woman to start a NASCAR Winston Cup Series race, and the first woman to finish a race in NASCAR's premiere series since Janet Guthrie did in 1980. Yet, even with this impressive record of accomplishment, she has not landed major sponsorship to pay for a full season on the top NASCAR circuit.

Louise Smith (1916–2006), known as the "First Lady of Racing," told me—on October 18, 1996, at her home in Greenville, South Carolina—that she began racing in the mid-1940s. She had a history of driving fast in town, proudly claiming that Greenville police could not catch her in her souped-up street car. Louise raced in competition for the first time at the Greenville-Pickens Speedway. Soon, she was traveling the South, East Coast, and even Canada to race nearly every night of the week except Monday during racing season, earning $100 for a win back. By contrast, Ryan Newman collected more than $1.5 million as the winner of the 2008 Daytona 500 (Results 2008). Her husband, Noah, owned an automotive business and prepared racecars for both her and moonshiners. "People had to run moonshine because nobody had any money, even people in business didn't have no money," Louise disclosed.

Bill France, Sr., NASCAR's founder and president, saw an opportunity to build the fan base for organized stock car racing and used Louise Smith to promote his races; in exchange for the promotional value, France paid "appearance money" just for showing up to race. Back then, it was rough in the pits—the area at the track where drivers park their cars and trailers. In the 1950s, drivers were not fined or arrested for fighting, as they are now. Louise Smith was right in the middle of it, reporting, "All of us would get to fightin' every once in awhile. If someone knocked you off the racetrack, you might as well get out fightin' because you're gonna fight as soon as the race ends. Sometimes it was pretty rough because they just didn't want a woman in there. But I'd go anyway. I was a NASCAR member and I could go if I wanted to go. They didn't scare me any, anyhow." Inducted into the International Motorsports Hall of Fame in 1999, she was a true ambassador for the sport. At the track called "Lou," Smith has been captured in a photograph leaning affectionately with one hand on the top of her car. Her posture is open—one foot up on the running board of her 1934 coupe, her pelvis square to the camera. Unlike some portraits of young women with automobiles from that era, this is not the sexy and submissive "sit on the hood of the family sedan" pose; "Lou" was in control.

Unlike Shawna Robinson and Louise Smith there are some women who follow the racing circuit to meet male drivers. Stock car racing's "pit bunnies," the equivalent of groupies who follow rock stars, have been around for years, according to Rich (2002: 141–142). They want tickets, autographs, and sex. Smokey

Yunick, well known as much for his rough character and womanizing as for his skills as a mechanic and automotive engineer, told me on September 23, 1996, about how many trophies he *used to* have:

"Turbo": "What do you mean 'used to have,' Smokey?"
Smokey: "I traded 'em."
Turbo: "For what?"
Smokey: "Pussy!"

Amateur Drivers

Like the above-mentioned drivers, Mary Green, Brenda Wickett, and Sandy Wenck have shared with me similar tales about the mindset of a racer and the challenges women overcome to be respected on the track (Thompson 2001.)

Figure 8 racing, a form of stock car racing, is just what it sounds: Cars drive clockwise around one turn, cross through what would be the infield at a circle track race, drive counterclockwise through the other turn, cross again in the middle, and do it all over again. The intersection of this lap is the point at which the traffic crosses. Brenda Wickett and Sandy Wenck both raced at the Warren County Fairgrounds in Indianola, Iowa, and at the Dallas County Fairgrounds in Adel, Iowa. In 2002, they drove in a class of cars called "Powder Puff," a division for women only.

Brenda Wickett comes from a racing family spanning three generations and maintaining six racecars. She demolishes the stereotype of "women drivers" as indecisive and inattentive, knocking it right off the track and explaining her driving technique: "Figure 8 racing is just playing chicken. I mean, as soon as you come out of the corner, you've got to look up and decide right then and there. If you change your mind you can cause a lot of problems. You can't hesitate." Wickett said it is a thrill to miss an oncoming car by a fraction of an inch. "You get out of it and think, 'YES!'" Saying it is possible for a woman to race in the Open division, which is dominated by male drivers, she added, "I don't see anything wrong with girls running with the guys. But I don't think any girl that runs with the guys had better expect any favors. You play chicken in the middle, and if you think, 'I'm a girl, they're gonna stop for me,' then no. I don't think that's right. If you want to run with them, then you're one of the boys."

Mary Green, a stock car driver at Sunshine Speedway in Pinellas Park, Florida, confided to me on September 20, 1996, that her first year in racing was rough, some male drivers calling her "Scary Mary." She proved her ability that season such that by her second year they called her just by her first name. Birgit "Junior" Wassmuth, a Ph.D. and Figure 8 driver, told me on October 4, 2008, that there are some women who always choose to compete in racing divisions where male drivers are predominant. Yet, she discussed one driver who brings her female partner to the track on race night, adding, "She may never wear high heels, but she's got hot wheels!"

Sandy Wenck, whom I interviewed on July 14, 2000, ran Figure 8 races in the Powder Puff and Senior divisions at both Adel and Indianola, Iowa, receiving trophies for winning races and earning a track championship at Adel. Still, she has not won as much money as her male counterparts: "I suppose it's because we're girls, but we run as fast as the guys. Any of us could run with the guys." Racing runs in her family, too. Wenck's daughter, Ashley, began driving in Figure 8 races at age 16, and her husband, Lanny, has raced Figure 8. Racing can be a bonding experience for a family. However, sacrifices must be made, as Sandy explained: "Lanny's middle daughter, Brenda, is getting married the 23rd of September [2000]. Well, that's a racing night. We did everything we could to try to get her to change the wedding date. Her wedding is at 7:00 o'clock that night. I said, 'Brenda, I love you dearly. I will be at the wedding. But as soon as you say 'I do,' I've got to go.' Lanny gets tired of racing because we have a farm, and he has his business, and he enjoys his time at home. But, no. Momma's gotta race!"

Not all women who race actually wanted to become drivers. Kathy Slorah had watched her significant other, Larry Conklin, race for years. Christmas morning of 1999, she woke up to find a stock car, a black #3 painted on it, just like her favorite driver Dale Earnhardt's NASCAR Winston Cup Series car, parked in the driveway with a big red bow wrapped around it. Larry had built the racecar for her, she told me on October 19, 2002. Slorah began driving in 2000, earning her first track championship in 2002 in the Powder Puff division at the Dallas County Fairgrounds in Adel, Iowa and eventually retiring as a three-time champion.

THE RACING FAMILY

Families of racers soon learn that the car comes first. Many racecar drivers refer to their cars as women and talk to them with a tone of affection. Divorce rates are relatively high for stock car drivers, who usually spend more time with their cars (their lovers) than with their families—a fact acknowledged at souvenir stands at race tracks across the country. One item for sale is a bumper sticker that says, "We interrupt this marriage for the duration of the racing season."

Many racers report they would rather spend money for a locked rear end than for new clothes for their kids, a house payment, groceries, or family vehicles (Alexander and Block 1980: 20, 39). Once, I overheard a professional truck driver talking about his stock-car-driving wife, stating, "I had enough money saved up for a down payment on a new work truck. But she's fed up with breaking down every weekend. Now she wants that NASCAR rear end. What am I gonna do? She's gotta race."

A hardcore racer, Butch Teague, helped me prepare my stock car one afternoon, but it took longer than expected. Finally, saying that he had to quit because his girlfriend was expecting him, Teague replied, "That's the problem with women. They don't understand how important this is. I make it clear to all my girlfriends. The racecar comes first. To hell with them." Racing becomes an obsession, a codependent relationship. It takes too much time and costs too much money. But racers cannot quit easily. Racing is not really addictive; it just gets into a racer's blood.

Sometimes, literally. Despite the sport's history of "being tough on marriages," stock car racing is a family sport that is often passed down through generations. Sons and daughters inherit their parents' racing knowledge. For example, the Petty family's history includes four generations of drivers—Lee, Richard, Kyle, and Adam; the Earnhardt family includes three generations of drivers—Ralph, Dale, and siblings Dale, Jr., Kerry, and Kelly (Earnhardt 2002; Green 2001). Daughters can inherit their fathers' race tracks. Brothers and sisters can race against each other. Some racing widows maintain the family business; for example, after Dale "The Intimidator" Earnhardt's death in a racing accident in 2001, Teresa Earnhardt maintained her role as CEO and president of Dale Earnhardt, the company founded by her husband, a seven-time NASCAR Winston Cup champion (DEI 2008).

When it comes to spectators, stock car racing is truly a family event. Infants and octogenarians are seen together attending weekly races at local tracks. It is common to see three or four generations sitting together. Some drivers get married at the track, as do some fans. Some drivers deliver messages to the crowd by using their cars as billboards—as I did once for my mother on Mothers' Day. And some diehard race fans request that their remains be buried at racetracks.

Another family aspect evident in stock car racing involves ownership of tracks across generations—evident in the movie *Grandview USA* (1984), where Jamie Lee Curtis operates a demolition derby track she inherits from her father. In real life, Bonnie Hill operated Sunshine Speedway in Pinellas Park, Florida, with the help of her husband. Her father owned the land and built the track that, years later, was closed to make room for a state highway (Cristodero 2004).

Jo Reynolds promotes Figure 8 races at the Warren County Fairgrounds in Indianola, Iowa; representing her family's third generation of involvement, she told me on July 14, 2000, that she is a member of the county fair board. Her father was the secretary/manager of the Warren County Fair until his death, and her grandfather was the building and grounds superintendent. Jo's involvement in racing helps satisfy her passion for maintaining and building the sense of community that this county fair provides to a part of Central Iowa.

Amid the family atmosphere at racetracks across the country, however, rogue males roam through the crowd wearing *Big Johnson* brand T-shirts. Many of these shirts are emblazoned with caricaturized illustrations of males surrounded by voluptuous Daisy Mae-type women wearing short shorts. Some examples of text on these T-shirts include the following:

- *Big Johnson Auto Parts. She may ask for a little header, but give her the whole crankshaft!*
- *If it has tits or tires, it's gonna' give you trouble! Big Johnson.*
- *Big Johnson Body Shop. We'll hammer any hole and fill every crack!*

CAR AND DRIVER

Custom-built stock cars seem to take on human characteristics. Car and driver have a physical relationship, almost like a mother and child. The cars are "skinned" with sheet metal, and systems that support the life of the car include gas lines, high-energy ignition systems, oil coolers, and air ducts for cooling brakes. Safety systems for the driver include strategically placed fire extinguisher nozzles and a two-way radio so the driver can communicate with his or her crew. Together these systems seem to serve as an umbilical cord—a vital link between car as mother and driver as fetus.

The car's suspension is adjusted to accommodate various tracks and driving conditions. "I.U.D."s (intrauterine/contraceptive devices)—rather, coil springs—are available in a variety of sizes and compression rates. The motor is constructed of parts that may be described by gender. Phallic pistons stroke the female cylinders. Petroleum-based lubricants are preferred. Well-tuned internal combustion at about 8,500 RPM creates the feeling of raw power (Alexander and Block 1980: 56). It is primal. It is pure sex.

Both drivers and mechanics usually refer to cars as female. Drivers often give names to their cars, such as Miss Sandra, Jeannie, or Big Bertha, talking to them with encouragements such as "Come on, girl. Let's go to the front." Joe Penland, a NASCAR regional champion who drove in South Carolina and Georgia in the 1960s would say, "Hey, Baby. Stay with me just these next few laps. Just stick with me" (Thompson 1996).

Some of these racecars are seriously seductive. They have sleek lines and nice curves. And some of these "girls" went to the races topless from 1957 to 1963—when convertibles raced (Kirkland and Thompson 1999: 18–19). A fresh coat of paint, reflective numbers, and plenty of decals may represent makeup, earrings, and even a well-placed tattoo. Add brand-new tires and you have a babe in black pumps flirting for a driver's attention.

Drivers are often seen touching their cars. They lean on the car, pat her, rub a fender, or sit on her hood. These are all forms of affection. They might rub the steering wheel, pat the dashboard, and purr, "Hi, Sweetie. Let's go racin'." These intimate displays are almost always positive. If a driver becomes frustrated or angry at his car, the language usually changes, and impersonal pronouns may be used. A neutral, non-gender-specific language might be adopted, such as, "It wouldn't run worth a damn, tonight," or "I can't believe this car won't run faster."

In the 1990 movie *Days of Thunder,* the cocky driver Cole Trickle (played by Tom Cruise) climbs into his car and says, "Let's see what this bitch can do." That's Hollywood talking. A real driver would say something like, "Let's see what she can do," or "Okay, girl. Let's see what you can do."

In a pre-race ritual that seems, at least for the purpose of this chapter, to resemble unrolling a condom over an erect penis, drivers typically dress head-to-toe in fire-resistant driving suits. They enter their cars by climbing through a window, as the doors have been welded shut. Then, they "strap in" to form a union between male driver (even if the driver is a woman) and the (female) car. Car and driver become one. The driver squeezes into a form-fitting seat with head and side supports. A five-point racing harness, designed to prevent him from sliding under the seat belt in case of a violent crash or rollover, embraces his shoulders and waist with a strap between the legs. Leather-palmed fire-resistant racing gloves and a crash helmet are donned. Lap and shoulder belts are tightened. The driver can move his feet, arms, and neck; everything else is immobilized. This is a form of bondage, really. But who is the master?

THE RACE

Because of their oval shape, stock car tracks are often called "circle tracks," often thought of as female. After all, this is where the female car switches gender roles. Once on the track, the racecar becomes male, thrusting himself upon the female track. The racing surface is either asphalt or dirt, so to prepare it for fast action, a dirt track is "wet down" with water before cars enter it.

The race itself is a rutting ritual. To establish dominance, drivers lock horns. Cars "enter the track," then line up in starting position. At local tracks, the faster cars line up in the back so that they have to pass the slower cars before assuming their dominant position in the race.

The beginning of a race can be quite erotic. There is a slow, warm-up lap. Motors rumble. Tires scrub back and forth to generate heat in the rubber; this is nothing less than foreplay. Shields on helmets are lowered. Shoulder harnesses are tightened one last time. Right feet become tense, ready to pounce on the accelerator. Glances are exchanged. Fenders smack. Bumpers thump. Tension builds. The pack closes up. The audience rises to its feet in anticipation. Nose-to-tail, the cars flex their muscles before the start. Motors heat up as RPMs gradually increase. Still rumbling but now forcibly restrained, they are building to a climax. Horsepower is under tight reign. The crowd feels the moment approaching. At last, the green flag drops.

Now! Motors scream. Horny young bucks unleashed at last, they are like sperm racing for the egg. They are flat out, haulin' ass! A popular T-shirt says, "Racing: No outs; no strikes; all balls." This is a male thing—a male thing that a lot of women understand.

WINS AND LOSSES

Second place is just the first loser.

—T-SHIRT DESIGN

Professional baseball players receive large salaries, earning the same amount whether they hit home runs or not. Professional stock car drivers, by contrast, receive relatively modest salaries and get a percentage of their winnings. Every week, the paycheck depends on the finishing position. In amateur racing, payoffs do not come close to covering expenses, even for a win.

Stock car racing is a contact sport. Not to cause injury, but to win—to gain a competitive edge. This is known as *rubbin'* or *bammin' 'n' frammin'*. Crashes can result from mechanical problems or territorial disputes. Sometimes wrecked cars resemble either a wrestling hold or rough sex; other times, they can appear almost graceful. For example, when two cars spin together, it resembles ballroom dancing at 150mph. When a car flips, it is ballet: *Glisser. À point. Pirouette. Jeté. Et finis.*

Sometimes, damage from an accident traps a driver in the car, and the Jaws of Life must be used to cut the metal and remove the driver, like a Caesarian delivery. At the end of the race, the checkered flag waves. Yin and yang; black and white; male and female; shared opposites. It means victory for one, subordination for the rest.

The failed hunter goes home hungry. There is some consolation—a little cash and a few points toward the overall season championship. But there is no photo, no interview with the media, and no jump in souvenir sales. Only one sperm gets the egg. There is only one alpha. In a seemingly tribal ritual, the victor appears to be awarded a woman—the trophy queen. Now the car goes into the background as the driver and the trophy queen pose for photos.

Before commercialization of the sport transformed her into a sterile brand-name-wearing advertising tool, the trophy queen often appeared as a vamp. She appears in the victory lane while the sweaty, dirty driver climbs out of his car. She wears hot pants, a bikini, or a tight-fitting mini-dress and high heels. A "Miss America"-style banner that says something like "Miss Englewood Speedway" drapes across her breasts. She greets the driver with a hug and a kiss and helps him hold his erection—the trophy, that is—while the photographer's flash breaks through the dusty air to record this happy union. One photo by Tom Kirkland, the track photographer at Darlington, South Carolina, depicts a happy couple on a pedestal, actually driver and trophy queen, standing on the roof of the race car (Kirkland and Thompson 1999: 56). A swarm of well-wishers surrounds the car like peasants catching a glimpse of royalty. "Miss Southern 500" of 1956 wears white gloves, a formal white gown, and white high heels. Her hair and teeth are perfect. The driver wears a white, though somewhat soiled, driving uniform. A round patch, the logo for his sponsor, Pure Oil Company, is sewn onto his left breast pocket; it says "Pure."

The 1960s saw the advent of beautiful women joining the winner in victory lane as professional product spokespersons. Linda Vaughan—"Miss Firebird," a bleached blond with disproportionately large breasts—was named for a brand of gasoline (Kirkland and Thompson 1999). Later, when representing Hurst brand high-performance transmission shifters, Vaughan was known as Miss Hurst Shifter. Tom Wolfe describes her in *The Last American Hero* (1965: 32):

> Starting time! Linda Vaughan, with the big blonde hair and blossomy breasts, puts down her Coca-Cola and potato chips and slips off her red stretch pants and her white blouse and walks out of the officials' booth in her Rake-a-cheek red show-girl's costume with her long honeydew legs in net stockings and climbs up on the red Firebird float. The Life Symbol of stock car racing! Yes! Linda, every luscious morsel of Linda, is a good old girl from Atlanta who was made Miss Atlanta International Raceway one year and was paraded around the track on a float and she liked it so much and all the good old boys liked it so much, Linda's flowing hair and blossomy breasts and honeydew legs, that she became the permanent glamour symbol of stock car racing.

By the 1990s, NASCAR's Miss Winston Cup had become a fully clothed, classy, moderately proportioned Barbie doll. She does not touch the winning driver, nor does she hold a phallic trophy. She just smiles for the camera, making sure the word "Winston"—the cigarette brand that sponsored NASCAR's premiere racing series from 1971 to 2003—is visible in all the photos. Miss Winston Cup is beautiful, yet not exploited.

Victory lane rituals are still practiced at most tracks. Yet, the trophy queen tradition seems to be fading away—perhaps because more women are driving and winning; perhaps because, for years, trophy queens and some male drivers' reactions to them have made drivers' wives jealous; or perhaps because female race promoters, who have inherited racetracks from their families, simply disapprove of it. In 2001, for example, at Farley Speedway in Farley, Iowa, a gray-haired granny handed the trophy to the winner and then stepped out of the way while the photographer recorded the moment.

CONCLUSIONS

Stock car racing, as evidenced here, is a rich area for the study of gender and language in sport; genders seem to appear in tandem, usually as male-female pairs but also with some gender-bending and role reversal. Women are participating in a variety of roles at every level of the sport. Beyond the scope of this chapter are stories about women who work as NASCAR officials, public relations professionals for race teams or for corporate sponsors of racing, performance engineers whose innovations contribute to speed and safety in the sport, corporate executives who may choose to sponsor a stock car racing team, and in many more capacities.

Since the 1940s, women such as Louise Smith have been involved in stock car racing. Yet, accomplished female drivers such as Shawna Robinson have struggled to break through the retaining wall (there are no glass ceilings in racing) to establish themselves at the top of their sport in the twenty-first century. Track operators such as Bonnie Smith embrace the legacy left to them by their fathers. Race team owners such as Teresa Earnhardt assume the mantle of corporate leadership when their husbands die.

However, historically, stock car racing has been a male-dominated sport. And distinct forms of gender-based segregation and discrimination persist, such as the Powder Puff division for women only. Today, there still is no talk of a stock car racing equivalent to the WNBA (Women's National Basketball Association) or the WUSA (Women's United Soccer Association). For now, souvenir stands at race tracks continue to sell bumper stickers that say, "WANTED: GOOD WOMAN... to push race car."

REFERENCES

Alexander, D. and Block, J. (1980). *The racer's dictionary*. Santa Ana, California: Steve Smith Autosports.

Big Johnson (2008). Racing. Available: (http://www.bigjohnson.com).

Chapin, K. (1998). *Fast as white lightning: The story of stock car racing*. New York: Three Rivers.

Craft, J. (1993). *The anatomy and development of the stock car*. Osceola, WI: Motorbooks International.

Crider, C. (1987). *The road to Daytona*. Daytona Beach, FL: Curtis Crider.

Cristodero, D. (2004, November 21). Full house sends off Sunshine Speedway. *St. Petersburg Times*. Available: (http://www.sptimes.com/2004/11/21/Sports/Full_house_sends_off_.shtml).

DEI (2008). Executive bio, Dale Earnhardt. Available: (http://www.daleearnhardtinc.com/content/corporation/bios.aspx)

Earnhardt, D., Jr. with Gurss, J. (2002). *Driver #8*. New York: Warner Books.

Fielden, G. (1992). *Forty years of stock car racing*, four-volumes. Surfside Beach, South Carolina: Galfield.

Gabbard, A. (1992). *Return to Thunder Road: The story behind the legend*. Lenoir City, TN: Gabbard.

Golenbock, P. (1993). *American zoom: Stock car racing from the dirt tracks to Daytona*. New York: Macmillan.

Grandview U.S.A. (1984). Directed by Randal Kleiser. With Jamie Lee Curtis and Patrick Swayze. Twentieth Century Fox.

Green, D. (2001). The Earnhardts: A winning family tradition. *AMI Auto World Magazine*: 40–46.

Hagstom, R. G. (1998). *The NASCAR way: The business that drives the sport*. New York: John Wiley & Sons.

Hodges, J. (1998, November). Moonshine to Mainstream. *Ambassador*: 44–47.

Howell, M. (1997). *From moonshine to Madison Avenue: A cultural history of the NASCAR Winston Cup Series*. Bowling Green, OH: Bowling Green State University Popular Press.

Kirkland, T., and Thompson, D. (1999). *Darlington International Raceway, 1950–1967*. Osceola, WI: Motorbooks International.

Menzer, J. (2001). *The wildest ride: A history of NASCAR (or how a bunch of good ol' boys built a billion-dollar industry out of wrecking cars)*. New York: Simon and Schuster.

Middleton, A. (2002, February). The last of the moonshiners. *Stock Car Racing*: 116–125.

Results (2008). 2008 official race results: Daytona 500. Available: (http://www.nascar.com/races/cup/2008/1/data/results_official.html).

Rich, R. (2002). *My life in the pits: Living and learning on the NASCAR Winston Cup circuit*. New York: HarperCollins.

Robinson, Shawna (2008). Available: http://www.shawnarobinson.info.

Thompson, D. R. (1996). Joe Penland: The story of a NASCAR champion. Paper presented at the Popular Culture Association Annual Meeting, Sports Division, Las Vegas, Nevada.

Thompson, D. R. (2001). Dangerous intersection ahead: Figure 8 racing at the Warren County (Iowa) Fairgrounds. (2001). Paper presented at the Popular Culture Association Annual Meeting, Sports Division, Philadelphia, Pennsylvania.

Wolfe, T. (1965, March). The last American hero is Junior Johnson. Yes! *Esquire*: 68+ [Note: This was later included in Tom Wolfe's *The purple decades: A reader* (New York: Berkley Books): 27–62].

PART III

SPORTS LITERATURE

CHAPTER SIX

All-skates, Witch Wool, AND A Blouse Full OF Lungs: Dan Jenkins' Use OF Masculine Sexual Language

JOHN MARK DEMPSEY

In his first novel, *Semi-tough* (1972), Dan Jenkins' protagonist, pro football star Billy Clyde Puckett, is surprised when his friend (and his future wife in a later novel), Barbara Jane Bookman, suggests that perhaps he should remove the "excessive vulgarities" from his tell-all biography. Billy Clyde reacts with righteous indignation: "I told Barb I had never heard or seen anything vulgar in my life, and I certainly wouldn't allow anything vulgar in my book" (Jenkins, 1972: 30), a trenchant comment establishing the major theme of Jenkins' series of sports novels: The real vulgarity is hypocrisy. It is a theme that continues to his most recent book: *The Franchise Babe* (2008).

Jenkins has filled his writing with blunt sexual language illustrating several theories related to the way masculinity is portrayed in our culture and the way young men purportedly think and speak. The sexual language spoken by Jenkins' characters serves several purposes or outcomes: to promote hegemonic masculinity (the promotion of traditional male cultural values), to assert a swaggering masculinity, to provide protection against emotional vulnerabilities, and to show defiance of convention. Most importantly, Jenkins uses frank sexual language to portray reality and to target hypocrisy in its many forms. In most instances, these purposes and outcomes overlap, so each scene involving sexual language may work on more than one level.

This chapter is based on rhetorical and literary scholarship, critical reviews of Jenkins' novels, and his e-mail replies to a series of questions posed by this author.

In addition to being a successful novelist, Dan Jenkins has been a prolific writer on football and golf for *Sports Illustrated*, *Golf Digest*, and *Playboy*. *New York Daily News* sports columnist and novelist Mike Lupica has said that Jenkins is as influential as any sportswriter in history (cited in Cohen, 1998). *Sports Illustrated* named *Semi-tough* as the seventh best sports book of all time (McEntegart et al., 2002). Already famed for his newspaper and magazine sports reporting, Jenkins pitched the Billy Clyde story to book editor Herman Gollob. "I'd publish anything with the title *Semi-tough*, even if it had blank pages," he replied—and the rest is sports literature history (Martin, 2008).

No one who has spent any time around male athletes, particularly football players, will find the sexual language in the comic novels of Dan Jenkins shocking, although the sheer volume of his profanities, vulgarities, and obscenities can be somewhat overwhelming. Jenkins' golf novels, such as *Dead Solid Perfect* (1974), are slightly less ribald because they deal with golfers, rather than football players; Jenkins has remarked that "their lives and language were different." But Jenkins finds the idea that the frank sexual talk in any of his novels might be "overwhelming" laughable. "By the way, how can the 'sexual content' of *Semi* have been 'overwhelming' to any grown-up who had ever been anywhere or known any real people?" he asked in a personal e-mail to me of January 24, 2002. In his view, the language and scenes in his novels represent merely a slightly distorted version of reality in pro sports. If the gentle reader is not hip to that reality, that is his or her own problem. Thus, Billy Clyde describes a sex party at his and Shake's apartment, fondly known as "Sperm City":

> One time there were these three spade hooks in attendance. They were hard-hitters and really good-natured. They let T.J. [Lambert, a particularly crude lineman] get them defrocked and boost them up on the mantel over the fireplace in the living room. I can still see them sitting up there with their legs spread, singing like the Supremes, while T.J. took turns eating all three. (Jenkins, 1972, p, 91)

The constant stream of sexual language in Jenkins' best-known sports novels—*Semi-tough* (1972) and *Dead Solid Perfect* (1974)—as well as his other sports satires mixes with similarly rough sexist and racially insensitive language to send a clear message: Politically correct language is not spoken here. If some hypocritical prig is offended, so be it.

Sexually explicit language becomes a badge of honor in the fast world of New York Giants' Billy Clyde Puckett and Shake Tiller in *Semi-tough*, and pro golfers Kenny Lee Puckett (Billy Clyde's uncle) in *Dead Solid Perfect*, and Bobby Joe Grooves in *The Money-Whipped Steer-Job Three-Jack Give-up Artist* (2001). As Lyons (1984: 93) has noted, Jenkins' uncompromising approach is to "wallow so deep in misogyny, scatology, bigotry and sacrilege as to leave readers just two choices: to fling the book across the room or to laugh out loud." These themes are also present in Jenkins' other sports novels: *Life Its Ownself* (1984), *You Gotta Play Hurt* (1991), *Rude Behavior* (1998) and *Slim and None* (2005).

Jenkins' writing demonstrates an excellent ear for sexual language. "All-skate [group sex] and stoves came from TV execs in Gotham," he told me in a January 24, 2002 e-mail. A "stove," in the words of Billy Clyde Puckett (Jenkins, 1972: 100), "was over thirty and preferably married. A Stovette was just under thirty, divorced, talked filthy, and tried to make up for all the studs she never got to eat because she got married so young." A "blouse full of lungs" (Jenkins, 1972: 98) refers to big breasts. "Side gash" (extramarital sex in *Money-Whipped*, 2001: 10) was a Big Band musician's term. "I steal shamelessly," Jenkins confessed in the same correspondence. "But 'semi-tough' was mine, and so were lots of others, like 'dead solid perfect,' which tour guys now say."

Semi-tough was published at time when the casual use of what used to be primly called "vulgar language" in the mass media of the 1970s was still relatively new. Like kids whooping it up on the last day of school, Jenkins made merry with the dirty words. Responding to my questions, Jenkins disavowed all motivations other than a devotion to realism:

> Frank sexual language [is] used because that's the way athletes talk, and I've only been around them for 50 years. Especially football and baseball players. But baseball players are even cruder. Every other word is "cunt."...I've never thought I write explicit sex. That's for others. My characters generally talk about it more than they do it, and usually in a funny way. I've never written an explicit scene where two people are humping, and I don't even like to read them. I mean, "He stroked her inner thigh and the earth moved," and all that bullshit. (January 24, 2002)

For the most part, critical reaction to his work was good. "Dan Jenkins has fashioned a lucrative career out of deflating the sports world, lampooning the excesses and foolishness of organized sport...doing so from a position of common sense, and, paradoxically, deep affection," David L. Vanderwerken (1987: 125) has written. "[He] has become our Mencken, outrageously and unabashedly prejudiced, jaundiced, eccentric, ornery." In a glowing review of *Semi-tough* for the *New York Times Book Review*, David Halberstam (1972: 2) wrote: "It is outrageous; it mocks contemporary American mores; it mocks Madison Avenue; it mocks racial attitudes; it mocks writers like me." Others may have been less enthusiastic about Jenkins' mix of sexual liberation, male chauvinism, and, sometimes, apparent bigotry. One reviewer (Spencer, 1972: 81) of *Semi-tough* found Jenkins to be a purveyor of "gridiron Archie Bunkerism." Reviewing *Dead Solid Perfect*, William C. Woods of the *New Republic* commented, "The people are so weird, the jokes so vile, the dialogue so infected with vindictive humor...you wonder whether Dan Jenkins' casual and contemptuous way of writing fiction isn't a valid new voice, so reactionary as to be truly avant-garde" (quoted in Kozikowski, Undated).

Jenkins' *Sports Illustrated* colleague Roy Blount called *Semi-tough* "the first raunchy sports book" (Ibid.), perhaps forgetting Jim Bouton's *Ball Four*, although Bouton's book on his playing days with the 1960s New York Yankees was non-fiction. Burt Reynolds and Kris Kristofferson starred in a movie adaptation of *Semi-tough* in 1977, and Randy Quaid starred in HBO's treatment of *Dead Solid Perfect* in 1988, helping the two novels make an even larger mark on American culture.

HEGEMONIC MASCULINITY

Some scholars may find the sexual language in Jenkins' novels as examples of hegemonic masculinity, defined by Connell (1990: 83–84) as idealizing the traditional masculine characteristics of toughness and competitiveness, while at the same time subordinating women and marginalizing gay men. The theoretical purpose is to maintain male social power. "Sport is a powerful institution through which male hegemony is constructed and reconstructed," Bryson (1987: 349) noted. For example, Trujillo (1991) found that media portrayal of real-life Texas baseball hero Nolan Ryan, who embodies the characteristics of male athletic power, the ideal worker, the family patriarch, the monogamous heterosexual, and the cowboy, represented hegemonic masculinity. Baseballs stuffed into the holsters on Ryan's hips in a magazine ad were seen as phallic symbols. Presumably, the media's characterization of Ryan was true enough, but it is the upholding of such characteristics, to the exclusion of others, that some scholars find objectionable.

While Ryan's portrayal may be an example of a positive form of hegemonic masculinity, Jenkins' use of sexual language could be seen as its negative counterpoint. Jenkins seems far too detached to earnestly promote traditionally masculine ideals, but the attitude portrayed by his characters may accomplish the goal anyway. For instance, some may see hegemonic masculinity in off-hand, swaggering comments that tend to belittle women. In *Life Its Ownself* (Jenkins, 1984: 54), a female television newscaster is not at all taken seriously as a journalist: "If she looked into the camera and said, 'The fire apparently started on the fourth floor of the tenement,' it came out as if she has said, 'Please fuck me, somebody.'" Or it might appear in even more belittling comments, such as this one from *Dead Solid Perfect* (Jenkins, 1974: 84–85) describing a prostitute's tattooed inner thighs: "On the inside of her right thigh was a sign with a little arrow pointing you know where. The sign read: 24-HOUR PARKING. On the inside of her left thigh was another sign with an arrow pointing down her leg. This sign said: THANK YOU.

CALL AGAIN." Jenkins' protagonists also frequently take potshots at gays, such as when Bobby Joe Grooves scornfully comments on "limpwrists" and "tugboat lesbos" holding hands in *Money-Whipped* (2001: 91). For his part, Jenkins disavows any attempt to slur women or promote traditional masculinity:

> I don't know about any hegemonic masculinity shit. I just write jock humor because I've been a jock and been around jocks my whole life, and we get it if no duncecap professors do... Most Texas women I know think my books are funny as hell. Even some of your "Up East" women do. What does it all mean? I have no fucking idea. I just type what strikes me as funny. (Jenkins, April 29, 2002)

Of course, Jenkins' use of the word "type" instead of "write" is deliberate and underscores his disdain for any sort of literary pretension. His characters certainly represent the well-established athletic ideal of masculinity, thus tending to promote the mainstream view of what it means to be manly. They tend to be capable of recognizing masculine foibles in themselves and others but still are physically tough, intensely competitive, and profoundly unsentimental. Rather than making a conscious or unconscious attempt to sustain male dominance, Jenkins says he is simply representing the attitudes of athletes he has known. Admiring Jenkins' ear for realistic male language in *Semi-tough*, Halberstam (1972: 22) has commented, "I cannot vouch for the locker rooms of the NFL, but it is the language of the U.S. Army."

Recently, some scholars have questioned the concept of hegemonic masculinity, arguing that it has been used too broadly; therefore, it could be argued that it is a mistake to make too much of hegemonic masculinity in Jenkins' work. Wetherell and Edley (1999: 337) have noted, "As social psychologists... we wonder about the appropriateness of a definition of dominant masculinity which no man may actually ever embody." Whitehead (1999) has observed that even women and gay men are capable of behaving in ways consistent with the concept of hegemonic masculinity. Indeed, Cheryl Haney, Bobby Joe Grooves' girlfriend in *The Money-Shipped Steer-Job Three-Jack Give-Up Artist* (2001) and soon-to-be ex-wife in *Slim and None* (2005, p. 8), insults Bobby Joe with dominating sexual language when she leaves him a note telling him the marriage is over: "You—out! And I'm putting a sign in the yard that says 'No More Shit-Brains Need Apply for Husband Duties Here.' Now, asshole. Adios your butt and your golf clubs down the road. I don't fuck for food anymore."

CONCEALING VULNERABILITIES

Victor J. Seidler (1989: 153–154) has noted that many young men, including athletes, may use blunt sexual talk as a way of concealing insecurities: "We refuse to experience parts of ourselves that would bring us into contact with our hurt, need, pain and vulnerability since these each threaten our inherited sense of masculinity." Of course, Jenkins rejects any notion that the athletes he has known and the ones he portrays in his novels speak the way they do out of any sense of vulnerability: "They don't consider themselves vulnerable to anything but a mean-ass linebacker" (January 24, 2002). Still, Bobby Joe Grooves feels it necessary to assert his heterosexuality, lest anyone doubt it: "Yeah, I like the ladies. I want to set that straight real quick. Too many people think golfers are limpos because we dress fancy instead of like roofers and dry-wallers" (Jenkins, 2001: 130).

Jenkins' characters hide their vulnerabilities in a "language of irony, disdain and cool," as described by Seidler (1989: 153–154). Such language is the stock-in-trade of Jenkins' characters. Their bravado expresses itself, for example, in a private rating system for women, as Billy Clyde described in *Semi-tough* (1972: 100–101): "A long time ago back in college at TCU, me and Shake and Barbara Jane to a certain extent had worked up this rating system for girls, or wool." The lowest rating, a "Ten," was a "healing scab...[she] had a bad complexion...but could turn into a barracuda in the rack."

A "Two," the second highest rating, was a "Her." "You might marry the same 'Her' twice. Or three times. Barbara Jane was a 'Her,'" Billy Clyde noted. There had never been a "One," although Barbara Jane protested that she was a "natural 'One.'" Besides having other qualities, a "One" makes her lover feel good about his sexual prowess. In Shake Tiller's words, she achieves orgasm "about every other time when she's getting fucked, but just as regular as a faucet when you eat her."

Paradoxically, while Jenkins treats sex and many women cavalierly, his main female characters are portrayed as bright and witty. In most ways, Barbara Jane Bookman and Cheryl Haney are the intellectual betters of Jenkins' male characters (Vanderwerken, 1987). For example, Beverly Tidwell, Kenny Lee Puckett's cerebral second ex-wife, perceptively comments on homes located beside a golf course that have been given cute, golf-related names: "My God, some people make golf their whole lives" (Jenkins, 1974: 113).

"I've always admired smart, witty women," Jenkins has confided to me (January 24, 2002). "I was basically raised by women—an 'Auntie Mame'-type mother, great grandmother, great aunts and cousins—and I always selected smart witty women to be pals with in high school and college and marriage. They do have the best lines."

Semi-tough has an entire chapter devoted to sex: "The Wool Market." In Jenkins' lexicon, "wool" is an all-purpose expression that can refer to a woman's pubic hair and/or vagina, an individual woman, or women as a group. For example, Billy Clyde finds himself in a Los Angeles nightclub, looking up at the dance floor from a pit-like alcove, when he discovers that the beautiful women ("witches") on the floor are not wearing undergarments. "So staring down at us was lots of slow moving, Southern California witch wool" (Jenkins, 1972: 98), Billy Clyde says laconically, referring to the women's not-so-private parts.

Messner (1992) notes the tendency of young athletes to fear making a commitment to women and, with it, surrendering control. The anxiety over the prospect of a permanent, serious relationship is obvious in Billy Clyde's comment about his girlfriend, Cissy: "To tell you the truth, I think she's deep down a pretty good wool and if it weren't for the fact that she's such a self-centered, spoiled bitch...I'd probably marry her" (Jenkins, 1972: 21). Shake Tiller discusses his reluctance to marry Barbara Jane Bookman: "I would forget one day to pick up bread for dinner or maybe I would forget to hang up my clothes. Or I might even forget to fuck her. Well, Barb, now being a legal wife, which would make her an *owner* of sorts, would say something about it" (Ibid.: 149–150). Knut Thorsson, a Scandinavian golfer, jokes, "Making love is what a woman does when you are fucking her!" (Jenkins, 2001: 74). And Kenny Lee Puckett's dark alter ego and fellow golfer Donny Smithern dismissively comments on his wife: "I could win me another won of those at [the] Houston [tournament], or the week after" (Jenkins, 1974: 92).

ASSERTING MANHOOD

Jenkins' observation that football players, golfers, and other athletes speak in blunt sexual language is not surprising. Scholars have documented the tendency of young males to use expletives, sexual and otherwise, as a way of asserting their manhood and supremacy:

> As an extreme form of slang, they [expletives] are typically used with the intention...to break norms, to shock, show disrespect for authority, or be witty or humorous....Because expletives contravene social taboos and are often used to shock people, or indicate contempt, they have become associated with power and masculinity in Western cultures. (de Klerk, 1997: 147)

All of these motivations are present in Jenkins' bawdy characters, but their desire to be seen as unambiguously masculine is especially strong. Apparently, the phenomenon of men asserting their masculinity through coarse language is universal. In a study of working-class Spanish men, Cos (1997: 96–97) noted the speaking habits that could apply to Jenkins' profane, unpretentious characters. In particular, Billy Clyde and Shake's paradoxical use of racist slang, combined with their enlightened attitudes toward minorities, supports Cos' observation:

> This style of masculinity presented itself as spontaneous, unsophisticated, somehow self-sufficient....The men tended to present their views and opinions as questions of taste or preference devoid of any underlying cause, elaborate intention or need for coherence. Their political beliefs, for instance, represented striking contradictions in terms of traditional categories such as combinations of racism and left-wing views.

Jenkins' use of blunt sexual language to establish the unquestioned masculinity of his characters fits with Umphlett's assertion (1986: 29) that American sports literature is part of a "tradition of sporting experience that originated in our ancestors' confrontation with the challenge of the frontier." Billy Clyde and Shake use blunt sexual language as an accent to their perpetual swagger. The Giants do not lose a game; rather, they get their "dicks knocked in the dirt" (Jenkins, 1972: 50). This is not the language of the timid, but of men who revel in excelling in a violent, uncompromising world.

When Jenkins' characters refer to themselves or to other men, it is often in sexual terms. Billy Clyde doubts the masculinity of a television actor he meets: "He had a real tough handshake like he was testing the stud hoss' grip, or tying to cover up the dicks he's swallowed" (Jenkins, 1972: 97). In *Money-Whipped*, a golfer who brags that he can look at a lingerie ad and get "a woodie a cat can't scratch" is nicknamed "Mule Dick" (Jenkins, 2001: 59).

Timothy Curry (quoted in Messner, 1992: 98) found that sexual talk among men often takes the form of "loud public performance," in locker rooms and elsewhere, as a way of establishing status among their peers. In *Life Its Ownself*, when an exceptional beauty makes her appearance in a bar, she is greeted with cries of "Face mask! That would be the ultimate compliment to the young lady from one of our freelance gynecologists" (Jenkins, 1984: 26). Any serious talk about male-female relationships takes place furtively on the fringe of a group, Curry noted. If it is discovered, the speakers are often ridiculed and taunted by other members of the team or group (Messner, 1992: 98). When Billy Clyde Puckett is asked about his girlfriend, he makes sure his friend doesn't get the idea he's serious about her: "She's a gotch-eyed, hump-backed, clapped-up Cambodian hooker who stopped over to help me work a pornographic jigsaw puzzle" (Jenkins, 1972: 47).

While Jenkins' characters portray a bewildered attitude toward women, their chauvinism does not extend to violence. In *Dead Solid Perfect*, Kenny Lee Puckett and two of his redneck high-school buddies enjoy a private striptease session performed by a mutual girlfriend, but when things get out of hand and his pals begin to terrorize the girl, Kenny Lee puts a stop to the would-be mayhem. "This bullshit's over. Come on, Troy. Put that damn knife away. Sandra, get your clothes on. It's gonna be okay," he declares (Jenkins, 1974: 81).

REALISM AND HYPOCRISY

Above all, Jenkins adamantly asserts that the language used by characters in his novels is realistic and accurately reflective of the way professional athletes speak. The protagonists of Jenkins' novels share another common trait besides their penchant for blunt talk: a profound distaste for hypocrisy in any form. In *Life Its Ownself*, Jenkins (1984: 49) writes, "Pretension is the greatest sin of all." "Hypocrisy and pretension are two of my major enemies," he has acknowledged to me (January 24, 2002), "and now I add political correctness, although, as you say, I was fighting PC before there was such a thing. PC makes me absolutely despise most university professors and administrations these days." Jesse Bier (quoted in Vanderwerken, 1987: 129) notes that satirists such as Jenkins are in rebellion against the "semi-official system of prettification and general soft-headedness... the indigenous mentality of the native middle class."

In choosing hypocrisy as a target, Jenkins is in good company. Numerous scholars have commented on it as a literary topic; for example, Fletcher (1990) has noted that Chaucer addressed hypocrisy through the character of The Pardoner in *The Canterbury Tales*. Ferreira-Ross (1992) observes that both William Shakespeare and Ben Jonson targeted Puritan hypocrisy as an antisocial force. Keller (1996) has written that Tennessee Williams lanced hypocrisy, in particular Southern attitudes toward homosexuality, and Durham (1967) observes that Mark Twain, one of Jenkins' favorite authors, criticized Christianity for nurturing hypocrites, rather than true Christians in *The Man That Corrupted Hadleyburg*. Jenkins himself has named as his "writing heroes" John Lardner (son of famed sportswriter Ring Lardner), Damon Runyon, S.J. Perelman, Raymond Chandler, and James Thurber (January 24, 2002).

Thomas Werge (1976: 17–18) has noted that Twain saw hypocrisy as a form of stealing or fraud, because it enables the hypocrite to take on a "false reputation or image." Making his own reference to Twain, Jenkins judges lack of pretension as the hallmark of his own writing. "As Mark Twain or somebody once said, the best humor is grounded in truth or fact. I've always thought I write romantic comedies and let my characters talk the way people I've known talk. Mostly Texans, I guess. Yeah, I do try to portray something comically that's grounded in reality.... I believe honesty works whenever you can find it" (Ibid.).

The sexual adventures in *Semi-tough* begin with a scene so repulsive that every other encounter in the book seems mild by comparison. It seems Jenkins' purpose in positioning the scene there is to inoculate the reader for the debauchery to come. Giants lineman T.J. Lambert, a man of prodigious flatulence, seeks to greet his bride on their wedding night as she enters the hotel bedroom with his "Class A boomer... so there wouldn't be no trouble about me fartin' around the house"

(Jenkins, 1972: 9). Presumably, it would be hypocritical to refrain from cutting loose in front of the wife. He strips and aims his posterior in the poor woman's direction, but instead of expelling methane, he drops a large load on the bed (Ibid.).

When I made a passing, facetious reference to Jenkins about T.J.'s "depravity," he steadfastly rose to his character's defense: "I don't think T.J. is depraved, for Christ's sake," Jenkins wrote, "He's much more likable than most linemen I was ever around. I mean, there were hulks who kept guns in their dorm rooms and shot at all kinds of shit, a guy who kept mad dogs chained in his room, guys who destroyed property for the sheer fun of it, and guys who liked to pick fights and beat the shit out of cops" (Ibid.). In other words, depravity in Jenkins' view is a word better used to describe deeds darker than honest, natural sexual (or excretory) activities.

Jenkins turns a jaundiced eye not just to the values of traditional morality, but also to those who flaunt their rejection of it. He describes a scene of "shapely adorables" surrounding a group of Hollywood-executive types, saying they "looked like they were primarily in the business of cock diving. They'd do that for a few years—until they snared a rich husband—after which they'd shop their way into middle age and spend most of their time worrying about what to wear to parties" (Jenkins, 2001: 74).

Interestingly, the type of people who presumably exemplify the hypocrisy that Jenkins' characters so despise rarely appear in his novels. Their existence is shadowy, mainly implied. Jenkins' protagonists exist in a world where they do exactly what they want and say exactly what they want, not only without apology, but without apology being demanded. It is as if the people who insist on adherence to conventional virtues are so inconsequential and irrelevant as to not merit even the passing attention of either Jenkins or his characters.

CONCLUSIONS

Dan Jenkins' novels are unfailingly honest representations of his points of view, refreshingly shorn of artistic pretensions; as such, they typify several prominent theories of how young male athletes speak and think. Jenkins rejects attempts to find deep philosophical or psychological meaning in his novels, and yet their uncompromising frankness supports the findings of rhetorical scholars who have commented that young men use ironic sexual language to conceal their vulnerabilities and fear of commitment. His characters also exemplify the observation that young men talk boldly about sex as a way of establishing status with their peers and support theories that the use of blunt sexual language is a way of asserting manhood.

Hegemonic masculinity is certainly prominent in *Semi-tough, Dead Solid Perfect,* and the other Jenkins novels, all of which advance a well-established standard of what it is to be manly. Still, the overarching theme of his work is a fierce contempt for hypocrisy in any form, sexual and otherwise. His unapologetically blunt sexual (and other politically incorrect) language is an unspoken challenge to more conventional souls, who are almost invisible in his novels.

As for Jenkins himself, the only claim he makes for his writing is a devotion to realistic language and dialogue. His sports-world characters realize that their world of throwaway relationships and easy sex is not the best of all possible worlds, but it is *their* world: a world of big money and high-rolling far beyond what they could have imagined growing up in simpler times and very modest circumstances. And so his cavalier treatment of sex is not only a rebuke of hypocritical uprightness, but also a weary shrug of resignation. As Billy Clyde Puckett observes in an unusually reflective moment, "Love could hold his own during depressions and wars, but if you gave people a little money and leisure time, love was in deep shit" (Jenkins, 1984: 47).

REFERENCES

Bryson, L. (1987). Sport and the maintenance of masculine hegemony. *Women's Studies International Forum* 10: 349–361.

Cohen, J. (1998, November). Grumpy old man. *Texas Monthly.* Available: http://web.lexis-nexis.com.

Connell, R. W. (1990). An iron man: The body and some contradiction of hegemonic masculinity. In M. A. Messner and D. F. Sabo (Eds.) *Sport, men and the gender order: Critical feminist perspectives,* 83–95. Champaign, IL: Human Kinetics.

Cos, J. P. (1997). Masculinities in a multilingual setting. In S.A. Johnson and U.H. Meinhof (Eds.) *Language and masculinity,* 86–106. Oxford, UK: Blackwell.

de Klerk, V. (1997). The role of expletives in the construction of masculinity." In S.A. Johnson and U.H. Meinhof (Eds.) *Language and masculinity,* 144–158. Oxford, UK: Blackwell.

Durham, J. J. (1967). Mark Twain comments on religious hypocrisy. *Revista de Letras* (10): 60–75.

Ferreira-Ross, J. (1992, April). The puritan hypocrite in Shakespeare and Jonson. *Unisa English Studies* (30: 1): 1–13.

Fletcher, A. J. (1990). The topical hypocrisy of Chaucer's pardoner. *The Chaucer Review: A Journal of Medieval Studies and Literary Criticism* 25 (2): 110–126.

Halberstam, D. (1972, September 17). Semi-tough. *New York Times Book Review* (77, 35): 2, 22.

Jenkins, D. (1972). *Semi-tough.* New York: Atheneum.

Jenkins, D. (1974). *Dead solid perfect.* New York: Atheneum.

Jenkins, D. (1984). *Life its ownself.* New York: Simon and Schuster.

Jenkins, D. (2001). *The money-whipped steer-job three-jack give-up artist.* New York: Doubleday.

Jenkins, D. (January 24, 2002). E-mail to author.

Jenkins, D. (April 29, 2002). E-mail to author.

Jenkins, D. (2005). *Slim and none.* New York: Doubleday.

Jenkins, D. (2008). *The Franchise Babe*. New York: Doubleday.

Keller, J. (1996, October). Tennessee Williams doesn't live here anymore: Hypocrisy, paradox and homosexual panic in the new/old South. *Studies in Popular Culture* (19, 2): 303–318.

Kozikowski, T. (Undated). Dan (Thomas B.) Jenkins. Available from Literature Resource Center: (http:galenet.galegroup.com).

Lyons, G. L. (1984, October 24). Way out of bounds. *Newsweek*: 93. Available: (http://web.lexis-nexis.com).

Martin, B. (2008, April 27). His ownself revealed: Dan Jenkins unplugged. *Charlotte Sun* (Port Charlotte, Florida): Sports, 2.

McEntegart, P., Wertheim, L. J., Menez, G. and Bechtel, M. (2002, December 16). The top 100 sports books of all time. *Sports Illustrated*: 128–148.

Messner, M. A. (1992). *Power at play: Sports and the problem of masculinity*. Boston: Beacon.

Seidler, V. J. (1989). *Rediscovering masculinity: Reason, language and sexuality*. London: Routledge.

Spencer, J. (1972, October 14). Review of *Semi-tough. Saturday Review* (81).

Trujillo, N. (1991). Hegemonic masculinity on the mound: Media representations of Nolan Ryan and the American sports culture. *Critical Studies in Mass Communication* (8): 290–308.

Umphlett, W. L. (1986). The literature of American sport culture: The emergence of a productive field of study and research. *Proteus* (3, 1): 28–33.

Vanderwerken, D. L. (1987). Dan Jenkins' needle. *Modern Fiction Studies* (33, 1): 125–133.

Werge, T. (1976). The sin of hypocrisy in "The Man That Corrupted Hadleyburg" and "Inferno XXIII." *Mark Twain Journal* (18, 1): 17–18.

Wetherell, M. and N. Edley. (1999). Negotiating hegemonic masculinity: Imaginary positions and psycho-discursive practices. *Feminism and Psychology* (9, 3): 335–356.

Whitehead, S. (1999). Hegemonic masculinity revisited. *Gender, Work and Organization* (6, 1): 58–63.

CHAPTER SEVEN

Football Hooliganism: A Rhetoric of Frustration and Honor

ANNE E. PRICE

Football (here, referring to the game called "soccer" in North America) hooliganism developed in England perhaps as long ago as the thirteenth century, and the British fans are today noted for being particularly destructive and violent. This chapter provides an interdisciplinary approach to the issues surrounding football hooliganism, serving as a primer for those unfamiliar with English issues of social class, football fan behavior, and studies of masculinity. It examines the working-class view of football hooligans in the novels of John King, who has provided us a glimpse of life from the hooligan's side of the lens—showing that violence in football team support is part of a rhetoric of personal honor, social class frustration, peer group solidarity, and recreation. To some extent, the hooligans in King's novels are presented as having a moral code and as being somehow reasonable.

The academic discussion around the phenomenon of football hooliganism includes perceptions of postmodernity, supranationalism, sport culture, and power. Eric Dunning and his colleagues at the University of Leicester have been central to the scholarship in this area and have in my reflections provided much insight into three of King's novels (see Bairner, 2006).

John King's *The Football Factory* (1997), *England Away* (1998a), and *Headhunters* (1998b) provide fictional narratives, with brutal realism, of the subculture of football hooligans in England. In the first of his novels, *The Football Factory*, we are introduced to the narrative with the words "Coventry are fuck all," which sets the tone for all three books. The dialect is that of West London, and the slang working class. The stories betray acceptance of and sympathy for football hooligans and their actions; in fact, the reader is left with a numbing sense that hooliganism can sometimes be dull and dissatisfying.

Looking at these novels, it is possible to extrapolate some understanding of the subculture of football hooligans—or, at least, a starting point for a sociology of it. Although fictional, the stories "pulsate with the intensity of inside knowledge…He knows what he's writing about" (Grant, 2000: 4). To paraphrase Raymond Williams (1981), John King's novels are works within which are continuities, tensions, conflicts, resolutions, innovations, and changes involving social practices and social relations. They provide us with an expression of a common culture, an example of Paul Willis's (1990) extraordinary in the ordinary. The novels are rich with characters, events, relationships, and language that provide opportunities for analysis of many kinds. Examples from the text are used here to illustrate specific points, but the focus here is John King's intriguing perception of football hooliganism as having normalcy.

In King's novels, hooliganism is seen not only as a means to exhilaration through a form of tribal warfare but also as an expression of resistance to social class structures, poverty, and bourgeois morality. From these stories, we have a clear sense that fighting among the fans is, in itself, a form of sport. Primarily, though, the hooligan is seeking honor within a stratified peer group system. King describes behaviors—notably, excessive drinking and fighting, the use of subcultural rhetorical styles, and indiscriminate sex. Unlike Willis (1990), who found that writing about these things caused him a dilemma, King makes no indication that the descriptions caused him any anxiety. John King reflects on the violence without separating it from prior and surrounding contexts, and it is this that makes it possible for the reader to perceive of hooliganism as a subcultural identity with subcultural acceptance.

A number of social and political phenomena have coincided in the evolution of this behavior. Attention is focused here on some frequently discussed components of the debate, phrased here as questions: Are hooligans "real" fans of football? Are hooligans unemployed and poor? Are hooligans defending their territory? And, are hooligans a threat to the public? What follows tries to answer those questions.

ARE HOOLIGANS "REAL" FANS OF FOOTBALL?

The football hooligans in John King's novels are Chelsea Football Club supporters. They give their undivided loyalty, appreciation, and attendance to every play of the game, and they know the team's history and potential. Their attachment derives from the community roots from which the game developed.

Football clubs were formed by working-class communities and, until relatively recently (historically speaking), football has been a sport for amateurs (Kidd, 1990). Unlike professional teams in Canada and the United States, which are franchises, football clubs in England cannot legally be bought or moved. They remain a part of the community in which they were created and as such retain a regional and social class affiliation. King's protagonists are participants in the fighting group of the club known as Headhunters.

The behavior of the "firm" (or fighting group) is not a demonstration of a lack of appreciation for football. It is, at least in part, a protest against a "bourgeoisification" of football. In Rogan Taylor's (1992) view, fans increased their activities of disorder in the 1960s at precisely the same time that the clubs were developing commercial departments and dismembering links between the fans and their clubs. Attempts to bring televised versions of football to the fans, according to Taylor, resulted in the hooliganism described in King's novels. The fans expect to be involved in the game's political structures in voluntary and democratic ways. When they are restricted in their involvement by organizational structures and by commercial agreements, many football fans feel that an essential right has been denied them. Of course, as Messner and Sabo (1994: 130) point out, "Simmering just below the surface of this seemingly egalitarian contest are the hatreds, prejudices, and antagonisms that result from social inequality."

Adding to this preexisting social tension, the U.K. football clubs of the 1960s and 1970s provided only weather-beaten and unsafe spectator stands, as well as overcrowded trains by which to transport supporters. Taylor (1992: 165) has asked, "What does the game expect of its supporters, when they have been chronically, badly (and unsafely) accommodated; poorly provided for; ignored or patronized in varying proportions?" Since that time, much has been done in response to the Taylor Report of 1990, requiring substantial changes, to try to keep hooligans away from the stadiums and to make seating arrangements safer for audiences.

However, Giulianotti and Armstrong (1997) have pointed out that changes in the physical components of stadiums have radically altered not only how fans interact but also which fans may attend a game. At different times, the segregation of groups of fans, perimeter fencing, all-seat terraces, and closed-circuit television have been instituted in order to eliminate fan violence. In doing this, clubs have tried to ensure that football spectatorship is accessible mostly to wealthier, often corporate, club members.

In addition, the physical space of the stadium, which once reflected wider socioeconomic gradations, has become commodified through sponsorship, advertisements, and corporate investment in the club (Ibid.: 3). Today, support for a team is evidenced in much more than scarves and club shirts. The most valued support is shown through corporate logos on stadium structures. In the 1960s and the 1970s, it seems, we were seeing class-defined, or at least financially defined, discriminations. Consider this comment from *Football and Raving* (1998):

> One football fan spoke to *The Guardian* recently complaining about his club jacking up seat prices, explained [*sic*], "I'm an old aged pensioner and have been following Chelsea since 1923," a Mr. Kennedy said. "A season ticket now costs £1,250. Last season we had reduced tickets in the same season for £600. A number of clubs know that if they put up the prices they will sell them anyway. Football is a drug."

Similarly, King's character Will Dobson in The Football Factory (1997: 54) reflects on rising ticket prices when he "educates" a female journalist in the ways of the hooligan:

> I had my best bylines during the hooligan era. All you needed was a half-decent photo and it didn't matter what you wrote. There was a lot of glory to be had back then. You couldn't fail. But that's progress I suppose. Then there was the Taylor Report and the clubs aren't stupid you know, they've increased their prices and blocked out a lot of people, priced the hooligans out of the game.

Apparently, hooligans are not the only people "priced out," but this detail tends to be overlooked in the enthusiasm for the bourgeoisification of football.

ARE HOOLIGANS UNEMPLOYED AND POOR?

It can be tempting, when observing large groups of violent men (and hooligans are virtually always men) to assume that they are expressing a rage deriving from unemployment and poverty; in fact, there is evidence to suggest that unemployment and poverty are likely to reduce the likelihood of violence rather than increase it (Canaan, 1996). The principle reason for this is that fighting is usually preceded by drinking, which costs money. That is not to say that all football supporters who drink become violent, but that virtually all football supporters who become violent have been drinking. Part of the anticipation for each mob encounter is enjoyed in the pub, as described in this itinerary: "Land at Heathrow at ten, meet the lads by eleven, a few beers and then turn the bastards over 5-0 . . . Chase the yids [Jews] down the Fulham Road after the game, then round off the day with a full session [drinking] and a curry" (King, 1998a: 213).

King's principle characters in The Football Factory are nearly all employed, even if they do not define themselves by their work. Their income makes it possible for them to drink heavily and to buy tickets and transportation for games.

Ex-hooligan and author Doug Brimson has written about his experiences. He and his brother claim to be fairly typical of the hooligan type, Doug having been one for seven years and having had an 18-year career in the Royal Air Force. His brother, Eddy, is a graphic designer. He says, as do other football hooligans, that they are intelligent people from the suburbs. In an interview in Britain's *Daily Mail* in 1998, Doug said (in Graff, 1998: 2),

> There isn't a profession I haven't met or known about [among hooligans]: lawyers, teachers, policemen, doctors, dentists, firemen, servicemen, City traders... We were fairly typical lads. I can't believe that now people are still coming out with: "But these guys are educated! They come from good homes! They've got good jobs! They've got families!" Where do you think the lads go when they're not at football? Back to some f—ing cave somewhere?

Joyce Canaan (1996: 122) found that working-class men fought "considerably less since becoming unemployed" and that "these young men tied this lessened interest in fighting partly to their unemployment." She provides this example:

> Steve, like Neil and Bob, maintained that fighting and employment were linked. He claimed that he knew many young men who engaged in violence at football matches. Some were "unemployed like, but most of them... [have] boring jobs, like, accounts and that." Thus young unemployed working-class men... could no longer afford to drink heavily in pubs or go to football matches.

Canaan thinks that drinking provides the courage to fight:

> The act which most confirmed it [masculinity]—fighting after drinking—also negated it because drinking, which gave one the daring to take on others and control one's body during a fight, also brought one to lose self-control and control over what one did to his antagonist. Thus it is not surprising that these young men repeatedly were called upon, and took up the challenge, to prove their hardness. (Ibid.: 120)

In order to prove their "hardness," these men drank to feel stronger and to have more confidence to fight. Unemployed football supporters, as we have seen, cannot afford the luxury of drinking.

If hooliganism is an issue of alienation, it seems to be more readily apparent in the lives of men engaged in boring jobs than in the lives of the unemployed. Melvin L. Kohn and Carmi Schooler (1983: 84) hypothesize that "being closely supervised, doing routinized work, and doing work of little substantive complexity will result in feelings of alienation." The attributes of this alienation, he says, are powerlessness, self-estrangement, normlessness, isolation (or cultural estrangement), and meaninglessness. In fact, it seems that there is also a "carryover from occupational experience to alienation in non-occupational realms" (p. 96). Thus, the employed working-class man, feeling alienated in the workplace and lacking control over the process of production, may feel and express alienation in home and leisure situations as well. Apparently, football hooligans are fighting to offset the attributes of alienation that, derived through employment, becomes increasingly apparent in a world of technological sophistication that distances the producer from the product.

ARE HOOLIGANS DEFENDING THEIR TERRITORY?

In the debate over the question of territoriality, there are two issues: The relationship of the hooligan to territory, and the relationship between violence and masculinity. Territorialism, in King's books, often takes the form of racial prejudice. At the bottom of many a bottle in his *England Away*, are reminiscences about the war (World War II) and evidence of the concomitant racism. John King's narrator, Tom Johnson, feels no hesitation in expressing racial stereotypes and biases:

> The Scandinavians and Danes are too fucking honest. They're too nice... So we just walk into their supermarkets and help ourselves... The Dutch and Belgians know what they're doing now, and the Germans don't fuck about. They've got the tradition. The Stasi and the Gestapo. When it comes to the Italians and Spanish, they hate the English... We hate the Latins but they hate us more. (1998b: 93)

The violence of the mob is not related to territoriality the way North American street gang violence is. In his ethnography of the Blades, a group of Sheffield United supporters, Gary Armstrong (1998) finds that this group of hooligans—whom he considers a postmodern tribe—is cohesive less by geographic territory than by the need to promote self-identity and self-definition.

The boundaries between groups are vague and ever-changing, allowing participants to be fluid and transient in their associations. As Williams, Dunning, and Murphy (1984: xxx) point out, groups from neighboring housing estates might be hostile to one another, but at football matches they "stand side by side in the cause of 'home end.'" Similarly, if the challenge is regional, then northerners will join forces against a collaboration of southerners. "Finally," they point out, "at the international level, club and regional rivalries can be subordinated to national reputation" (Ibid.). King's Tom Johnson, a football fan from Chelsea in London, observes,

> England's full of shit towns. Places like Barnsley and Sheffield. They can't compare with London. We're out on our own and don't belong with the rest of England.

> Northerners hate us and we return the compliment....It's two countries in one. Different ways of thinking. Though when you get to a football ground we're all the same really...Mind you, go see England away and Northerners turn human. A bit like Blade Runner in a way. Android lads from Yorkshire take on new identities when you're in Poland or some other East European slave state...You know you're fighting blokes with the same attitudes, but it doesn't stop anything. If you sat down and analyzed it you'd end up doing fuck all. You can't apply logic. (1997: 123–124)

The patriotism of the football supporter abroad is notorious, but at those times the display of the Union Jack has been associated with racism and intolerance. King's characters in *England Away* object to this portrayal and compare their flags to the Union Jack dresses of the Spice Girls. The narrator says, "Our pride is in our history and culture. That's the way things are and one day the thought police will be tagging the flags and only selling them to pop stars and the upper classes" (1998b: 45).

In this fluid definition of territoriality, King's principle characters, with whom the reader comes to empathize, develop specific expectations of one another in their display of group loyalty. But also contested is the terrain of masculinity. These two notions are co-mingled when the narrator tells us, "With football you make a choice. It's no easy option. You don't want to bottle out [appear cowardly] in front of your mates, and the more your reputation develops, the more pressure there is to perform" (1997: 105). That is, the choice to participate in violence is an individual one, made to establish an identity with the group. This is not unlike the "choice" to participate in hazing rituals or rites of passage.

Another example of self-denial for the sake of the group is evident when watching a game of football. For a team supporter, it is considered inappropriate to applaud good play by the opposing team. This hiding of positive feelings about others is an expression of mob solidarity. King's narrator observes, "There's no room for that kind of behaviour. No chinks in the armour. You have to stand firm and dedicated, always loyal. Present the world with a united front" (1997: 108).

Clearly, hooligans would rather appear united in the face of opposing forces than identify themselves as individual troublemakers. Taylor (1992), however, sees the need for group solidarity somewhat differently. Having researched fans from over a hundred years of football history, he finds that "supporters need a kind of membership that works at local and national levels to involve them more deeply in football's fabric" (p.187). But, he thinks, to the extent that the clubs have disavowed the fans, the fans have retaliated with mob action.

According to Gary Armstrong (1998: 306), the hooligan group's raisons d'être include "display, style, experiences of emotion, and creating community." In this, territoriality is tied to masculinity. Canaan (1996: 121) says that "hardness (or softness) could extend beyond a young man's bodily bounds to those of his territory. This is not surprising since these young men perceived their territory as being central to their identities." Many of the more shocking actions of the principle characters in King's novels clearly satisfy personal needs as well as peer group norms. One of those needs being met is for a feeling of self-worth, which is closely associated with masculinity within the working-class culture, entailing proof of one's ability to fight and to drink. "Frank," a 26-year-old lorry driver and self-confessed hooligan, is quoted by Williams, Dunning, and Murphy (1984: xxvi) as saying, "I go to a match for one reason only: the aggro. [aggravation]. It's an obsession. I can't give it up. I get so much pleasure when I'm having aggro that I nearly wet my pants." Similarly, King's (1997: 24) fictional hooligans express the same obsession, qualified by the standards of the group:

> You have to keep your wits about you when you're looking for a ruck [fight]. Get pissed and you're on for a kicking, not to mention a threatening behavior charge... The cream of the club knows the score and leaves the pissheads to make lots of noise... You can be twice as tasty without the show. Just do the business and piss off before you're spotted.

ARE HOOLIGANS A THREAT TO THE PUBLIC?

King makes it clear that there are standards in selecting the people who are targets of the hooligans. The hooligans go to great lengths to track down the "fighting mob" of the opposing team. If King's fictional characters reflect reality, the hooligans do not intend to hurt members of the general public. While looking at the passengers on a train, the narrator in *The Football Factory* observes, "There's small mobs, kids and decent citizens. Older geezers with lion tattoos and granddads who remember Bobby Tambling and Jimmy Greaves like it was yesterday. There's nothing aboard to compare with us though and we get a few nervous looks... We wait for the next train" (p. 25).

They are not interested in "bothering women" or in spoiling their day by fighting with "little hooligans [teenagers]." What they want to do, with like-minded hooligans, is to experience the "rush" of the fight with equals. In finding his opponents, King's narrator (1996: 28) declares, "You can feel the tension and I'm buzzing. Been looking forward to this all week. Washes away all the boredom and slaving over hot cardboard boxes." The link to the alienation experienced in workplace is clearly apparent here, and the fights associated with football are not a generalized rampage against the middle class or the political system. The hooligans who have jobs generally want to keep them. They attack the police only when the police prevent them from fighting the opposing mob; their rage and exhilaration are turned toward their peers. In this way the feelings are reciprocated and validated. Honor can be claimed. Giulianotti and Armstrong (1997: 4) have observed that,

> as Bourdieu recognizes, honour can only be legitimately claimed through challenging, or responding to the challenge of, an equal... There is nothing to be gained and often "face" to be lost in disputing honour with non-equivalents, such as "ordinary supporters" or those considered incapable of violence.

While "ordinary" supporters and passersby may feel intimidated by these groups, they probably should not fear that the violence might be directed toward them. Rival hooligans are recognizable to one another. They seek out each other, and only each other.

Left-wing academics and social workers are dismissed with just as much disdain as are police and right-wing politicians. Michelle Watson, a social worker, is described as "keen and sincere and working for the state" (King, 1997: 113). John King's portrayal of her is of a patronizing middle-class do-gooder when he writes,

> At times Michelle despaired of the working-class people with whom she dealt each day... They had no idea of directing their anger and aggression in the cause of class solidarity, preferring to drink themselves near to a state of coma and then fight each other over trivialities... Those football hooligans she'd read about were avoiding the issues... Sport was the ultimate indignity of a capitalist society, resting as it did on the importance of competition, the wastage of resources, concentrating people's energies away from the class struggle towards silly games. (Ibid.)

The social worker failed to see mob violence as an expression of subcultural unity. The violence of the hooligan is not portrayed as a political action by the participants, except to the extent that one says, "It's freedom of choice because I'm doing it for myself, not because the wankers in power tell me... Mob-handed [collectively] we can do whatever we want" (King, 1997: 105). There are a number of assumptions in this that seem to be begging the question. One might wonder how much freedom there is in fulfilling the expectations of the peer group and how much freedom can be enjoyed by a violent collectivity. Even so, it seems clear that collective action is taking place.

However, the social worker in these novels is described as failing to see a collective, and as simply interviewing a number of poor people. One of these was Albert Moss, a pensioner, whose poverty is described without embellishment: "The winters were getting harder the older he became. He couldn't afford the heating bills and the doctor had told him to eat a high-protein diet. But protein cost money" (Ibid.: 112). Through Albert Moss and others, we are painted a picture of poverty and unemployment in Britain that seems to provide a motivation for hooliganism; however, if Brimson is accurate in his perception of hooligans as educated employed men from the suburbs, this perception is misleading.

What does seem clear is that King resents the motivations and methods of the middle-class people who intervene in the lives of the poor. Michelle, the social worker, also saw Billy Bright who, as he understood it, had been made redundant "by the captains of industry who spent their time bleating on about national identity and then invested British resources overseas" (Ibid.: 116). In Michelle's view, he was "a deformed neo-Nazi" with "the short hair and black combat jacket she had seen on TV reports covering fascist activity in Brick Lane" (Ibid.: 114). In his view, she was "a right Trotskyist," and "these people [social service workers] talked about the working-class but didn't have a clue what the working-class was all about... [They are] Dykes and Marxist theorists with mortgages and framed university degrees next to the futon" (Ibid.: 116).

Through the social worker, the reader is provided a context for the poverty and underemployment of Londoners. We see the community and its lack of hope for an improved future. Framed in this way, the antisocial actions of hooligans become a form of political commentary, if not political action. This reconceiving of the activities of the mob contradicts prior assessments of the role of the sports spectator in society. Allen Guttmann (1980), who could have been a model for the character of Michelle, has suggested that sports serve to distract the proletariat from what he sees as its real task; he says, "The rage and anger which should be directed against the ruling class is turned instead against the opposing team; the loyalty and emotional involvement which should be part of one's class consciousness is wasted on the home team" (p. 276).

As we have seen, though, the violence is not so much against the opposing team as it is against other hooligans, who take on the role of enemy in a very ill-defined way. John King's novels imply that the rage and anger to which Guttmann refers are indeed turned against the ruling class. That class, however, is perceived by hooligans as police, social workers, politicians, and others who would seek to confine their actions and limit their opportunities. The rage is expressed through fighting people in similar social positions to themselves. This raises a number of questions about both political action and fighting: perhaps the hooligans are being turned in on themselves through corporate dominance of football and social control mechanisms.

On the other hand, as Conley (1999) implies, perhaps hooligans are simply engaging in a recreation, and no political motivation can be attributed to their actions. They may behave in self-destructive ways after drinking, but nothing deters the ongoing ritual of meeting together to drink to excess. Incomes are not invested in the future, or in attempts to escape the community; instead, they are spent on drinks at the pub, or on trips to support the local, regional, or national team where hooligans enjoy a fight. In doing these things, the principal characters in King's novels reaffirm the identity of their subculture and reject the identities of other social classes.

CONCLUSIONS

John King's novels give us insight into the behaviors of hooligans as well as a glimpse into the biases of the author. It appears from King's novels that hooligans value their own language and culture more than anything else, and they perceive them as parts of their personal identity and their community connectedness. They also value elements of masculine identity that the middle class prefers to suppress. Although onlookers may be afraid that the unfettered fury of the mob may be turned against them, the evidence here seems to suggest that this is highly unlikely. The football hooligan in King's novels is responding to the frustrations of his life and the expectations of his peers by attacking only other hooligans.

The football world has changed somewhat in the last ten years partly because of the ongoing development of the European Union. In addition, there has been an increasing employment of football players of various ethnicities, thus introducing aspects of cultural diversity into UK football clubs. Employment legislation now prescribes equal opportunity practices, and the clubs promote community-based activities and antiracism (Woodward, 2007). To some extent this involves the clubs and fans in self-regulating football identities. Although "those who fail to comply are denied access to their object of desire, football" (Ibid.: 774), diversity has allowed for a renegotiation of identities for clubs and fans.

The landscape of football fandom has also been changed in recent years by new technologies and the uses of Internet club sites, satellite television, blogs, and discussion boards to develop fandom physically removed from the games (Williams, 2007). Transformations are still in process for all concerned: legislators, clubs, media, and fans. There are growing national and international tensions in response to globalization that affect not only politics and capitalism but also, increasingly, culture. It seems reasonable to suppose that these changes will affect football fans in a number of ways, but since globalization has spawned new regionalisms we are probably yet to see the demise of the hooligan.

REFERENCES

Armstrong, G. (1998). *Football hooligans: Knowing the score.* Oxford: Berg.

Bairner, A. (2006, October). The Leicester School and the study of football hooliganism. *Sport in Society* (9, 4): 583–598.

Canaan, J. (1996). "One thing leads to another": Drinking, fighting and working-class masculinities. In Mac an Ghaill (Ed.), M., *Understanding masculinities*, 114–125. Buckingham, UK: Open University Press.

Conley, C. (1999, Fall). The agreeable recreation of fighting. *Journal of Social History* (33, 1): 57–72.

Football & raving: 2 become 1. (1998). Available: (www.dancesite.com/arc/05June98/news3.htm). http://www.display.co.uk/watford/reviews/books1/html

Giulianotti, R. and Armstrong, G. (1997) *Avenues of contestation: Football hooligans running and ruling urban spaces.* Available: (www.hmse.memphis.edu/WPSLC/Nov'97.htm).

Graff, V. (1998, June 19). Hooligan turned author: You've got us wrong. *Daily Mail.* Available: (worldcup.soccernet.com/u/soc... cup98/covers/columns/graff61988.htm).

Grant, I. (2000). *Blind, stupid, and desperate.* Watford FC Site. Available: (www.display.co.uk/watford/reviews/books1/html).

Guttmann, A. (1980). On the alleged dehumanization of the sports spectator. *Journal of Popular Culture* (81): 275–282.

Kidd, B. (1990). The Men's Cultural Centre: Sports and the dynamic of women's oppression/men's repression. In Messner, M. A. and Sabo, D. F. (Eds.). *Sport, men and the gender order*, 31–43. Champaign, IL: Human Kinetics Books.

King, J. (1997). *The football factory.* London: Vintage.

King, J. (1998a). *England away.* London: Jonathan Cape.

King, J. (1998b). *Headhunters.* London: Vintage.

Kohn, M. C. and Schooler, C. (1983). *Work and personality: An inquiry into the impact of social stratification.* Norwood, NJ: Ablex.

Messner, M. A. and Sabo, D. F. (1994). *Sex, violence and power in sports.* Freedom, CA: Crossing.

Taylor, R. (1992). *Football and its fans.* London: Leicester University Press.

Williams, J. (April 2007). Rethinking sports fandom: The case of European soccer. *Leisure Studies* (26, 2): 127–146.

Williams, J., Dunning E., and Murphy, P. (1984). *Hooligans abroad.* London: Routledge & Kegan Paul.

Williams, R. (1981). *Culture.* London: Fontana.

Willis, P. (1990). *Common culture.* Boulder: Westview.

Woodward, K. (July/September 2007). On and off the pitch. *Cultural Studies* (21, 4–5): 758–778.

CHAPTER EIGHT

Gender, Cross-dressing, AND Sport IN Lewis Nordan's *The All-Girl Football Team*

ROBERT SIRABIAN

In traditional male sports fiction and nonfiction about baseball, such as Roger Kahn's *In the Catbird Seat* (1974) and *Where Have All Our Heroes Gone* (1974), the experience can help father and son bridge their generational differences and express feelings for one another, even though baseball's pastoral yearnings may not always be appreciated by the younger generation. Ironically, the sentimentalism and nostalgia of Kahn's stories contrast with the physical play of women athletes today. As a *New York Times* article (Araton, 2008) about a WNBA court fight between Candace Parker (Los Angeles Sparks) and Plenette Pierson (Detroit Shock) points out, "A sports culture that historically has preferred its female athletic icons pony-tailed or pixie-framed... could stand a little reconditioning on the appeal of strong, aggressive women, who not only can dunk but can dish it out" (Araton, 2008). With the popularity and continued growth of women's athletics, what were once exclusively masculine values of sport—toughness, competitiveness, self-confidence—have become athletic values defining individual participants, including young girls/teens (e.g., Frost, 2000; Murdock, 2007; Schinto, 1995).

Ideally, "athlete" refers to qualities of the individual rather than connoting separate masculine or feminine traits. In practice, however, gender divisions in sport at all levels are well entrenched, raising issues for sports commentators and fans alike (Fuller, 2008). The revealing "bikini uniforms" worn by female beach volleyball players compared to those worn by men at the 2008 Beijing Olympic games raises questions about functionality versus marketing. While sport mirrors social concerns and issues, constructed through mainstream cultural and linguistic practices, it also has the capacity to transform social and individual perceptions.

Lewis Nordan's short story *The All-Girl Football Team* (1986) offers an examination of relationships between gender identity, language, and sport. The central character and unnamed narrator, Sugar Mecklin, is a 45-year-old man describing his participation in an all-girl football game at age sixteen. High school girls, fully dressed in football equipment, play the game while he, with other boys, participates as a cheerleader—causing him to reevaluate his masculine identity, his father's masculinity, and his evolving understanding of femininity. The narrator's father participates in a Womanless Wedding, taking parts such as bride, mother of the bride, and flower girl. In an ironic twist, he passes down to his son not a tradition of love for a game, but a tradition of dressing up like a woman, understanding what it is like to feel "beautiful." Ultimately, the story raises questions about how gender identity is constructed and defined as father and son bond over the ritual of dressing as a woman.

Identity issues concerning gender link to understandings of sex and masculine/feminine binaries. Not to be equated with sexuality, "sex" refers to biology and nature, "natural" gender identification, and social construction of gender. Assumed natural connections between sex and gender are not as natural as social norms would dictate since "a gender cannot be said to follow from a sex in any one way" (Butler, 1990: 10; see also Sedgewick, 1990). Sport unequivocally grounds our understanding of gender in terms of sex differences, encouraging women to play their *own* sports, suited to their bodies and biological limitations.

Women dressed as male athletes and men cheerleaders in *The All-Girl Football Team* undermine traditionally rooted distinctions. As Laurence Senelick (1992: ix) suggests, "Gender exists only in so far as it is perceived," clothing a key visual marker of gender identity. Cross-dressing has a long history in theater, everyday life, and religions of many cultures, offering opportunities to subvert perceptions and conventions. Sport shares an affinity with theater and performance, as athletes adorn uniforms and roles both on and off the field—all part of playing the game. Sport has plots, characters, and themes to excite audiences and involve them in the action. Focusing on the body, shaped through training, sport participates in the production, reiteration, and transformation of norms.

Nordan's mock football game parodies and subverts traditional gender differences, cross-dressed players and cheerleaders suggesting that gender construction can be undermined and challenged. "The body is not the ground, but the figure," Marjorie Garber (1989: 181) has noted. The narrator/cheerleader's maturation results from his realization of identity beyond gender, a motivation for challenging how the body can be trained to move and look. Further, the fantasy element adds humor and theatricality. On the other hand, according to Judith Butler's (1993: 12) notion of performativity, "sex" is not determined by a free subject playing a role, is "not a singular act" but a reiteration (through discourse) of norms it "conceals or dissimulates," and can create or produce what it names.

Can the female sporting subject exist outside of language as an entity that can actively challenge and resist gender norms as well as invent new (self-)identities? Nordan suggests she can. The fantasy of *The All-Girl Football Team*, the interaction of the private imagination with the social world, represents a "space of possibility" (Garber, 1992: 17) where the (female) sporting subject is independent. Sport allows the fashioning of "fantasy" into actuality.

THE FEMALE SPORTING BODY AND FEMININE IDENTITY

The narrator's class decides to play an all-girl football game, the ostensible purpose being to raise money for some school project: "The idea was for the junior and senior girls to put on uniforms and helmets and to play football against each other" (Nordan, 1986: 114). Maybe the males pushed the idea, both for a joke and to fulfill a teen sexual fantasy of watching girls play a contact sport. But another component is added at the suggestion that the boys dress up in cheerleading costumes. Soon, "everybody" agrees to add a homecoming too. The narrator objects—"'It's a silly idea'" (Ibid.: 116), but with encouragement from his father, he reluctantly accepts to dress as a cheerleader for the game.

The two components of the event—the game and the cheerleading—reverse socially constructed gender roles structuring and organizing sport, particularly around masculine values, with implications moving beyond simple humor or parody. Alisa Solomon (1993, p. 145) points out, "If men dressed as women often *parody* gender, women dressed as men, on the other hand, tend to *perform* gender." Marjorie Garber (1989: 165–166) raises a related question: "If 'woman' is culturally constructed, and if female impersonators are conscious constructors of artificial and artifactual femininity, how does a 'female impersonator' differ from a 'woman?'" Both suggest that gender itself is a masquerade, a putting on of "uniforms" that focuses on representation.

In Nordan's story, uniforms challenge the 16-year-old narrator's thinking about representations of sex and gender. He explains his attraction to the game, which focuses on players' bodies: "The idea seemed even better when I first saw the girls in uniform. They were beautiful. Hulda Raby had long legs and boyish hips and large breasts, and when she was dressed in our school colors and was wearing pads and cleats and a rubber mouthpiece, I thought no one on earth had ever had such a good idea as the all-girl football team" (Nordan: 114). Barred from the locker room, the narrator imagines the girls inside: "I saw them strip dirty tape from their ankles and remove the Tuff-skin with alcohol. I smelled the pungency of their skin. I watched them walk through the locker room wearing only their shoulder-pads, nothing else, the padding stained with sweat. I watched them soap up in the shower and play grab ass and snap each other with towels" (Ibid.: 114–115). The sexual fantasy invoked here results from his view of female players as strong, sexualized objects combining feminine sexuality and male power, symbolized by the football equipment and masculine bonding in the locker room. Moreover, the eroticized elements are predicated on the female players' ability to touch one another freely without stigma or censure. Christian Messenger (1990: 186) notes that "men may 'touch' only with objects (bats, balls, helmets, padding, equipment) that regulate violence [...]. A male player may have soft hands, but he cannot touch other men with them." The freedom and unity of the girl players reveal a lack of inhibition typical in the male locker room, where snapped towels and grabbing are often forms of intimidation that reaffirm masculine values. The narrator's favorite moment is when the girls come out of the locker room after practice:

> Nadine Johnson came out, the quarterback. She had short hair and it was still wet and slicked back like a man's. Hulda Raby had blonde hair that hung down to her hips. [...] She toweled it roughly with a white locker room towel and then flung her hair back over her head so that it hung down her back again. She dropped the towel behind her, arrogant, and she seemed to know that someone would pick it up for her. It was my joy to rush across the lot and place the towel into a bin of soiled linens. (Nordan: 115)

For him, the girls are most attractive when masculine power and control are sexualized in feminine bodies as objects of desire, revealing limitations of masculine power. Unlike baseball's pastoral myth, football is heroic when one emphasizes hyper-real images of power and strength. Whereas the female athletes in all-girl teams reveal a comfort and confidence as individuals bonding as a team, male athletes often remain distanced from one another, their identity and power often predicated on aggression and violence, "[punching] each other's arms and [making] jokes" (Ibid.). The all-girl athletes are framed as feminine: "I feared them and I loved them" (Ibid.: 114), and later, more cryptically, "I envied them their womanhood" (Ibid.: 115). Cross-dressing, as seen in Sydney Pollack's *Tootsie* (1982), becomes a site of power, a space of possibility challenging not only the gender binary but also the idea of category. Gender identity is constructed from, among other cultural meanings, sex or biological differences that are often accepted as natural or fixed. Judith Butler (1993: 1–2) offers an explanation of why "sex" is not fixed in the body:

> ["Sex"] is a regulatory ideal whose materialization is compelled, and this materialization takes place (or fails to take place) through certain highly regulated practices. In other words, "sex" is an ideal construct which is forcibly materialized through time. It is not a simple fact or static condition of a body, but a process whereby regulatory norms materialize "sex" and achieve this materialization through a forcible reiteration of those norms. That this reiteration is necessary is a sign that materialization is never quite complete, that bodies never quite comply with the norms by which their materialization is impelled.

"Sex," Butler suggests, is a process materialized through norms and regulatory ideals that must be reiterated because the body resists them. Nordan's narrator views the players as "women"—beyond adolescent qualities of "girls," implying maturity and mystery. Whereas men dressed as women reaffirm the male as "universal" (Solomon, 1993: 144), women who dress and act like men challenge the masculine standard by showing it to be not universal, but mutable. Cross-dressing as (male) football players, the "girls" reveal that gender characteristics are not clearly definable, challenging and confounding the assumed natural direction of sexual desire—male to female or female to male—determining (heterosexual) identity.

While the narrator attempts to define the players in all-girl teams through his gaze, they can control him, defining themselves through his desire; rather than assuming traditional qualities of passiveness, vulnerability, and weakness, the players participate in the heroic myth that football invokes, exhibiting a presence of athletic strength and ability. Cross-dressing uncovers the difference between what is seen and what is stated or known, a theatrical self-reflexivity. Whereas sport may provide women the opportunity to define themselves by gaining power and strength, much of sport still fosters the body as object to be watched and defined along split gender lines. Traditional sports culture maintains clear divisions between masculinity and femininity, often reinforcing gender logic to demonstrate women as inferior or that "muscles are good but too many muscles are unfeminine" (Coakley, 2007: 246). Female bodybuilding, the most startling example, exemplifies how sports can become a "manifestation of the will to be visible" (Heywood, 2000: 80). In *Sporting Females*, Jennifer Hargreaves (1994: 289) observes that "women are involved in the dialectic of cultural struggle—they are manipulated *and* resistant, determined by circumstances *and* active agents in the transformation of culture. Sports, like other forms of culture, are deeply contradictory."

CROSS-DRESSING AND MASCULINE IDENTITY

Although the narrator of *The All-Girl Football Team* thinks he has discovered the all-girl players' "womanhood" and understands his father's masculinity, these seemingly stable categories defining his identity prove to be tenuous gender markers, and dressing as a female cheerleader further confuses it. The authority and power usually associated with maleness is merged into "woman-ness," representing a capacity for beauty and strength combining masculine and feminine qualities in the figure of the "woman." This conception comes close to the myth of feminine mystery as explained by Simone de Beauvoir (1952), a subjective response to the lack of an objective understanding of a woman as human and individual. Here, "woman" is not a specific player but a representation of an idea.

Although the narrator questions his own masculine identity, his father's masculinity is never in question: "My father was all man. His maleness defined him to me" (Ibid.: 113). But in the story's second twist on the tradition of sport and father/son relationships, the father passes on his knowledge of drag-dressing rather than sharing a passion for sports. Eventually, by dressing as a cheerleader and participating in the game, the narrator learns that there may be a possibility beyond the masculine or the feminine.

While a Womanless Wedding as a concept may mock women, the attitude of the narrator's father suggests more than mockery, as does the narrator's dressing up as a cheerleader. Sport can enforce masculine standards of behavior and homophobic attitudes about men being "too feminine" or expressing emotions. Dressing up as a cheerleader, the narrator challenges these attitudes by subverting typical gender norms and redefining what is "natural" or "normal." His "uniform" consists of women's false breasts and lacy underwear in lieu of shoulder pads and a jersey. When he looks at the bathroom mirror, he sees himself as a fool and still feels like a boy. His understanding of womanhood is still set in opposition to his conception of masculinity. What he fails to realize—his father's message—is that cross-dressing can challenge and subvert gender norms defining identity. The cross-dressed figure invokes "a space of possibility" (Garber, 1992), a site in which to create alternatives to traditional gender identity, to envision new identities free from regulatory norms that stem from society and its institutions. His father's sports equipment, symbols of masculinity, and his father's manhood are still powerful markers defining the narrator's idea of maleness. Dressing like a woman does not make him feel beautiful because he thinks his appearance is artificial—cosmetics and false breasts being only surface changes. Drag is a masquerade for him; he still feels "like a boy," a feeling reinforced by his "stiff and aching" penis (Ibid.: 118). Masculinity, as he understands it, is also artificial.

When he arrives at the game, however, and begins to jump up and down performing cheers, the narrator explains that there was "something about the football field" and the surroundings that tell him who he is (Ibid.: 119). His epiphany occurs when he begins to understand that it is the land he loves, and he comes to a new understanding of beauty: "Suddenly I knew that my father was right, that I did feel beautiful, except that now beauty had a different meaning for me. It meant that I was who I was, the core of me, the perfect center, and that the world was who it was and that those two facts were unchangeable" (Ibid.: 120). All things are possible.

The landscape further reinforces the idea of security as something recognizable and unchanging to which he is connected. Caught up in the game, he participates in cheers and revels in his femininity—waving his pom-poms, tossing his hair, imagining himself as "a cheerleader at the center of the universe" (Ibid.). He has a revelation about his body: "My cock, beneath the lacy underpants, was what it had always been, this odd hard unpredictable equipment I had been born with, and yet it was also a moist opening into the hidden fragrance of another self that was me as well.... I stood on the sweet sad brink of womanhood, and somehow I shared this newness with my father" (Ibid.). That his penis is "unpredictable equipment" underscores the link of identity with masculinity and sport, while female "equipment" allows an imaginary hermaphroditic transformation. The brink of womanhood is both "sad" and "sweet" because it offers a new potential articulation of (sexual) identity lying outside traditional gender markers, but this identity is also "unpredictable."

Although sport is in the background of the story, it maintains a relevant presence as a site where the body can change, both physically and mentally. Yet, a question remains: Can sport create an individual (female) subjectivity that escapes the dualistic gender scheme and still articulates and controls its own identity?

GENDER REPRESENTATION AND IDENTITY WITHIN SPORT AND SOCIETY

The most imaginative twist in *The All-Girl Football Team* comes when the narrator realizes that as a "woman," he is a lesbian—an act revealing the relationship between performance and gender, allowing him the opportunity to push his gender speculations outside of socially acceptable sex and gender norms. While the idea of being a lesbian can destabilize traditional gender divisions by revealing their inability to account for nontraditional sexuality, within the male/female binary framework lesbianism forms a forbidden "outside" that reinstates heterosexual norms. Although earlier he had felt isolated from the game, he becomes absorbed in cheerleading: "I knew that I was a beautiful woman and that because of this I had a chance of growing up to be as fine a man as my father" (Nordan, 1986: 122). Dressed in drag, he embodies the possibility of identity outside of gender categories.

Soon, though, the narrator hates the idea that he has erotic thoughts and feelings about boys in drag. Rather than lusting after the all-girl players, he chooses Tony Pirelli dressed in drag, even swearing that his false nipples hardened at the thought. Playing the role of a lesbian is an act that points to gender itself as a role. As in games, gender rules—not always visible or consciously recognized—are culturally mapped out. Feeling like a fool because, as a lesbian, he has violated the rules, he ultimately retreats to his masculinity: "I was not a woman. I did not feel like a woman. I was not in love with a boy. I was a boy in costume for one night of the year, and was my father's child and the child of this strange southern geography" (Ibid.: 125).

The all-girl football game presupposes a subject as player, but the assumption of a subject who exists prior to gender and sex identifiers fosters the essentialist belief in sex and gender differences. When the narrator states, "I was a cheerleader at the center of the universe" (Nordan, 1986: 120), or "I believed I was a lesbian. What else could I call myself" (Ibid.: 124), or "I stood on sad, sweet brink of womanhood" (Ibid.: 120), the act of naming creates his identity. And this naming repeats gender conventions that already define or reaffirm gender norms. He cannot discover a natural identity within himself because it is not there; it is produced performatively, as Butler (1993) suggests, by discursive practices that dictate identity. He can only move from boy to woman to lesbian and back to boy. Discourse has the authority to name that which it creates, and that naming is a recirculation of norms that grant authority.

Acknowledging that organized sport is a commercial activity, Shari Dworkin and Michael Messner (2002: 25) raise the following question: "Does this mean that women's agency in sports and other physical activities is a dead end that should be abandoned by feminist activists? Absolutely not. We think that sport is like any other institution: We cannot abandon it, nor can we escape from it. Instead, we must struggle within it." Although "agency" is used broadly here, it invokes the sense of an individual subject who has the freedom and ability to shape identity, contest regulatory conventions and the application of language, and affect an outcome within institutions such as sport.

When the narrator concludes that he is neither a woman nor lesbian, he arrives full circle, only now his understanding of his identity has changed. Although he says his epiphany about gender identity comes by way of "magic," there are contradictions connoted by "beautiful," "wise," and "sad," along with "doomed with joy." These realizations are ultimately tied to the narrative frame itself. It is the adult speaker who narrates the events that took place when he was sixteen, and the gap between adulthood and childhood is telling. As an adult, the narrator tends to dismiss his speculations and feelings as fantasy. "Perhaps one's gender presentation," muses Jennifer Blessing (1997: 14), "and responses to those of others are determined by how one thinks (consciously/unconsciously) one *ought* to look at a given moment." Within various moments throughout the story, particularly at its conclusion, the narrator envisions how he should look. He controls his performance in terms of how others view him, as does his father. His desire to never grow old and for his love to last forever confront conceptions of (sexual) identity that are shifting and individualized.

While the female athlete might try to achieve independence from prescribed roles within sport, its structures emphasize compliance to a collective feminine norm. The same is true for male athletes, who are often forced to obey masculine norms—competition, aggression, pain. The player's challenge is establishing an individual identity free from prescribed codes and conventions. In Jennifer Levin's *Water Dancer* (1982), Dorey Thomas, a competitive swimmer who is also a lesbian, is caught between gender codes that carry conflicting expectations, and she struggles to achieve an authentic and autonomous identity. As Sharon Carson and Brooke Horvath (1996: 318) argue, she learns that "her humanness [is] a condition that is both masculine and feminine" (Ibid.). This type of freedom can be isolating, particularly for the female athlete. Only by "making the water and the world allies rather than adversaries," a condition of the masculine arena of contest, can Dorey create "a place for herself in the world" (Ibid.: 319).

The narrator of *The All-Girl Football Team* tries to make his place, too. But his attempt to make "allies" is still ongoing, particularly in the final image of what seems to be conventional high school dancing. Margaret Morse has argued that "exercise prepares a freely-moving subjectivity which can be active in the world. As such it contradicts long-prevailing notions of feminine passivity and stasis" (quoted in Hall, 1996: 58). The players in all-girl teams cannot be easily categorized as feminine or lesbian, just as the narrator cannot easily categorize himself. As the cross-dressed figure highlights the performance of gender, so does sport emphasize that gender is a game in which the subject plays against the effects of language that define what is normal and natural.

The All-Girl Football Team offers a fanciful, humorous view of gender and sports, framed by a father/son relationship. But the story more pointedly speculates about the possibility, particularly through sports, of moving away from fixed notions of identity to more open and flexible ideas about gender—that gender is representation, and that reinventing and redefining gender norms allow for new definitions and understandings of individual identities. In another story from Nordan's collection, *John Thomas Bird*, gender roles are reversed. The introspective but insecure Molly, with her "gargantuan jugs and freckled butt," rescues the Adonis-like J.T. when they go swimming during a date. Molly struggles with her self-image as a woman compared to her dumb, appearance-obsessed date. The story's "role reversal... dramatizes the arbitrary nature of sexual role-playing" (Johnson, 1989: 416). As in *The All-Girl Football Team*, "masculine" and "feminine" can be understood as variable, nonexclusive identifiers, "man" and "woman" as individuals who dress up for each new game and undress thereafter.

REFERENCES

Araton, H. (2008, July, 25). Women who can dunk and duel. *New York Times*. Available: (http://www.nytimes.com).

Blessing, J. (1997). *Rrose is a rrose is a rrose: Gender performance in photography*. New York: Museum Books.

Butler, J. (1990). *Gender trouble: Feminism and the subversion of identity*. New York: Routledge.

Butler, J. (1993). *Bodies that matter: On the discursive limits of "sex."* New York: Routledge.

Carson, S., and Horvath, B. (1996, Fall). Sea changes: Jennifer Levin's *Water Dancer* and the sociobiology of gender. *Aethlon* (14, 1): 311–321.

Coakley, J. J. (2007). *Sport in society: Issues and controversies*, 9th ed. Boston, MA: McGraw Hill.

de Beauvoir, S. (1952). *The second sex*. H. M. Parshley. Trans. and Ed. New York: Knopf.

Dworkin, S. L., and Messner, M. A. (2002). Just do... what? Sport, bodies, gender. In Scraton, S. and Flintoff, A. (Eds.), *Gender and sport: A reader*, 17–28. London: Routledge.

Frost, S. (2000). *Throw like a girl: Discovering the body, mind, and spirit of the athlete in you!* Milwaukee, WI: Gareth Stevens.

Fuller, L. K. (2008). *Sportscasters/sportscasting: Principles and practices*. New York: Routledge.

Garber, M. (1989). Cross-dressing, gender, and representation: Elvis Presley. In C. Belsey and J. Moore (Eds.), *The feminist reader*, 2nd ed., 164–181. Malden, MA: Blackwell.

Garber, M. (1992). *Vested interests: Cross-dressing and cultural anxiety*. New York: Routledge.

Hall, M. A. (1996). *Feminism and sporting bodies: Essays on theory and practice*. Champaign, IL: Human Kinetics.

Hargreaves, J. (1994). *Sporting females: Critical issues in the history and sociology of women's sports*. London: Routledge.

Heywood, L. (2000). Ghettos of obscurity: Individual sovereignty and the struggle for recognition in female bodybuilding. In Frueh, J., Fierstein, L. and Stein, J. (Eds.), *Picturing the modern amazon*, 72–85. New York: Rizzoli International.

Johnson, G. (1989, Summer). Wonderful geographies. *Georgia Review* (43, 2): 406–416.

Kahn, R. (1974, August 5). In the catbird seat. *Sports Illustrated* (41): 34–40+.

Kahn, R. (1974, October). Where have all our heroes gone. *Esquire* (82, 4): 141–143+.

Levin, J. (1982). *Water dancer*. New York: Simon and Schuster.

Messenger, C. (1990). *Sport and the spirit of play in contemporary American fiction*. New York: Columbia University Press.

Murdock, C. G. (2007). *The off season*. New York: Houghton Mifflin.

Nordan, L. (1986). *The all-girl football team*. Baton Rouge: Louisiana State University Press.

Schinto, J. (1995). *Show me a hero: Great contemporary stories about sports*. New York: Persea Books.

Sedgewick, E. K. (1990). *The epistemology of the closet*. Berkley, CA: University of California Press.

Senelick, L. (Ed.) (1992). *Gender in performance: The presentation of difference in the performing arts.* Hanover, NH: University Press of New England.

Solomon, A. (1993). It's never too late to switch: Crossing toward power. In Feris, L. (Ed.), *Crossing the sage: Controversies on cross-dressing*, 144–154. London: Routledge.

Tootsie (1982). Director: Sydney Pollack.

PART IV

BROADCAST MEDIA REPRESENTATIONS

CHAPTER NINE

Media, Masculinity, AND *The World's Strongest Man*: Exploring Postmodern Sports Programming

GINA DADDARIO

A quick perusal of the television section of a daily newspaper, sports cable website, or even *TV Guide* will reveal a television programming phenomenon prompted by ESPN in 1995 with its airing of the eXtreme Games (X-Games). A series of physically demanding events intended to challenge traditional notions of sport, the X-Games are comprised of sports that renegotiate what Heino (2000) describes as issues of race, gender, and social class, as well as cultural domination and resistance.

The eXtreme Games were coined after Generation X, demographic nomenclature derived in the early-mid 1990s to categorize individuals born in the 10–15-year period after baby boomers entered adulthood. Gen Xers are characterized as self-oriented, self-sufficient, and outcome-based—descriptors that might also characterize the X-Game sporting culture. Extreme sport forms typically involve some combination of blades, bikes, and boards. For example, there are both winter and summer versions of mountain biking, one involving snow and the other involving dirt. Other sports include skateboarding, street luge, motocross, surfing, wakeboarding, kayaking, rock climbing, cave diving, kite surfing, among many others. These sports are potentially violent in nature and involve a high level of adrenaline, danger, and risk. And, as Puchan (2004) notes, they also involve gravity, ingenuity, and technology.

As these sports become increasingly more extreme in nature, the sporting body too is pushed to the extreme, as in a sport like motocross (dirt bike racing) that puts the body at high risk of injury and even death. Messner, Dunbar, and Hunt (2000) observed that reckless speed and violent crashes are dominant images depicted and replayed in extreme sports programming; specifically, they find that commentators use claims such as "he's on fire" or "he's going huge" to elevate the levels of excitement when an athlete puts himself at greater risk than his opponents (p. 389). Yet, the high-risk nature of extreme sport is also one of its qualities that appeals to its young male audience.

CHARACTERISTICS OF POSTMODERN SPORTS

An understanding of extreme sports programming requires an awareness of emerging postmodern sports forms as cultural recombinations or juxtapositions of earlier and/or existing sports. The eXtreme Games are comprised of "vertigo" sports or those that "disorient, thrill, or otherwise disequilibriate" the participant (cited in Rinehart, 1998, p. 398), such as skateboarding, bungee jumping, in-line skating, and sky surfing.

Since the eXtreme Games debuted on ESPN in 1995, the sports themselves have enjoyed numerous nomenclatures. Rinehart (1996, 1998) uses the terms "alternative sport," "avant-garde sport," "extreme sport," and even "outside sport" somewhat interchangeably to refer to them. Other identifiers include "trash sport," "adrenaline sport," and "pseudo-sport" (Kohn & Sydnor, 1998) as well as my own pedagogical terms "fringe sport" and "hybrid sport." Most recently, programmers and critics began using the terms "action sports" and even "Gen Y sports" to refer to the genre and its new generation of viewers (Bennett & Henson, 2003). Whatever the terms, these contemporary sport forms share several common characteristics; three of these will be examined below.

One characteristic of postmodern sport is that it is highly commodified, enjoying a significant level of commercial appeal and corporate sponsorship. As Rinehart (1996) argues, mass production and commodification have become "inextricably linked though temporally separate" in the life cycle of any contemporary sport (p. 170). Essentially, no sport can survive as a television commodity without establishing its own "brand" that includes at its base a corporate sponsor, niche audience, and generic identification. In terms of sponsors, the X-Games, as they have come to be branded, attract advertisers such as Adidas, Mountain Dew, and Taco Bell (Bennett, Henson, & Zhang, 2002). The niche audience for ESPN's X-Games and NBC's Gravity and Gorge Games now includes Gen Y males between the ages of 10 and 24 who are presumed to have a buying power of

$250 million (Bennett, Henson, & Zhang, 2002). Finally, the postmodern sport brand is identified, in part, by its high-risk nature and individualized competitive orientation. Ironically, critics argue that snowboarding, due to its staggering growth and successful branding efforts, has revolutionized the extreme sport world by becoming mainstream (Puchan, 2004).

A second characteristic of postmodern sports is what Gitlin (1998), Miller and Real (1998), Rail (1998), Real (1996, 1998), Rinehart (1998), and others refer to as the pastiche nature of their performances. Similar to a pastiche art form, a pastiche sport form brings together different sporting styles to create a "nostalgic blend" of past and present (Miller & Real, 1998, p. 19). The blend becomes its own simulacrum or a copy of "something of which there is no original," just infinite replications of a hybrid form (Ibid.). In postmodern sports programming there are two forms at play: the sport pastiche itself, such as street luge or sky surfing, and the mediated one (i.e., how a sport form is constructed for the television medium), with the latter allowing for many kinds of rhetorical images and narrative texts to be woven together.

Similarly, a postmodern sport integrates "unlikely combinations" of sports, often resulting in a "schizophrenia of styles" (Real, 1996, p. 239) that tend to be non-original in nature and evocative of the past rather than of the present—that is, until the present is assimilated into the past as a critical component of contemporary sporting culture. In a cultural history of snowboarding, Heino (2000) suggests that rather than aligning themselves with the dominant ski culture, snowboarders trace their origins to surfing, skateboarding, and "gangsta" culture.

Rail (1998) argues that a schizophrenic style offers its participants, both athletes and spectators, a new type of "subjectivity, experience and culture" (p. 144). Today, some sports are hybrid combinations of other sports: street luge combines snow luge and skateboarding, whereas sky surfing combines wave surfing, sky diving, and snowboarding. Essentially, postmodern sports have emerged as a hybrid of two or more familiar spectator sports where the cultural similarities, more than the subjective and experiential ones, link the sports together. Heino (2000) observes that despite the common apparatus and technique used in surfing and skateboarding, it was snowboarding's collective challenge to the "symbolic order" (p. 178) that provided the common bond among its participants.

Sometimes the hybrid form combines sport with a non-sporting activity as in the case of chess boxing. As the name suggests, chess boxing combines several rounds of pugilism with a game of chess or what founder Iepe Rubingh calls the "number one fighting game" with the "number one thinking game" (McGroarty, 2008).

Outside of cable sports programming aired on channels such as ESPN and ESPN2, there is probably no better venue for viewing the postmodern sports phenomenon than the Olympic Games. Spectators can enjoy two weeks of mediated events that cultural critic Frederic Jameson characterizes as a "random cannibalization of all the styles of the past" (cited in Miller & Real, 1998, p. 23). This is evident in the telecast's rhetorical and genre style, which includes combinations of both masculine and feminine narrative forms where sport meets soap opera, long shot meets close-up, and action meets intimacy. It is also evident in the Olympic events themselves as one sport is "consumed" by or rather subsumed within another sport. Synchronized diving, introduced at the 2000 Games and obviously intended as a feminine hybrid spectator sport, combines elements of diving and synchronized swimming. Even beach volleyball, introduced as an Olympic sport at the 1996 Games, brings together elements from sport and voyeuristic media—from traditional volleyball and *Playboy* magazine.

A third characteristic of a postmodern sport is that it often takes place outside of a mainstream venue—on a dirt motor track rather than in a 100,000-seat stadium—and airs on a channel outside of a mainstream media venue, such as on ESPN2 or TNN rather than ABC, CBS, or NBC. With a programmatic mix of traditional sports and extreme sports, ESPN2 was specifically spun off ESPN to target younger, more active viewers. For example, the debut eXtreme Games was the most-watched sports program among 18–34-year-olds (Rinehart, 1998). A decade ago, extreme sport events ranked seventh among 8–17-year-old boys' favorite sports programs (Messner, Dunbar, & Hunt, 2000). More recently, a study on Generation Y viewing behavior found that middle and high school males preferred watching action sports on television over the traditional sports of basketball and baseball (Bennett, Henson, & Zhang, 2002).

Both Rinehart (1998) and Puchan (2004) argue that alternative sport form has been little examined. Therefore, the remainder of this chapter will focus on the programming success of a long-running postmodern sport spectacle that has spanned the Gen X and Gen Y audiences, *The World's Strongest Man Contest.* Appealing to television audiences since 1977, the *World's Strongest Man* is only one of many sports programs that found success on ESPN2 by using its action sport brand to attract a male niche audience. First, I will argue that women's sports programming, rather than action sports, should have found a place on emerging cable channels such as ESPN and ESPN2 that initially offered a mediated home for marginalized sports fare. Second, I will identify the characteristics of a postmodern sports form followed by a case study look at *The World's Strongest Man Contest.* However, these will be preceded with a brief look at the status of women's sports programming in order to situate postmodern sport's programmatic place among mainstream sports programming.

FEMINIST SPORTS CRITICISM

The popular press heralded the 1996 Atlanta Games as the "Year of the Woman," as the United States' women's softball, soccer, basketball, swimming, and gymnastics teams accounted for many of our country's gold and silver medals. This momentum was paralleled in the mid-1990s with two active basketball leagues: the American Basketball League (ABL) and the Women's National Basketball Association (WNBA), as well as one fast-pitched softball league and a soccer and ice hockey league. Just two years later, however, the ABL declared bankruptcy and folded up in the middle of its third season, while the Women's Professional Hockey League and the National Soccer Alliance stalled.

While there are several possible reasons for the inability of women's sports to thrive nationally to date, one is obviously related to its failure to secure desirable television airtime and a critical viewing audience. Sean McManus of CBS Sports observes that there is little room for women's teams on the broadcast networks' schedules because both of these crucial variables are missing (cited in Goldstein, 1999). However, cable sports channels would seem to be a logical outlet for televising women's sports, as they expanded exposure for many kinds of sports programming. Green and Collingwood (1997) observed that, prior to the emergence of ESPN2 and the SportsChannel, only "known quantities, like the NFL, NCAA men's basketball, and the Professional Bowlers' Association had any chance of being seen regularly on television" (p. 28).

Cable television was intended as a "natural" outlet for sports programming from its onset as it could devote more airtime to the kinds of non-mainstream sports that had either been marginalized by the larger networks and confined to local stations or not extended its airtime at all (Bellamy, 1998). Presumably, women's sports should have fit this criterion, as their coverage had long been limited, if not nonexistent, on both local and national broadcast stations. Duncan and Messner (1994) found that the sports segments of local newscasts overwhelmingly favored men's sports with only about 5 percent of the total airtime devoted to female athletes or women's sports.

Even with the proliferation of cable sport news shows, these patterns remain unchallenged. In a study on reporting differences of men's and women's sports on CNN and ESPN, Tuggle (1997) found a void in women's sports reporting. Specifically, he examined ESPN's *SportsCenter* and CNN's *Sports Tonight* and found that the two daily programs combined devoted approximately 95 percent of their stories to male athletes and sports and 5 percent to female athletes. In a similar analysis of sports-centered programming, Messner, Dunbar, and Hunt (2000) found that when examining ESPN's *SportsCenter* alone, the results were even lower with only 2.9 percent of its news time devoted to female athletes. The authors found that when women did appear in extreme sports programming, it was typically in stereotypical roles, as sexy "masculinity-validating" props (Ibid., p. 383).

These findings suggest that despite the emergence of regularly aired cable sports programming, there has been no significant change in the amount of coverage extended to women's sports over the last two decades. If anything, the coverage has diminished. Further, extreme sports coverage appears to be among the most male-dominated within the sports genre. This kind of programming trend is counter to the marketing force driving the expansion of sports cable channels. Rather than devote more time to those women's sports that have been marginalized by broadcast channels (which includes almost all women's sports outside of golf, tennis, ice skating, and NCAA women's basketball), the sports cable media devote more air time to men's competitive or recreational sports that have enjoyed minimal coverage by broadcast channels—from fishing to billiards to rodeos. It also has helped spawn and support a whole new genre of television spectator sport that includes postmodern sports.

THE WORLD'S STRONGEST MAN CONTEST: A CASE STUDY

According to the assumptions laid out here, cable sports channels should be devoting at least some of their 24/7 airtime to women's sports; however, the channels have chosen not to do so. Instead, programming hours are filled with a mix of sports, some of which fall within the category of postmodern sport and/or extreme sport as well as mainstream sport and sports news. The remainder of this chapter examines some of the textual dimensions of postmodern sport in its consideration of what a postmodern sport program looks like in terms of its production techniques, rhetorical strategies, and narrative conventions.

This analysis looks at the final 1999 title competition of the *World's Strongest Man Contest* that was produced in Malta and sponsored by Met-RX, manufacturer of a sports protein bar. This particular episode focused on the last leg of an international competition that had originally involved 30 participants, including five Americans, but had now dwindled down to the last 10 finalists from Finland, Norway, Canada, Sweden, Hungary, Scotland, Denmark, and Iceland. The finals involved seven events—with such visually evocative titles as Super Yoke, Dead Lift, Boat-Pull, Atlas Stones, Plane Pull, Giant Log Lift—and a final medley. The Dead Lift event involved lifting concrete dumb-bells while the Atlas Stones event involved lifting five round stones on a rock wall. Obviously, both weightlifting events were contrived and cannibalized in an Athenian-like context with an unveiled allusion to the past. The most visually intriguing yet thematically incongruent event undoubtedly was the Plane Pull that took place on a runway at the Malta International Airport and required contestants to pull an 83-ton, 148-passenger Air Malta 737 Jet. Harnessed to the plane at the waist and bent nearly at a 45-degree angle, the contestants had to pull the plane in a straight line, 25-meters down the runway. The fastest time would determine the winner.

The Plane Pull competition, in particular, appears to be the quintessential postmodern sport pastiche. It is an ideal example of what Miller and Real (1998) refer to as a familiar yet unrecognizable simulacrum of something of which there is no original. Earlier in the telecast, contestants competed in a boat pull event that evoked images of ancient Herculean mariners; however, the plane pull evoked no parallel imagery. Instead, it was a commodified, highly technologized, and even ironic sport form: Olympian-strong athletes towing a commercial airliner.

The *World's Strongest Man* celebrates the questionably attained human body in a contest of not so much body against body but body against technological forms, from commercial aircraft to kitchen appliance—a human tractor-pull to a foot-race where the runners compete with refrigerators strapped to their backs. The imitative nature of these events draws from existing sport forms and television genres; specifically, they appropriate elements from track and weightlifting as well as from television reality shows, such as the new *American Gladiators*, a modernized simulacrum of the 1990s original.

The *World's Strongest Man* contest is truly a visual spectacle that takes traditional masculine sport forms and frames them for television using a postmodern aesthetic. The production approach borrows slightly from the Olympics that, as a sport telecast, come closer to resembling "live" action sports in real or simulated time. Rather than indulge in lengthy (in terms of television time) pre-taped human-interest profiles such as those in the Olympic telecasts, the *World's Strongest Man* inserts clips of its contestants from pre-taped interviews and reduces the encounters to a brief comment or two of either self-bravado or self-defeat. Unlike the Olympic productions, the *World's Strongest Man,* rather than favor slow camera dissolves in the production of the interview segments, employs quick cuts and low-angular shots to frame its athletes. It tends to frame the behemoth contestants in micro close-up shots that "sever" their heads at mid-brow as their brute strength literally bursts them out of the frame.

These techniques borrow more from MTV's quick-cut, angular-shooting production style than from a soap opera's slow-dissolve, close-up method. Similar to the Olympic Games, the *World's Strongest Man* uses these techniques to target a gender-specific sports audience. However, rather than target females for a two-week long Olympic spectacle, it targets a young MTV-viewing male audience accustomed to quick often disorienting frame cuts and sound-bite responses.

Consequently, this MTV rhetorical style suggests that postmodern sports programming has spawned a new television genre. According to Mary Ellen Brown (1994) in *Soap Opera and Women's Talk*, if a new genre can make use of a genre tradition that is already popular with the audience in question, then it has a higher probability of success. Postmodern sports programming appears to be making use of several existing genres, such as the mainstream sports genre, the Olympic genre (a hybrid genre in itself), the music video genre, and the reality genre, to appeal to an audience that is primarily adolescent male and yet increasingly mainstream.

CONCLUSIONS

This chapter considers where sporting spectacles, such as *The World's Strongest Man Contest*, are situated in the programming landscape of television sports. The narrative and spectatorial dimensions of these particular events are found to have helped shape a new sports programming genre: the postmodern sport. Not surprisingly, postmodern sport tends to appeal to adolescent and young adult male audiences since competitive events such as street luge, sky surfing, and motocross racing are hybrids of high-risk masculine sports that provide commentators with exciting "color" discourse and spectators with vicarious thrills. Many of these telecasts rely on violent visual images of spills and crashes causing gruesome injuries that are aired repeatedly in instant replays.

Although masculine in nature, some of these sports share characteristics with sports considered feminine, such as figure skating, gymnastics, and even diving, as they revolve around individualized performances where athletes compete against a posted score rather than an opposing team or a singular opponent. With this particular competitive orientation, postmodern sport might help challenge the masculine hegemony that shapes our perceptions of competition as a direct confrontation between teams or opponents. In turn, this shift might facilitate interest in and acceptance of less traditional mediated sport, including many women's sports.

As for the spectatorial dimensions, postmodern sports such as ESPN's eXtreme Sports and *The World's Strongest Man Contest*, as analyzed here, embrace a mix of production styles, with roots in both the past and the present. In some cases, the style is hybrid in nature, combining presumed mediated representations of feats from ancient Greece with 1990s production techniques and new millennia sporting themes. In some specific sporting events, the style is a mutant of sorts—a simulacrum of images where there seems to be no original, such as the Plane Pull.

Looking at the programmatic dimensions of postmodern sport, one can conclude that although cable sports channels "ought" to be devoting more coverage to women's sports, they have opted to extend airtime to postmodern (and other male spectator) sports instead. In fact, although cable channels devote far more coverage to sports than their broadcast counterparts in any given week, they extend no more than 5 percent of that coverage to women's sports. With the capability to engage in narrowcasting and niche programming, cable television could have been a natural outlet for sports that are underrepresented on commercial broadcast television, including women sports; however, the industry opted to expand its sports coverage to an array of men's sports, including purely recreational and postmodern ones.

As the postmodern sports genre begins to "feminize" traditional notions of competition, perhaps sports critics should begin calling for the emergence of a feminine postmodern sports programming subgenre. Figure skating was headed in that direction several years ago when a barrage of skating entertainment programs aired regularly on prime time broadcast television. Considered by some critics (Stoloff, 1995; Wiegman & Zwinger, 1995) to be a hybrid comprised of athleticism and artistry, figure skating borrows elements from dance, theatre, and music, emphasizing artful choreography, sequined costumes, and instrumental songs. The melodramatic spectacle involving skaters Tonya Harding and Nancy Kerrigan that consumed audiences prior to the 1994 Olympic Games spawned several figure skating "variety specials" airing under such titles as *Rock 'n Roll Figure Skating* and *Battle of the Sexes on Ice*. The former is an "American Bandstand" on ice, while the latter incorporates elements of boxing, with its skating routines divided into "rounds."

However, interest in figure skating has waned over the past few years after it saturated coverage of the 1998 Winter Games. More recently, Olympic audiences have been captivated by women's team sports, such as soccer, basketball, and softball. This study suggests that postmodern sport has expanded demographically the audience for television sport by attracting adolescent males to its young to middle aged adult audience. Like football, boxing, hockey, and other sports that cater to male viewers, motocross racing, sky surfing, and bungee jumping can be potentially violent as they pose a high risk of danger and injury to its participants; this characteristic is not as prominent (or made prominent by the media) in women's sports.

Perhaps it is time for cable programmers to expand the demographic dimensions of their sporting audiences even wider by extending air time to underrepresented sports, such as women's sports. These could be a hybrid of sports with less emphasis on risk and more on the aesthetic form, resulting in a postmodern subgenre appealing to a more gender-inclusive audience.

REFERENCES

Bellamy, R. (1998). The evolving television sports marketplace, In L. Wenner (Ed.). *MediaSport* (pp. 73–87). London: Routledge.

Bennett, G. and Henson, R. (2003). Perceived status of the action sports segment among college students. *International Sports Journal 7* (1): 124–138.

Bennett, G., Henson, R. and Zhang, J. (2002). Action sports sponsorship recognition. *Sport Marketing Quarterly 11* (3): 185–196.

Brown, M. E. (1994). *Soap opera and women's talk: The pleasure of resistance.* Thousand Oaks, CA: Sage.

Duncan, M. and Messner, M. (1994). Gender stereotyping in televised sports: A follow-up to the 1989 study. Los Angeles: Amateur Athletic Foundation.

Gitlin, T. (1998). Postmodernism: What are they talking about. In A. Berger (Ed.), *The postmodern presence: Readings on postmodernism in American culture and society* (58–73). Walnut Creek, CA: Altamira.

Goldstein, M. (1999, Jan. 18). Few leagues of their own. *Business Week*. p. 74.

Green, D. and Collingwood, H. (1997). Toss up. *Working Women, 22* (4): 26–29.

Heino, R. (2000). New sports: What is so punk about snowboarding? *Journal of Sport and Social Issues, 24* (2): 176–191.

Kohn, N. and Sydnor, S. (1998). How do you warm-up for a stretch class? In G. Rail (Ed.). *Sport and postmodern times* (21–32). Albany, NY: State University of New York Press.

McGroarty, P. (2008, July 16). New sport combines boxing and chess. Associated Press. Available at http://www.azcentral.com/sports/ heatindex/articles/2008/07/16/20080716chessboxingON.html.

Messner, M., Dunbar, M. and Hunt, D. (2000). The televised sports manhood formula. *Journal of Sport and Social Issues, 24* (4): 380–394.

Miller, G. and Real, M. (1998). Postmodernity and popular culture: Understanding our national pastime. In A. Berger (Ed.), *The postmodern presence: Readings on postmodernism in American culture and society* (17–34). Walnut Creek, CA: Altamira.

Puchan, H. (2004). Living "extreme": Adventure sports, media and commercialization. *Journal of Communication Management 9* (2): 171–178.

Rail, G. (1998). Seismography of the postmodern condition: Three theses on the implosion of sport. In G. Rail (Ed.), *Sport and postmodern times* (143–162). Albany, NY: State University of New York Press.

Real, M. (1996). The postmodern Olympics: Technology and the commodification of the Olympic movement. *Quest, 48* (1): 9–24.

Real, M. (1998). MediaSport: Technology and the commodification of postmodern sport. In L. Wenner (Ed.), *MediaSport* (14–26). London: Routledge.

Rinehart, R. (1996). Dropping hierarchies: Toward the study of a contemporary sporting avant-garde, *Sociology of Sport Journal, 13* (2): 159–175.

Rinehart, R. (1998). Pecking orders within alternative sport at ESPN's 1995 *The eXtreme Games. Journal of Sport & Social Issues, 22* (4): 398–415.

Stoloff, S. (1995). Tonya, Nancy, and the bodily figuration of social class. In C. Baughman (Ed.), *Women on ice: Feminist essays on the Tonya Harding/Nancy Kerrigan spectacle.* (225–240). New York: Routledge.

Tuggle, C. A. (1997). Differences in television sports reporting of men's and women's athletics: ESPN SportsCenter and *CNN Sports Tonight*. *Journal of Broadcasting and Electronic Media,* (41): 14–24.

Wiegman, R. and Zwinger, L. (1995). Tonya's bad boot, or, go figure. In C. Baughman (Ed.), *Women on ice: Feminist essays on the Tonya Harding/Nancy Kerrigan spectacle.* (225–240). New York: Routledge.

CHAPTER TEN

Xclusion AT THE Winter X Games: The Marginalization OF Women Athletes IN Alternative Sport

JOY CRISSEY HONEA

The world of sport is continually changing. Amidst the grumbling of fans tired of overpaid professional athletes complaining about their salaries and the rising number of children who have "burned out" on organized sports participation by their teen years, alternative sports have exploded. Individual, alternative sports were usually activities that initially existed outside of formal sports organizations, and participants were young people who, for one reason or another, did not fit into traditional ones such as baseball and football. Since the mid-1990s, however, participation rates for alternative sports such as skateboarding, snowboarding, and BMX (bicycle motocross) have increased dramatically while interest in traditional sports has been waning.

Sociologists and sports scientists have begun to study these previously alternative sports, much of their interest focused on how their organization, goals, and values often differ from those of more mainstream sports (Eitzen, 1999; Rowe, 1995). One of the crucial differences between alternative and mainstream sports is that alternative ones have historically been more likely to be possessed of an insider requirement; that is, there is often a lifestyle associated with participation in the activity, and participants are expected to dress and act in certain ways as members of its subculture. Attendant with this lifestyle requirement comes a countercultural element, participants explicitly or implicitly rejecting "mainstream" values and norms, particularly those associated with materialism and competition. However, despite rejection of many dominant values, the cultures associated with alternative sports are frequently highly traditional in their construction of gender and gender differences: Male participants are viewed as the norm, and female participation is often discouraged or ridiculed. As alternative sports have gained popularity, girls and women have increasingly begun to participate (Olsen, 2001). Although males continue to dominate in such sports as skateboarding and BMX, women make up increasing numbers of participants in snowboarding. This study examines the 1999 Winter X Games, hosted by the cable television sports network ESPN, as a way of investigating the construction of gender in an alternative sport. ESPN's X Games was the first widely televised alternative sporting event, and it remains the most popular and well known. The research analyzes both the organization of the event and the use of gendered language to gauge levels of acceptance of female participation at alternative sporting events in general and snowboarding in particular to examine differences in media presentations of male and female performances.

THE EMERGENCE OF ALTERNATIVE SPORTS

Alternative, or action sports, are generally defined by what they are not: mainstream. Though they differ greatly from each other, alternative sports can be loosely defined as participant controlled and directed, individually focused, with less emphasis on competition than traditional sport, and in general possessed on an "insider requirement." In other words, they are more likely than mainstream sports to encompass their own subculture (Rinehart, 1999). Some alternative sports have been labelled "extreme," which originally seems to have meant they involved risk-taking that more traditional sports did not (such as BASE jumping—parachute jumping from fixed objects such as bridges or buildings, and cliff diving); basically, the media have adopted the term *extreme* to encompass any sport that is not considered a sports staple on television.

The popularity of these alternative sports has been on the rise in recent years. All-sports television networks such as ESPN and Fox Sports have been instrumental in exposing them to the public, targeting young males in particular. Television ratings are slipping for traditional sports, the 2008 World Series having the lowest rating in its history and *Monday Night Football* audiences continually getting smaller—about half of what they were in the 1970s. Alternative sports, on the other hand, are gaining in popularity, especially with young viewers. The audience for "extreme" sports on ESPN increased 119 percent between 1994 and 1998 (Greenfield, 1998), and a 2003 study of the growth of action sports conducted by the University of Florida found more students preferring actions sports than any other traditional ones; further, American Sports Data found skateboarding the second most popular sport choice of young people (Walter, 2005). This popularity is also reflected in participation rates: According to the National Sporting Goods Association (NSGA), between 1996 and 2001 participation rates for skateboarding and snowboarding were higher than those for any other sports, at 106 and 72 percent respectively, while traditional sporting activities such as football and basketball actually witnessed declining participation rates (NSGA, 2002).

Although sports such as skateboarding, snowboarding, and BMX are relative newcomers to the world of commercial sport, researchers have begun to examine them for both their unprecedented popularity as entertainment and their potential as sites of resistance to dominant ideology (Beal, 1995; Beal and Weidman, 1998, Crissey, 1999; Rinehart, 1999). Participation in alternative sports is often associated with membership in specific subcultures, emphasizing values antithetical to many mainstream sports ethos. For example, while most mainstream sports focus on head-to-head competition, alternative sports put more emphasis on individual achievement and aesthetic pursuits, and while the majority of mainstream sports are controlled and directed by governing bodies or other umbrella organizations, alternative sports are usually controlled and directed by the participants themselves.

In her work on skateboarding, Becky Beal (1995) found that skateboarders engaged in daily practices of resistance to a dominant cultural emphasis on elite competition and outsider control of sports. The subjects of her study de-emphasized elite competition by praising other skaters for not being competitive and asserting that individuals who did try to compete with each other were "uncool." They maintained participant control of the sport by refusing to participate in contests sponsored by a local skateboarding association and by saying there were no objective criteria by which to judge a particular trick or style of skating. Beal found that "the opposition of skateboarders to the [association]-sponsored contest is an overt and explicit example of the daily and more subtle resistance to the values and norms associated with corporate bureaucracies and corporate bureaucratic sport. Skateboarders resisted the values and norms of elite competition, and authority as expert, by encouraging cooperation and creating a participant-controlled activity" (p. 264).

Despite the largely anti-establishment orientation of most alternative sport subcultures, some dominant norms and values remain unchallenged—particularly regarding gender relations. At ESPN's X Games, arguably the most publicized alternative sporting event, only 15 percent of the competitors in 2000 were female and, of the three most popular events (skateboarding, BMX, and inline skating), only inline skating featured a women's division, and there were 6 female competitors as compared to 20 in the men's division (Kang, 2000). Though this has improved slightly since then, most notably with the inclusion of women's motocross in 2008, the X Games remain male-dominated. Male participants might attribute this to the difficulty of the activities, but others call it a case of classic sexism—on the basis of instances such as the reference to female skaters as "Skate Betties." Perhaps the alternative sport in which girls and women have made the most headway is snowboarding.

FROM ALTERNATIVE TO MAINSTREAM: THE EVOLUTION OF SNOWBOARDING

Twenty years ago, the sport of snowboarding and its adherents could have been characterized as quite similar to skateboarding, its equipment sold primarily at skate and surf shops. The tenets of the snowboarding lifestyle reflect the values of skateboarding: A grassroots activity privileging artistic expression over competition, controlled by participants, and requiring a commitment to both the sport and the lifestyle. To outsiders, snowboarders were "the curse of the slopes—reckless, rude, and bad for business" (Neville, 1998).

Today, snowboarding is the fastest-growing winter sport in the United States. While in 1987 there were fewer than a half million snowboarders, the National Sporting Goods Association (nsga.org) reported that, after peaking at a high of 6.57 million in 2004—outranking skiers for the first time in history—participation rates levelled out at 5.1 million in 2007. In terms of corporate involvement, the global retail market for snowboarding equipment increased by 40 percent a year throughout the 1990s (Neville, 1998). The exposure of snowboarding in the media has been phenomenal. Following its debut in the 1998 Winter Olympic Games, snowboarding programming began being aired on ESPN, ABC, Fox Sports Network, and MTV. Indeed, it is the focal point of ESPN's annual Winter X Games, the big air snowboard competition being the finale. In addition, ESPN added the big air competition to its summer X Games in 1998, making snow in 80-degree weather because of spectator interest. Participation rates have mirrored media interest, with an increase of 33 percent in a one-year period in the mid-1990s (Greenfield, 1998).

Still, snowboarding's role remains ambiguous. To a certain degree, the sport is still directed by individual participants. The lack of a unified governing body is a testament to the uncertain position of snowboarding in mainstream athletics. And, despite its popularity, the sport has not lost its alternative reputation. Like in other alternative sports, the culture of snowboarding emphasizes participant control and individuality, de-emphasizing elite competition (Crissey, 1999).

Although snowboarding seems to challenge dominant values such as competition and material rewards, it is similar to other alternative sports in that it does more to reinforce traditional gender roles than to challenge them. As in skateboarding and BMX, male narratives about the underrepresentation of women tend to center on essentialist arguments about the qualities the sport requires, such as a body structure possessed only by males or a "mental attitude" that snowboarding demands (J. Dugan, cited in Anderson, 1999.) These types of claims, along with sexist language such as the term "Bunnies" for female snowboarders, serve to discourage women's full participation. Girls and women continue to be underrepresented, comprising only 26.3 percent of all participants (NSGA, 2007).

Kristin Anderson (Ibid.: 76) argues that the alternative nature of snowboarding means that the construction of gender in the sport is different than it is in mainstream, organized sports: "[It] does not involve the sex-segregated teams, regulated structure and exclusive participation policies." She suggests that male snowboarders construct the sport as a masculine practice through a variety of social practices, including sporting a "street punk" style of dress, adopting an aggressive and superior attitude, emphasizing the danger of their sport, and stressing their heterosexuality (see also Heino, 2000). Its organization and events such as those at the Winter X Games provide evidence of perpetuated gender inequality. Event organizers and commentators also play a role in maintaining male dominance in snowboarding.

THE WINTER X GAMES: A CASE STUDY

The annual X Games and Winter X Games are showcases of popular alternative sporting events produced, hosted, and presented by ESPN. Having debuted in 1995 as "The eXtreme Games," they gathered hundreds of athletes from around the world competing in skateboarding, motocross, inline skating, BMX, and, at one point, street luge (racing down streets laying on sleds with wheels.) The network uses varying filming techniques such as "helmet cams" and "bike cams" and presents the events in tape-delayed 30-minute action-packed segments in order to liven the events and entice its target market of 18–34-year-old males (Burgi, 1995). The debut X Games offered nearly $400,000 in prize money and reached 65.5 million homes (Hoffer, 1995) and was so successful that ESPN added the Winter X Games two years later. Corporate sponsors included Coors, AT&T, Mountain Dew, Taco Bell, Nike, Chevy Trucks, and Advil. The third annual Winter X Games, held in January 1999 in Crested Butte, Colorado, featured ice climbing, snowmobile racing, snow mountain bike racing, ski boarding, free skiing, and snowboarding. It drew over 500 competitors from around the globe and offered thousands of dollars in cash and prizes, including a new Volkswagen Jetta to "the most extreme athlete in the Games." Over four days of competition, they drew an estimated 30,000 spectators, most of whom were young, white, and male. The event was also aired on television, both on the host network and on its partner network, ABC, organized into 30–60-minute segments that were tape delayed and broadcast a day or more after the live competition.

METHODOLOGY

Data was gathered solely by the author, using two methods: The first method was participant observation, using personal time and funds during the four-day period. Notes were recorded by hand and photographs were taken. No formal interviews were conducted and my status as a spectator limited the areas to which access was granted, though entry to most areas was not problematic due to the outdoor nature of the event. Any personal comments were either overheard in a public venue or offered in informal conversation by individuals who were aware that research was being conducted. The second method of data-gathering was an analysis of the television coverage of the X Games events. Videotape recordings were made of all coverage on both ESPN and ABC; later, notes were made on gender-related material and coded accordingly.

Both the live events and the recorded broadcasts were analyzed using two indicators of gender inequality at the X Games: (1) how the events were organized at the live event and in televised coverage and (2) the use of gendered terminology by hosts, commentators, and participants. The results of the study are presented below.

GENDERED ORGANIZATIONAL PATTERNS

Although the alternative sports featured at the 1999 Winter X Games are individual and not team sports, sex segregation nevertheless occurred as a result of the organization of events into male and female divisions. Of the six sports featured at the Winter X Games (ice climbing, snowboarding, ski boarding, free skiing, snow mountain bike racing [biker X], and snowmobile racing [snowcross]), all featured men's divisions and four included women's. There were no women's divisions for snowcross or ski boarding and, while women did participate in skiing events, of the those subdivisions (skier X, free ski, and skier "big air"), only skier X contained a women's division. Snowboarding, on the other hand, contained four subdivisions (boarder X, slopestyle, halfpipe, and "big air"), and there were women's divisions of each. To break it down further, there were a total of 11 events for male participants and 7 for females, although all four snowboarding events were open to both. The disparity in events open to women versus those to men is the most evident indication of gender inequality at the X Games. Although spectators and some participants made comments such as "chicks don't dig motocross," there seems little empirical evidence to support this position. The dramatic increase in female sports participation rates after the passage of Title IX, supports the claim that girls and women *are* interested in participating in male-dominated sports and will do so if the opportunity is available (Coakley, 2000). Another organizational method relegating women to a secondary role was the order of events: Both at the live events and in television coverage, women's events were held first, when crowds were smaller. Television also followed the same ordering pattern. Although crowd size was not an issue with the televised version, as ESPN rarely focused the cameras on groups of spectators, the positioning of women's events before men's still privileged male athletic performances according to the formula of audience "warm up." A third organizational method employed by ESPN also served to reinforce the notion that alternative sports are a male domain: Essentially all the hosts, interviewers, and commentators were male, with the notable exception of the famous mountain biker Missy Giove, who sat in with male commentators during the men's biker X. Male voices were the overlay for all events: a man interviewed individual participants and a man hosted the entire televised event from a room called "The Cyber Café," where invited male competitors and commentators came to chat—even if occasionally bringing along a wife or a girlfriend. Together with the limited number of female athletes at the Games and the second-rate time slots garnered by women's events, the total narration of the events almost entirely served to reinforce the implication that the Winter X Games, if not snowboarding itself, was an event made by men, for men. Sexualized images and gendered language further marginalized women participating in the Games.

GENDERED LANGUAGE AND IMAGES

The fact that there were both men's and women's divisions for each of the four snowboarding events at the Winter X Games allows for comparison of the language used to refer to each, and to characterize male and female performances. There were marked differences. First, although ESPN was careful in naming events, using the term "women" rather than the often-used "ladies," hosts and commentators often excluded the "men's" part of the title for male events, simply saying, for example, "Boarder X," while always mentioning when an event was women's. It may be appropriate to denote whether an event is from a men's or women's division, but it is nevertheless sexist to use the male event as the referent—defining the women's as "other" and assuming male participation as the norm. Despite ESPN's officially referring to female events as "women's events," commentators often used the term "ladies" or "girls" to refer to them—an infantilizing terminology subordinating women by implying that they are childlike, or less than fully adult athletes.

Actual performances by athletes were also characterized in gendered terms. Discussing performances of male snowboarders, commentators declared, "That was huge," or "What a risky trick." Men's performances were more likely to be characterized as powerful, daring, and committed, while women's were more likely to be described as graceful, clean, and smooth. In the women's big air contest, one participant's jump was described as "a neat, floaty, feminine charge trick." Additionally, commentators spent a great deal of time discussing how one particular course was intimidating to female riders, while no mention was made of males having any concerns about it. One commentator stated that the women were "having trouble going over the step-up jump and had to change course," while another simply asserted that some of the women were "a little freaked" about the course. No mention was ever made about a male participant's being nervous or intimidated, while these were quite common characterizations of women.

If a woman's performance was deemed to be especially good, commentators would often compare her to men; one was congratulated by the interviewer with, "I haven't seen one *guy* do that!" Another commentator said of the women's big air competitors, "They ride so tough that you could mistake them for guys." Again, the implication is that "real" snowboarding is done by men; males are the referent, and if women are accomplished at the sport, they are being "like guys." Perhaps the most obvious example of the androcentric nature of snowboarding at the Winter X Games was the name of an obstacle on the slopestyle course: a large handrail on which tricks were performed during snowboarding runs was called "the sex change"—a reference to the dangerous nature of the handrail implying that if a contestant did not perform a trick properly, *he* might fall on the rail and damage his genitals.

Despite gendered language that firmly defined snowboarding as a masculine pursuit and the comparison of female athletes to their male counterparts when their performances were especially competent, commentators held a discussion in which they analyzed the role of women in snowboarding, arguing that it was a good thing that women did not ride "like men." One offered the observation that female snowboarders were more "lovey-dovey" than males, while another summed up the gist of the discussion: "Girls used to ride like guys...That died and I'm glad...They are more feminine in their style." This characterization of women as different from men in their athleticism is yet another assertion of the inherently male nature of the sport, the insinuation being that women cannot truly ride like men, so it is better that they develop their own style. In addition, it may relieve some men's fears that they might actually have to compete against women who, if they rode "like guys," might be able to beat them. Finally, descriptions of women's performances as "feminine" or "beautiful" serve to define males and females in terms of traditional gender roles, wherein men are the actors and the subjects, while women are the commodified items of beauty, the objects. This is especially evident in the sexualized language used at the Games.

Throughout the televised version of the Winter X Games, there was a recurring theme placing men as the adored, athletic winners and women as the prize that these men "won." One contestant (a ski boarder), in an interview, when asked, "Do you get a lot of girls ski boarding?", replied, "It's not about the chicks…but it's great that they come along!" A commentator pointed out the benefits of winning the men's slopestyle contest: "You get the ladies [and] you get the gold" and the winner of the men's snowboarding big air was celebrated as a "ladies man." These comments reinforce the narrative that successful men "get" women and that women are not acting human beings but are, instead, objects—part of the bounty a man can win in a sporting event. Women participants themselves were not immune to objectification, and their performances were often sexualized. While comments about femininity and grace during a performance might be excused as innocent, commentators went even further to make remarks on the physical attributes of contestants. The winner of the women's snowboarding big air was congratulated for having "the most beautiful eyes in snowboarding," and the commentating crew for the snowboarding events said that they loved their job because they were able to "hang out with the foxy ladies of snowboarding." The most glaring example was a segment that ESPN called "The Softer Side of X," subtitled "X Unfiltered—Chicks Rule!" This was a segment, several minutes in length, purported to feature female snowboarding participants, yet there was little footage of actual athletic performance, as most visuals consisted of participants doing stunts: Doing the can-can in a row of flailing legs, helping each other tie bows in their number jerseys, and discussing how they are all good friends and are more supportive of each other than the men are to one another. The segment appeared to be aimed more at male viewers interested in attractive young women than at highlighting the athletic achievements of these snowboarders.

The cumulative affect of the use of gendered language during snowboarding events, the definition of women's performances as different from men's, and the sexualization of female participants was that the Winter X Games painted a picture of highly traditional gender roles. Female participants were accepted as contestants so long as they did not challenge male supremacy in alternative sports.

They were "cute, beautiful and feminine," even if they were not the best snowboarders. The covert message being that women's participation in the sport was acceptable as long as they were pleasant to look at and enjoyable to be around. They were objects rather than subjects. Hosts, commentators, and participants used these strategies to maintain male dominance in snowboarding and to neutralize any threat that women's involvement might contain.

CONCLUDING REMARKS

The 1999 Winter X Games provided evidence that, despite the encouraging indication that alternative sports may challenge dominant ideologies supporting competition and external rewards and that it may help provide a vision for new and better ways to organize sports, these sports do little to challenge traditional gender relations. Methods of organization, including the lack of women's divisions in many sports and the privileging of male event coverage, as well as gendered terminology and sexualized rhetoric used by hosts, commentators, and participant serve to maintain male dominance in alternative sport.

There was, however, at least one indication that X Gamers were aware of gender inequalities. As mentioned above, the contest promised to award a new automobile to the "most extreme athlete at the Games." At both of the first two Winter X Games, the award had gone to a male participant, but at the 1999 Games a woman won. Unfortunately, the appearance that a woman had managed entirely on the strength of her skills to be deemed "more extreme" than her male counterparts was shattered when the announcers pointed out that the prize was awarded to the woman after she had actually asked if they "were finally going to give it to a woman." This qualification lessened the impact of the award and, again, gave the message that women were second-status at the X Games.

Within the world of sport, it appears that female athletes are making greater strides in mainstream sports than they are in the less-institutionalized realm of alternative sport; in fact, in winter 2002, International Olympic Committee (IOC) members contended that their traditional sports were more progressive in terms of gender equality than were alternative sports. IOC member Anita DeFrantz of the United States pointed out that, of the 2,400 athletes who competed in Salt Lake City, about 49 percent were women. Still, the 2002 Winter X Games featured only 28 percent women (Ruibal, 2002).

There is some evidence that ESPN is addressing these disparities. The company announced that its 2009 Winter X Games will feature equal prize money for both males and females for the first time ever; in addition, the number of women participating in the Winter X Games has increased. By 2007, women comprised

31 percent of all competitors (Lakowski, 2007). While the emergence of alternative sports is encouraging because it presents us with new and different models of organizing sports participation, fewer overuse injuries, and less burnout, current alternative sports clearly do not provide a panacea. This is particularly true in the case of girls and women. Though some make the case that sexist undercurrents in sports such as snowboarding are being actively contested and reframed by female participants (Thorpe, 2008), this is not sufficient to challenge male privilege in the sport. Any new, alternative model for sports must not only challenge the dominant ideologies outlined above but also confront the historical legacy of female exclusion from and marginalization within the sporting world.

REFERENCES

Anderson, K. L. (1999). Snowboarding: The construction of gender in an emerging sport. *Journal of Sport and Social Issues* 23 (1): 55–79.

Baird, W. (1993). *Recreation conflict between skiers and snowboarders*. Ft. Collins, CO: Unpublished Masters thesis, Colorado State University.

Beal, B. (1995). Disqualifying the official: An exploration of social resistance through the subculture of skateboarding. *Sociology of Sport Journal* 12 (3): 252–267.

Beal, B. and Weidman, L. (1998). The skateboarding image: An analysis of the industry's impact on the participants' view of authenticity. Paper presented at the annual meeting of the International Sociology of Sport Association, in conjunction with the World Congress of Sociology. Montreal, Quebec.

Burgi, M. (1995). Don't try this at home. *Mediaweek* 5 (24): 24.

Coakley, J. J. (2000). *Sport in society: Issues and controversies* (7th edition). Boston, MA: Irwin McGraw-Hill.

Crissey, J. (1999). *Corporate co-optation of sport: The case of snowboarding*. Ft. Collins, CO: Unpublished Master's thesis, Colorado State University.

Eitzen, D. S. (1999). *Fair and foul: Beyond the myths and paradoxes of sport*. Lanham, MD: Rowman & Littlefield Publishers.

Greenfield, K. T. (1998). A wider world: Who needs the NBA anyway? Smaller Sports are luring young viewers and fresh advertising. *Time* (November 9): 80–81.

Heino, R. (2000). What is so punk about snowboarding? *Journal of Sport and Social Issues*. 24 (2): 176–191.

Hoffer, R. (1995). Down and way out. *Sports Illustrated* 83 (1): 42–43.

Kang, Y. P. (2000). Men rule at the X(Y) Games. *Wired* (August 17). Available: (http://www.wired.com/news/culture/0,1284,38154,00.html).

Lakowski, T. 2007. Xpanding opportunities. *Women's Sports Foundation* (January 30). Available: (http://www.womenssportsfoundation.org/Content/Articles/Issues/Equity-Issues/X/Xpanding-Opportunities.aspx).

National Sporting Goods Association (NSGA). (2002, November 22). Skateboarding and snowboarding lead 5-year participation growth. Available: (http://www.nsga.org/public/pages/index.cfm?pageid=525).

Neville, Lee. (1998). Board crazy. *U.S. News & World Report* 124 (5): 8.

Olsen, Marilyn (2001). *Women who risk: Profiles of women in extreme sports.* New York: Hatherleigh.

Rinehart, R. (1999). Emerging arriving sport: Alternatives to formal sports. In Coakley, J. J. and Dunning, E. (Eds.). *Handbook of sports studies*, 504–520. London: Sage.

Rowe, D. (1995). *Popular cultures: Rock music, sport and the politics of pleasure.* Thousand Oaks, CA: Sage.

Ruibal, S. (2002). X Games vs. Olympics. *USA Today* (January 17): C1.

Thorpe, H. (2008). Foucault, technologies of self, and the media: Discourses of femininity in snowboarding culture. *Journal of Sport and Social Issues* 32 (2): 199–229.

Walter, N. (2005). Growth causing mixed responses: Professionals weary of action sports' popularity. *Colorado Springs Gazette* (July 10).

CHAPTER ELEVEN

The Jim Rome Show AND Negotiations OF Manhood: Surviving IN "The Jungle"

MAUREEN MARGARET SMITH

Although I have never been in a men's locker room, I have taken my peeks here and there and have seen my share of televised accounts of victorious men celebrating and losers commiserating after some Big Game. For me, as a female, the men's locker room has been out of bounds and, while some women reporters have gained access, it has not exactly been a warm, welcoming environment. Timothy Jon Curry (1991: 119) describes the men's locker room as a "bastion of privilege and a center of fraternal bonding"; his accounts of one team's exchanges there confirm popular culture images of these male sanctuaries as sacred sites for bonding. Still, I find myself wanting to hear the dialogue, the words these men use to define their identities, and the ways in which they bond. While such an opportunity is unlikely, for me sports talk radio (although some may argue it is not the same) works as an *audio locker room*—addressing themes such as fraternal bonding, competition, and "doing gender through homophobic talk" (Ibid.) almost 24/7 in our sport media–saturated airwaves.

SPORTS TALK RADIO

Sports talk radio has become increasingly more popular over the last decade, with nationally known hosts dominating the AM airwaves, as well as their small town counterparts adding their two cents. The radio ratings company Arbitron reports how sports talk draws an audience of 41.8 million at least once a week and, "with some 150 national all-sports stations, the format accounts for advertising revenues of $2.2 billion, along with broadcast rights fees of $443 million" (Fuller, 2008: 88). There is a growing body of literature analyzing sport talk radio as the industry grows and establishes a devoted following (Douglas, 2002; Eisenstock, 2001; Ghosh, 1999; Goldberg, 1998; Haag, 1996; Lefkowitz, 1996; Mariscal, 1999; Nylund, 2001, 2004, 2007; Zagacki and Grano, 2005). Similarly, sport bars have been explored as a site of male bonding in an unconventional "sport" setting focusing not only on athletes but also on sport fans (Crawford, 2004; Curry, 1998; Eastman and Land, 1997; Kraszewski, 2008; Rein, Kotler, and Shields, 2006; Wenner, 1996). Much more has been researched concerning male bonding and sports as a dominant site for defining masculinity (Beal, 1997; Bird, 1996; Bryson, 1987; Burtsyn, 1999; Connell, 2000; Curry, 1991; Davis and Carlisle Duncan, 2006; de Garis, 2000; Drummond, 2008; Farr, 1988; Kidd, 1990: Kimmel and Kaufman, 1995; Lyman, 1987; Messner, 1990, 2002; Messner, Dunbar, and Hunt, 2000; Nelson, 1994; Sabo, 1985; Sabo & Panepinto, 1990; Smith and Beal, 2007; Stempel, 2006; Whitson, 1990).

Research focusing on fan behavior and identity is equally relevant and continues to be a topic of scholarly inquiry (Eastman and Land, 1997; Eastman and Riggs, 1994; Gantz and Wenner, 1995; Grossberg, 1992; Giulianotti, 2002; Lewis, 2001; Real and Metchikoff, 1992; Wann, Melnick, Russell, and Pease, 2001. Curry (1998: 120) posits that sport is "an ideal place to 'do gender,' where men are able and encouraged to display masculinity in a socially approved fashion," helping to maintain hegemonic masculinity. It is my intent to gain a greater understanding of the ways in which men use sports talk radio to define themselves as men and, in very powerful ways, maintain the power and privilege of hegemonic masculinity.

There are hundreds of different sports talk radio programs across the nation, to which hundreds of thousands of sport fans tune in on a daily basis.

THE JIM ROME SHOW

The Jim Rome Show will serve here as a site for critical exploration of uncontested debates and, most significantly, as a replication of dominant ideological beliefs and values under the guide of "sports talk." Also known as "The Jungle," it has a large male audience, operates a website (www.jimrome.com), sells merchandise (such as T-shirts and hats), performs "tour stops" nationwide, and serves as a site for predominantly male debate about sport and, oftentimes, societal issues.

Jim Rome's syndicated three-hour show airs daily 9am to noon Pacific time (noon to 3pm EST) during weekdays on over 200 radio stations nationwide to over two million faithful listeners. As host, he conducts interviews with athletes and coaches and regularly fields calls from listeners; in interviews, he is generally non-confrontational and always stays on the good side of the guest. Unlike the guests, who receive star treatment, however, callers can engage in no dialogue: They are simply given the opportunity to speak, to either finish their "take" or get hung up on; then, Rome dissects the call, usually humiliating the caller, who is now listening to the host's reaction. There is no debating, no exchange of ideas—simply action and reaction. With its own vocabulary, known as "gloss," *The Jim Rome Show* makes for an excellent subculture worthy of analysis.

Rome's entry into sports talk radio began on ESPN2's *Talk 2*. In 1994, during a live broadcast of an interview with quarterback Jim Everett, Rome referred to his guest as "Chrissy," alluding to the female tennis player Chris Evert and, thus, challenging the quarterback's masculinity; predictably, a fight ensued—helping to define Rome as an "in your face" host whose view is *the view* and all others, in his words, "suck." Named one of the top 100 most powerful individuals in sports by *The Sporting News* (#79, in 1999), he has made a cameo appearance in Michael Jordan's *Space Jam*, appeared in a music video for Blink 182, appeared on *Arliss* (HBO's series about sports agents), cut his own CD ("Welcome to the Jungle"), and hosted FOX Sports Net's *The Last Word with Jim Rome* (a 30-minute daily television show); he is currently doing a daily show on ESPN: *Rome is Burning*.

The Jim Rome Show extends beyond the airwaves, his lexicology providing a "smacktionary," a vocabulary combining "East Coast jargon, ghetto jargon, California surfer talk among other exotic dialects" (Perrin, 2000: 113). The phrases or words are almost always insulting, if humorous to those creating and using them. Callers might read from a script laden with "gloss" as evidence of their cultural knowledge of their trusted leader (Rome) and his Rome-speak. By way of example, "clones" are "an excessively imitative fan of Rome's show," and Rome is the "Pimp in the Box," the "Huge One," "Van Smack," and the "King of Smack."

Professional athletes are usually given names highlighting unpleasant facial features, underscoring too manly or feminine qualities, or dealing with run-ins with law enforcement. For example, football player Bam Morris is "Bong Morris," tennis player Arantxa Sanchez Vicario is "a raunchy chick from the barrio," and former NFL quarterback John Elway is "Mr. Ed" while Olympic figure skater Nancy Kerrigan is "Edna" because of their resemblance to horses. Likewise, Rebecca Lobo, former WNBA player, is "Roger Lobo," Christian Laettner of the NBA is "Christine," the NBA's Portland Trailblazers are the "Jailblazers," and convicted murderer and former NFL player Rae Carruth is "the Green Mile."

Sometimes the names are racial. NBA player Nick van Exel is "gangsta hooper," boxer Julio Cesar Chavez is "the Myopian Mexican," and the city of Cleveland has been called "Ku Klux Kleveland." Cities are given renames: Omaha (NE) is "Bugaha," Sacramento (CA) is "Suckramento," and Rochester (NY) is "Crapchester." Even some regular callers have been tagged with nicknames, such as "Irie Craig," and "J.T. the Brick," the latter having gone on to start his own talk radio show largely as a result of his winning Rome's first "Smackoff," a contest to judge the best caller.

Tour Stops have become popular spin-offs of the radio show, acting essentially as a "live show" without the callers. Attracting over 20,000 fans at some stops, Rome rewards for "banging their monkey" (translation: letting *The Jim Rome Show* know that your city wants a tour stop, or voicing your support of the show by calling your local affiliate). The stops serve as another site for the reproduction of hegemonic masculinity through male bonding in a sport setting; further, the inclusion of alcohol introduces comparisons between sport bars and tailgating. No balls are thrown, no scores are kept, and there are no ticket fees, but fans are given the opportunity to meet and socialize in a form of "group viewing," providing them with "a greater sense of connectedness and membership in a group than watching in private" (Eastman and Land, 1997: 165). Such events allow "airwave" communities the opportunity to bond with other clones—what Kathryn Ann Farr (cited in Nelson, 1994: 108) refers to as dominance bonding, "a process of collective alliance through which the group and its members affirm and reaffirm their superiority."

The alcohol consumption typically includes drunkenness—another type of male ritual. "The male ritual of 'drinking each other under the table' is rooted in heavy drinking as a symbol of greater masculinity" (Wenner, 1996: 74–75). Similarly, sporting events and tour stops serve as space for displaying masculinity. "Much of the cultural power of sports is linked to its functioning as a male rite of passage and the role sports spaces and places play as refuge from women," Lawrence Wenner (1996: 78–79) has noted.

SPORTS TALK RADIO AS THE ABRACADABRA TO OPEN THE DOOR

Several themes addressed in the literature help to establish a framework for understanding the relationship between sports talk radio and American male sport followers, demonstrating it as a legitimate site of study. Specially, topics examined prior to and within the analysis of *The Jim Rome Show* include the following:

- within the sporting arena, how men define and maintain masculine identity;

- male bonding;
- misogyny and violence against women;
- sexualizing of females and female athletes;
- white male privilege and subsequently, how white masculinity is defined.

Sports are serious entertainment for American men and, in many ways, being a fan is an extension of being a part of the team—it means staying in the game, maintaining access to the privileged world of sport. Sporting events "become symbolic struggles, passion plays reenacted daily to define, affirm, and celebrate manliness" (Nelson, 1994: 5; see also Burstyn, 1999; Connell, 2000; Messner, 2002). Borne out of this ever- increasing fan base is an industry responsive to the growing needs of sport spectators, from 24-hour sport channels to sport websites to television and radio shows reinforcing patriarchal lessons. "Televised games and box scores and multimillion-dollar contracts inform boys that male games are valued, and that they, as men-to-be, are valued. From the manly sports culture, boys (and girls) learn that men's games are valued more than women's games; that men are more valued than women... But boys seem to fall in love with spectator sports as an integral part of falling in love with the masculine privilege that their fathers symbolize" (Nelson, 1994: 106; see also Burstyn, 1999; Connell, 2000; Messner, 2002).

Many men attach deep personal meanings to "being a sports fan"—especially on sport talk radio, which "announces, informs, pontificates, moralizes, politicizes, commercializes, and commodifies—as it entertains" (Goldberg, 1998: 213). It also serves to reinforce beliefs and opinions in a forum enabling listeners to be part of a larger, more powerful "team" of people sharing similar values and ideals. "Sports talk radio plays a central role in producing this uniformity—a uniformity in style of expression, of opinion, of team support... There's something abstractly ethnonationalistic about the enterprise. Supporting one's team today has taken the place of what it was once like supporting one's country, right or wrong. Sports talk radio is the propaganda machine of the new fan-aticism" (Goldberg, 1998: 216). As Nylund (2001) points out, sports talk radio is not a forum for two-way dialogues, nor an opportunity for a caller to ask questions or respond to the host comments.

Mariah Burton Nelson (1994: 5) has acknowledged the significant relationship between men and sport when recognizing the importance of "having" a team; for male fans, "to identify with successful manly athletes is to feel successful and manly oneself, to feel a part of the dominant male culture. Millions of men affirm their manliness and manly ties by betting on sports, discussing sports, arguing over sports, agonizing over decisions such as, 'Should I root for Baltimore, where I grew up, or Cleveland, where I live now?'" She states, "Men use sports talk to establish their niche in the gender hierarchy." Even if the male's last at-bat was as a young Little Leaguer, his ability to communicate the sports language is critical to his adult male acceptance: "Sports talk is considered by men to be legitimate social and business conversation" (Ibid.: 108). Curry (1991: 120) supports these ideas, viewing sports as "an arena well suited for the enactment and perpetuation of the male bond."

The type of verbal "one-upsmanship" that is common talk among sports fans ("I know more statistics, have more knowledge, 'know' sports better than you") is a form of competition for non-athletes and athletes alike. Sport fans are "competing to establish who is most informed. It's... an oral contest. This competitive conversation simultaneously establishes both hierarchy (who wins the argument; who has the most information) and unit: we are men, talking about men's interests" (Nelson, 1994: 109). This behavior is frequently apparent on *The Jim Rome Show* when callers have their "take" racked (Rome's term for a call deemed good enough not only to hang up on, but also to be entered into the "call of the day" contest), encouraging outrageous submissions.

METHODOLOGY

Using data from a content analysis of *The Jim Rome Show*, along with detailed fieldnotes gathered using ethnographic research methods at a "Tour Stop" in Oakland, California, three themes are discussed:

1. Definitions of Manhood;
2. Women and *The Jim Rome Show*; and,
3. Representations of Race: Blackness and White Masculinity.

Combined, the research materials and analyses provide us a rich understanding of the powerful impact one sports talk radio host has on listeners and how the radio show, its host, and the content serve to maintain and reinforce definitions of manhood in American society.

Theme #1: "Fellas are already picking out their scrunchies for next year": Jim Rome and definitions of manhood

On a daily basis, Jim Rome and his callers aim to define manhood and what "real men" do. Clearly, they do not play soccer, jump rope, stand trial for the murder of their wife, play softball against women, "come out" as gay men, or whine about a coach, but they *do* play *real* sports, have good "takes," hold athletes accountable, and care about sports.

A significant subtheme of Rome's discussions around masculinity focuses on discussions of male genitalia and sexual activities. He has reported being approached by a company to promote penile implants, but his agent turned town the offer by stating that his client did not do commercials, joking about his affiliation with such a product and asking, "Can you imagine me pimping these things? 'Hi. I'm Jim Rome. I've got a miniature crank, but with this product...'"

Homoerotic undertones are hard to miss at the tour stops. Men go to see him, to see professional athletes, pose for pictures with each other in compromising positions, slap each other's fannies, and to spend time with their male friends. They bask in a setting celebrating their masculinity through sport, sports talk, and sex talk. When asked why they attend tour stops, a majority of men gave me these responses: "To hang out with my friends"; "To get drunk"; "Rome is God"; and "to escape my wife." Several authors have written extensively on the homosocial environment that sport consumption allows and encourages (Butterworth, 2006; Curry, 1991, 1998; Nelson, 1994; Nylund, 2001, 2004, 2007; Wenner, 1996).

Theme #2: "*That* kicker from Duke": Women and *The Jim Rome Show*

That kicker from Duke was Heather Mercer, who was awarded a large settlement in her sexual discrimination lawsuit against the university; for Rome, she represented the encroachment of women into forbidden football territory. Women should not be playing football, and they certainly should not get money from a school because of "discrimination." This case is representative of how female athletes—actually, females in general—are discussed on *The Jim Rome Show*. The host and his callers practice routine sexism reinforcing women as other/intruder and as out of place in the sport arena. Wenner (1996: 82) has commented that one of the promises of sport is to provide places that are "naturalized refuge from women. These places become progressively more public but remain in what is a fundamentally male preserve. The early stages, in the locker rooms and on the playing fields or courts, are marked by overt sexual segregation with women as the 'other.'"

Rome displays a general disdain for a number of female athletes, routinely commenting that track and field medalist Marion Jones needed dental work, that tennis player Monica Seles is part of the rodent family, and that basketball player Rebecca Lobo is "horsey." Another example of how women are treated on *The Jim Rome Show* involves discussions of domestic violence, Nicole Simpson, the murdered ex-wife of football player O. J. Simpson, being a common target.

At the Oakland tour stop, Rome's verbal treatment of women manifested itself in several ways. As I drove into the parking lot accompanied by a female friend with "big hair," a large group of men pointed to us and happily yelled, "A Raiderette is here!" referring to the cheerleading squad for the Oakland Raiders.

Later, the crowd in the front started cheering, throwing Rome off his routine. A blonde, big-breasted woman was walking down the aisle and the crowd went crazy before Rome finally noticed her, then asked his audience, "What's up? Never seen that before?"

The Raider fans had a T-shirt with the message: "Fuck KC... rape em... no lube"—painting a violent picture of the ways sexual language has been used to send messages. It also presents a powerful example of how some men enact the lessons they learn during their consumption of sport—lessons of dominance and power. For example, David Shields (1999: 28), in a diary he kept during an analysis of race in the NBA, reflected on how his consumption of male athlete behavior influenced his sexual behavior with his wife: "We make love, though that's not quite the right term—it's more like fucking: a rough physicality that I realize later that is my attempt to imitate the athletes I spend so much time watching and thinking about."

Theme #3: "O. J. Did It": White masculinity redefined in "The Jungle"

The majority of men attending tour stops are Caucasian, although some men of color also attend. Because radio lacks the visual element, it is uncertain what the racial makeup of Rome's listeners is, although one might presume, both correctly and incorrectly, a caller's ethnicity based on topics, comments, and patterns of speech. Although black male athletes tend to dominate (not necessarily in numbers, but in performance), their portrayal on *The Jim Rome Show* routinely relies on stereotypes of them as criminals and gangsters (for portrayal of Latinos, see Mariscal, 1999).

Ironically, although many white men cheer black athletes on the field or court, that admiration tends to be limited to athletic performance. Dennis Perrin (2000: 63), believes that white men have a hard time celebrating black athletes: "Whenever a black athlete celebrates a score, the little Klansman inside most American white men stands and clenches his jaw. Every hip-shaking, head-tossing, fist-pumping display sends even 'civilized' Caucasians into redneck fits of disgust... In fact, this happens more to white-collar types than to actual rednecks for the simple reason that the latter openly shows his hates and fears. Since nothing is repressed, there is no need for release, at least not the kind that doubles up those who hold it all in" (see also Simons, 2003). Callers often show their disdain for black athletes—how they carry themselves on and off the field. When Allen Iverson of the Philadelphia 76ers produced a rap album prior to an NBA season, Rome was critical of his lyrics, telling his listeners, "Violence against women and gays is not OK."

During my time listening to the radio show and attending Rome's tour stop, the specter of O. J. Simpson loomed large, many fans listing him as their favorite topic. Rome's website listed Orenthal (Simpson's given name) jokes and sold merchandise capitalizing on the former football player's alleged criminal activity, including a hat worn by a white male that read "O. J. Did It." A Hispanic fan sported a T-shirt mocking the MasterCard commercial: "Leather glove: $10.00; Household steak knife: $29.00; Italian leather shoes: $300.00; Committing a heinous act and getting over: PRICELESS. There are some things money err O. J. can't buy, for everything else there's Orenthal." When Terrell Owens, San Francisco 49er, ran his touchdown ball to midfield and placed it on the Dallas Cowboy star in an act of taunting his opponents, Rome tagged him with the nickname "Terrellenthal." When Carolina Panther Rae Carruth was found guilty of murdering his pregnant girlfriend, he was called "Raenthal" and "The Green Mile." Green Bay Packer Mark Chmura, a white athlete, was charged with having sex with a minor, which included him sitting in a hot tub at a prom party—earning him the nickname "American Chewy."

CONCLUSIONS

When Jim Rome welcomes new listeners to his show, he often reminds them that they need to give the show a couple of weeks before deciding whether they really enjoy it. He encourages them to listen, get used to the smack, and acknowledges that the show is something of an acquired taste, conceding that sometimes the language might be difficult to understand for a new listener, and that only by listening can they become a part of the jungle.

After listening to the show for an entire month, attending two tour stops, and engaging in countless conversations with faithful listeners, I think I have been able to successfully immerse myself into the jungle. Such entrance into a private club is much easier when the meeting space is audio. Acceptance and assimilation at a tour stop was more challenging, where I was reminded that the consumption of sport (those activities that Rome and hegemonic masculinity deem sport) remains a male-dominated space. Thus, the language spoken exists to serve the common interest of men. "Sexist comments, like racist comments, can get men fired in some circles. But not in sports. In the manly sports world, sexism is a badge of honor, a common ground, a familiar language," Nelson reminds us (1994: 84). Although Curry (1991: 133) focused specifically on locker rooms, he found that "years of participating in such a culture desensitizes athletes to women's and gay rights and supports male supremacy rather than egalitarian relationships with women." Moreover, such talk is "likely to have a cumulative effect on young men because it reinforces the notions of masculine privilege and hegemony, making that world view seem normal and typical" (Ibid.).

Behaviors that in a workplace or other social settings might be unacceptable found reward and praise when exhibited in calls or at the tour stops. Despite infrequent comments by Jim Rome that reveal a tolerance for difference, such as his criticism of Iverson's lyrics against women and gays, his show ultimately serves as a site for men to feel empowered in a world where, in fact, they have little power. Most men have no power in sport; they may express a desire to be athletic or participate in fantasy leagues where they can pretend to be owners, but ultimately their power lies in their consumption of activities that serve to perpetuate their need for belonging, to become a part of the sports world.

Jim Rome is not breaking any barriers. One behavior that may set him apart from other media is his public call for the accountability of professional athletes when they commit acts he deems as unacceptable, whether specific crimes or acts of bad sportsmanship. This is one quality listeners find attractive about Rome, considering him a channel for their voice calling for accountability of athletes. Jim Rome serves as their representative in the exclusive world of sport.

POSTSCRIPT AND POST-POSTSCRIPT

Every once in a while, like a junkie seeking a fix, I turn my radio to *The Jim Rome Show* and check in to assess the "state of the nation." Recently, I happened to hear him comment soon after the birth of his first child—a son named Jake—that he would never play soccer. After all, soccer is not a *real* sport. I realized that little had changed; beyond the impact Rome has on his listeners, his son will undoubtedly be socialized in such a way that tells him what sports *real* boys play.

When Rome returned to Sacramento for another tour stop, he promised more if the Sacramento Kings were to beat the Los Angeles Lakers for the NBA championship. After waiting in line with several drunk men, and a much larger contingent of females (some of whom would flash their bare breasts at the urging of their male partners in exchange for rowdy cheers), I was not surprised to hear that O. J. was out, Tonya Harding was in, strippers and big breasts had replaced the discussion of penis size, and the men in attendance still *love* their "Romey."

More recently, I turned to Rome once again to see how "The Jungle" was doing. Rome's son Jake plays on a soccer team, his show is now available on iTunes for subscribers, and O. J. Simpson was again a topic of conversation after his arrest and conviction for breaking into a Las Vegas hotel room. Race continues to be a topic of interest for Rome and his listeners—from the number of Division I football coaches to NFL wide receiver Plaxico Burress' shooting himself in the leg. Women are still appreciated for their sex appeal (think beach volleyball players). And manhood is still debated on a daily basis, from the masculinity of NFL quarterbacks who are yet to win "the big one" to the suspicious masculinity of NFL kickers and punters to male cheerleaders to fathers who provide their sons with steroids, and then back to Rome, who continues to be "the man."

REFERENCES

Beal, B. (1997). The Promise Keepers' use of sport in defining "Christlike" masculinity. *Journal of Sport & Social Issues* (21): 274–284.

Bird, S. (1996). Welcome to the men's club: Homosociality and the maintenance of hegemonic masculinity. *Gender & Society* (10): 120–132.

Bryson, L. (1987). Sport and the maintenance of masculine hegemony. *Women's Studies International Forum* (10): 349–360.

Burstyn, V. (1999). *The rites of men: Manhood, politics, and the culture of sport*. Toronto: University of Toronto Press.

Butterworth, M. L. (2006). Pitchers and catchers: Mike Piazza and the discourse of gay identity in the national pastime. *Journal of Sport and Social Issues* (30): 138–157.

Connell, R. W. (2000). *The men and the boys*. Berkeley, CA: University of California Press.

Crawford, G. (2004). *Consuming sport: Fans, sport, and culture*. New York: Routledge.

Curry, T. J. (1991). Fraternal bonding in the locker room: A profeminist analysis of talk about competition and women. *Sociology of Sport Journal* (8): 119–135.

Curry, T. J. (1998). Beyond the locker room: Campus bars and student athletes. *Sociology of Sport Journal* (15): 205–215.

Davis, N. W., and Duncan, M. C. (2006). Sports knowledge is power: Reinforcing masculine privilege through fantasy sport league participation. *Journal of Sport and Social Issues* (30): 244–264.

de Garis, L. (2000). Be a buddy to your buddy: Male identity, aggression, and intimacy in a boxing gym. In McKay, J., Messner, M. A., and Sabo, D. F. (Eds.), *Masculinities, gender relations, and sport*, 87–107. Thousand Oaks, CA: Sage.

Douglas, S. J. (2002). Letting the boys be boys: Talk radio, male hysteria, and political discourse in the 1980s. In Hilmes, M. and Loviglio, J. (Eds.), *Radio reader: Essays in the cultural history of radio*, 484–504. New York: Routledge.

Drummond, M. J. N. (2008) Sport, aging men and constructions of masculinities. *Generations*. 32 (1): 32–35.

Eastman, S. T., and Land, A. M. (1997). The best of both worlds: Sports fans find good seats at the bar. *Journal of Sport & Social Issues* (21): 156–178.

Eastman, S. T., and Riggs, K. E. (1994). Televised sport and ritual: Fan experiences. *Sociology of Sport Journal* (11): 249–274.

Eisenstock, A. (2001). *Sports talk: A journey inside the world of sports talk radio*. New York: Pocket Books.

Farr, K. A. (1988). Dominance bonding through the good old boys sociability group. *Sex Roles* (18): 259–277.

Fuller, L. K. (2008). Sportscasters/sportscasting: Principles and practices. New York: Routledge.

Gantz, W. and Wenner, L. (1995). Fanship and the television sports viewing experience. *Sociology of Sport Journal* (12): 56–74.

Ghosh, C. (1999, February 22). A guy Thing: Radio sports talk shows. *Forbes*.

Giulianotti, R. (2002). Supporters, followers, fans, and flaneurs: A taxonomy of spectator identities in football. *Journal of Sport and Social Issues* (26): 25–46.

Goldberg, D. T. (1998). Call and response: Sports, talk radio, and the death of democracy. *Journal of Sport & Social Issues* (22): 212–223.

Grossberg, L. (1992). Is there a fan in the house? The affective sensibility of fandom. In Lewis, L. (Ed.), *Adoring audience: Fan culture and popular media*, 208–236. New York: Routledge.

Haag, P. (1996). "50,000 watt sports bar": Talk radio and the ethic of the fan. *South Atlantic Quarterly* (95): 453–470.

Kidd, B. (1990). The men's cultural centre: Sports and the dynamics of women's oppression/men's repression. In Messner, M. and Sabo, D. (Eds.), *Sport and the gender order: Critical feminist perspectives*, 31–43. Champaign, IL: Human Kinetics.

Kimmel, M. S. and Kaufman, M. (1995). Weekend warriors: The new men's movement. In Kimmel, M. S. (Ed.), The politics of manhood: Profeminist men respond to the mythopoetic men's movement (and the mythopoetic leaders answer), 15–43. Philadelphia, PA: Temple University Press.

Kraszewski, J. (2008). Pittsburgh in Fort Worth: Football bars, sports television, sports fandom, and the management of home. *Journal of Sport and Social Issues* (32): 139–157.

Lefkowitz, D. (1996). On the mediation of class, race and gender: Intonation on sports radio talk shows. *University of Pennsylvania Working Papers in Linguistics* 3(1): 207–221.

Lewis, M. (2001). Franchise relocation and fan allegiance. *Journal of Sport and Social Issues* (25): 6–19.

Lyman, P. (1987). The fraternal bond as joking relationship: A case study of the role of sexist jokes in male group bonding. In Kimmel, M. S. (Ed.), *Changing men: New directions in research on men and masculinity*, 148–163. Beverly Hills, CA: Sage.

Mariscal, J. (1999). Chicanos and Latinos in the jungle of sport talk radio. *Journal of Sport and Social Issues* 23(1): 111–117.

Messner, M. (1990). Men studying masculinity: Some epistemological issues in sport sociology. *Sociology of Sport Journal* (7): 136–153.

Messner, M. A. (2002). *Taking the field: Women, men, and sports.* Minneapolis, MN: University of Minnesota Press.

Messner, M. A., Dunbar, M., and Hunt, D. (2000). The televised sports manhood formula, *Journal of Sport and Social Issues* (24): 380–394.

Nelson, M. B. (1994). *The stronger women get, the more men love football: Sexism and the American culture of sports.* New York: Harcourt Brace.

Nylund, D. (2001). *Heterosexism, homophobia, and sports talk radio.* New York: GLAAD Center for the Study of Media and Society.

Nylund, D. (2004). When in Rome: Heterosexism, homophobia, and sports talk radio. *Journal of Sport and Social Issues* (28): 136–168.

Nylund, D. (2007). *Beer, babes, and balls: Masculinity and sports talk radio.* Albany, NY: State University of New York Press.

Perrin, D. (2000). *American fan: Sports mania and the culture that feeds it.* New York: Morrow/Avon.

Real, M. R. and Metchikoff, R. A. (1992). Deep fan: Mythic identification, technology, and advertising in spectator sports. *Sociology of Sport Journal* (9): 323–339.

Rein, I., Kotler, P., and Shields, B. (2006). *The elusive fan: Reinventing sports in a crowded marketplace.* New York: McGraw-Hill.

Sabo, D. (1985). Sport, patriarchy, and male identity: New questions about men and sport. *Arena Review*, 9 (2): 1–30.

Sabo, D. F., and Panepinto, J. (1990). Football ritual and the social reproduction of masculinity. In Messner, M. and Sabo, D. (Eds.), *Sport and the gender order: Critical feminist perspectives,* 115–126. Champaign, IL: Human Kinetics.

Shields, D. (1999). *Black planet: Facing race during a NBA season.* New York: Crown.

Simons, H. (2003). Race and penalized sport behaviors. *International Review for the Sociology of Sport* 38(1): 5–22.

Smith, M. M., and Beal, B. (2007). "So you can see how the other half lives": MTV "cribs" use of "the Other" in framing successful athletic masculinities. *Journal of Sport and Social Issues* (31): 103–127.

Stempel, C. (2006). Televised sports, masculinist moral capital, and support for the U.S. Invasion of Iraq. *Journal of Sport and Social Issues* (30): 79–106.

Wann, D. L., Melnick, M. J., Russell, G. W., and Pease, D. G. (2001). *Sports fans: The psychological and social impact of spectators.* New York: Routledge.

Wenner, L. (1996). The sports bar: Masculinity, alcohol, sports and the mediation of public space. In Drucker, S. J. and Gumpert, G. (Eds.), *Voices in the street: Explorations in gender, media, and public space,* 74–75. Creskill, NJ: Hampton.

Whitson, D. (1990). Sport in the construction of masculinity. In Messner, M. and Sabo, D. (Eds.), *Sport and the gender order: Critical feminist perspectives,* 19–30. Champaign, IL: Human Kinetics.

Zagacki, K. S. and Grano, D. (2005). Radio sports talk and the fantasies of sport. *Critical Studies in Media Communication* 22 (1) (March): 45–63.

PART V

VISUAL MEDIA REPRESENTATIONS

CHAPTER TWELVE

Put Me in, Ms. Coach: Sexual Rhetoric in the Locker Room

MEGAN CHAWANSKY

This chapter explores the sexual rhetoric embedded in locker room interactions among men, examining its implications for women coaches seeking to lead men's teams. It uses the films *Wildcats* (1986) and *Sunset Park* (1996) to argue that the misogynist and homophobic locker room rhetoric utilized by athletes can create a hostile climate for women attempting to embark on coaching careers within men's sports. In addition, an analysis of the potential for disrupting misogynist and homophobic locker room rhetoric takes place through an examination of the strategies utilized by the women coaches within these films.

BACKGROUND/METHODOLOGY

> Cable news has always been the Wild Wild West for journalists: mostly men report the news with a smile, a swagger and a wink. They're the bad boy brothers to the straight-laced network news people, whipping out their virtual six-shooters, mouthing off with their flip and fiery words and wearing their rebel attitude like a badge of honor. It's a smelly locker room with the doors wide open.
>
> —Sandra Kobrin, *Cable News' Locker-Room Mentality* (2008)

On March 27, 2002, days before the Women's Final Four collegiate basketball tournament would proceed in San Antonio, Texas, National Public Radio

(NPR) featured a segment concerning the status of collegiate women coaches on its *Morning Edition* show. The topic at hand provided a new twist on the issue of gender equity within intercollegiate athletics; for once, the focus was not on how to increase opportunities for women to compete, but instead on who should be coaching them. According to Linda Jean Carpenter (a former Brooklyn College physical education professor who has tracked the status of female athletes and coaches since the passage of Title IX), now, more than ever, female athletes have opportunities to compete in intercollegiate athletics. However, the number of female coaches has not experienced the same growth, as currently only 46% of the coaches of collegiate women's teams are female, an all-time low (Murray, 2002).

The debate around this issue is contentious to say the least, and those interviewed for NPR's *Morning Edition* represented both sides of the debate. Geno Auriemma, head coach of the women's basketball team at the University of Connecticut, told NPR's Cheryl Corley that gender should not be a factor in hiring decisions, and that the best coach should be hired. But Rene Portland (the then head coach of the Penn State women's basketball team) says that gender does and should matter, and that despite her 26 years of experience as a head coach, she is not a likely candidate for a men's basketball coaching vacancy solely because of her gender. She told NPR's Corley, "What happens on the men's side [of basketball] is important. I think I can only apply for 50 percent of the jobs and men can apply for 100% [of coaching vacancies]" (Corley, 2002). Auriemma disagreed, "What happens on the men's side is irrelevant" (Ibid.).

Auriemma's sentiments beg the question: What exactly does or would happen on the "men's side" if women were given the opportunity to coach men? What are the pitfalls and possibilities when women enter men's sports as coaches? An investigation of this via an examination of the films *Wildcats* (1986) and *Sunset Park* (1996), two great examples, a decade apart, provides an insight into how this issue has been framed in the mainstream media. These two films, in which women coach and lead men's teams, provide a glimpse into what happens when female coaches tread on "male" turf.

The examination of these two films foregrounds the misogynist and (hetero)sexually charged locker room rhetoric and the "real life" implications of this for women seeking to attain coaching positions within men's sports teams (see Araton, 2004; Fornoff, 1993; Fuller, 1992). Similar to findings in the article "Depiction and Characterization of Women in Sport Film," my work suggests that, within these films, not only is "women's athletic prowess trivialized…by their [the films'] comedic themes and attentions to heterosexual attractiveness," but also that the locker room rhetoric contributes to a hostile environment, one that potentially discourages women from attempting to break the glass ceiling within men's sports (Pearson, 2001: 103). Like Pearson, I agree that "these findings...raise intriguing questions regarding the messages communicated through sport films" and seek to counter Auriemma's suggestion that what happens on the "men's side" need not be considered (Ibid.). In considering the potential for and possibilities of disrupting the (white) male patriarchal hegemony of sport through these female coaches, this analysis of locker room rhetoric within *Wildcats* (1986) and *Sunset Park* (1996) reveals a decidedly unchanged environment despite the presence of women in coaching capacities.

THE LOCKER ROOM

For this analysis, it is important to briefly consider the symbolic importance of the locker room itself. According to Disch and Kane (1996), the locker room proves a sacred, albeit complex space for male athletes. In their examination of incidents surrounding the sexual harassment of *Boston Herald* reporter Lisa Olson, who was harassed while working within the locker room of the National Football League's (NFL) New England Patriots, they explore the "supposed" gaze of Olson, the sexual harassment that ensued, and its connection to compulsory heterosexuality. In addition, Disch and Kane (1996: 347) deconstruct the mystical locker room by noting,

> Far from being a castle in which players simply and unquestionably rule, the locker room is the place where their bodies are suited up to be invincible; consequently it is also a place where those bodies can be vulnerable...in the locker room, as on the playing field, male physical superiority is not a biological given but an ideological construct that must be produced by *ritual performances that promote male narcissism and exclude male vulnerability*. (Italics mine)

The locker room, then, provides a unique space within the realm of sport wherein myths and truths about gender and sexuality are both created and challenged (Miracle and Ress, 1994).

This analysis seeks to examine the rhetoric embedded within these "ritual performances" of masculinity that emphasizes heterosexual male prowess, excludes femininity, and denigrates non-heterosexual behavior. An analysis of sexual rhetoric within the locker room comes from examining two films in which a woman is chosen to lead a male sports team and, therefore, must often share this mystical space with her team. In addition, this analysis exists to explore the possibilities of disrupting misogynist and homophobic locker room rhetoric by means of embodied female leadership and visibility.

To situate this analysis, Timothy Jon Curry's study of locker room talk segments is utilized. In his study of "two teams...at a large Midwestern university with a 'big time' sports program," Curry (1991: 189) observed the teams at practice, in competitions, and, most importantly for this analysis, during their time in the locker room. It was in the locker room where he compiled his data: talk segments from conversations among the members of the team, which were then analyzed via a pro-feminist perspective. He identifies two major themes that emerged during the course of his study. First, conversations about status and competition, primarily regarding athletics and women, occurred frequently. Another tendency was for athletes to perform heterosexuality by talking about women as objects and inserting homophobic language. In addition to noting these themes, Curry observes that resistance to this type of talk was limited: "It is important to note that no one ever publicly challenged the dominant sexism and homophobia of the locker room. Whatever oppositional thoughts there may have been were muttered quietly or remained private." (p. 199). Furthermore, Curry suggests that "sexist locker room talk is likely to have a cumulative negative effect on young men because it reinforces the notions of masculine privilege and hegemony, making that world view seem normal and typical" (Ibid.).

THE LOCKER ROOM IN FILM

One can use the themes from Curry's (1991) study to examine locker room dynamics in major motion pictures. *Sunset Park* (1996), a film about physical education teacher Phyllis Saroka (played by Rhea Perlman) and her ability to lead the Sunset Park high school boys' basketball team to the city championship, opens with a scene in the locker room. The players are changing into their practice gear, excited about the prospects of a new season and a new coach. Shorty, the team's point guard, speaks to Butter, the team's best player, "Yo, Butter. When you gonna start passing that rock [the basketball]?" Butter replies, while high-fiving his teammates, "Man, talk to me after you get your first piece of punani"[1] Another teammate chimes in to chide Shorty, "Ahh, Shorty…ya still ain't got no ass yet?!" Shorty attempts to defend himself by protesting, "Stupid. I got mad females on mine." This, we find out later in the film when Shorty reveals his virgin status to Coach Saroka, is not true, but the scene itself is demonstrative of the competition and status attainment that can take place within the confines of the locker room. Butter's interactions with his teammates suggest that "getting punani" indicates one's masculinity and heterosexuality and, therefore, one's athletic ability. If one "gets punani," one deserves and gets "the rock."

Similarly, *Wildcats* (1986), the Warner Bros. film that depicts the program turnaround orchestrated by Molly McGrath, a Prescott high school teacher (played by Goldie Hawn), features a number of locker room conversations revolving around male sexual prowess. In fact, McGrath's first encounter with the team not only relies on sexual rhetoric but also includes visual cues of male sexual virility. Before McGrath is about to enter the chain-linked door that leads to the locker room where she will meet her team for the first time, she pauses, as if to brace herself for her entry into this unfamiliar turf. When she finally sees the team, she is greeted not by athletes ready to practice, but rather with a heavy dose of sexual harassment. The entire team stands before her, shoulder pads and jerseys in place, but sans pants and with their helmets held in front of their genitals.

As McGrath attempts to regain her composure, Trumaine, the team's self-proclaimed "ebony lover" speaks first: "We're suited up and ready to play, coach." As the rest of the team laughs and mumbles their support, they simultaneously raise their helmets to their heads, exposing themselves further to McGrath. "Be on the five in field minutes," a visibly disturbed McGrath stammers. McGrath leaves the locker room and rests her head heavily against the closed door. "Oh, God," she sighs, rolling her eyes and looking skyward. The team has struck early, clearly marking their territory and sending this message: the phallus rules this locker room.

Sunset Park (1996) and *Wildcats* (1986) also contain locker room scenes wherein the players discuss the sexuality of their coaches. Although both discussions are considered within the confines of hetero-normativity, the approaches are significantly different and noteworthy because of the ever present concern over the sexual orientations of women athletes and coaches. In *Sunset Park* (1996), the discussion begins while the players dress in their locker room, getting ready for that day's game. Butter says to no one in particular, "Go in her [Coach Saroka's] office...what do you see on the wall?" He responds to his own question before anyone can answer: "Got a picture of Bruce Lee with his shirt off, kid." Shorty is not sure where Butter is headed: "So what?" he asks. "So," Butter replies, "Coach likes brothers." Drano, another teammate chimes in: "Bruce Lee is Chinese, stupid." Butter retorts, "Bruce Lee is half black, half Chinese, kid. Look at his name. Bruce Lee. That's a black man's name, bro." At this point, the players are distracted and the conversation is interrupted by the entrance of "Busy Bee," a teammate who was in the hospital recovering from a gunshot. The conversation is ambiguous; with the uncertainty surrounding whether the student athletes are laughing at Butter or his comments, it is unclear as to how to read Butter's monologue on race and the politics of naming. However, of interest to this discussion is the commentary on the sexuality of Coach Saroka, and the way in which an attempt to confirm her as a heterosexual woman plays out. A consideration of Coach Saroka's sexual orientation within a non-heterosexual framework might serve to expand the chasm that exists between Saroka and her players by virtue of her gender.

In *Wildcats* (1986), the (hetero-)sexualization of Coach McGrath also takes place, but the rhetoric veers from an examination of McGrath's sexual orientation to an explicit discussion of her as a sexual object. Upon entering her office prior to the third day of practice, McGrath finds it vandalized with spray-painted slanders such as "Get out pussy" and "McGrath sucks." Instead of instilling fear, these slurs incite McGrath, and she storms down the hallway to the team locker room. The screen then splits and the spectator observes Trumaine and his teammates joking and jovially speculating on how and when McGrath will quit after she sees what they have done to her office. Trumaine feigns disinterest in her departure and asserts, "Well I hope she stays 'cause I figure I only got a few more days 'til I get my hands on her. Look, she knows I got ten pounds of danglin' fury [*he motions to his genitals*] just waitin' for her. Shit, I know she wants it. I can tell by the way she looks at me." At this point, McGrath storms in: "Put your pants on and listen up." Trumaine smirks and greets his head coach with a casual "Hey baby. We were just talking about you." His tone positions McGrath not as a subject or an authority figure, but rather as an object in a heterosexual fantasy that he controls. To be able to control her in this capacity far outweighs any control she may exert as the head coach of the football team on which he plays.

Not only do both films talk about their coaches as potential partners of men, but also it seems as if the student athletes (or both films' representations of stereotypical "dumb jocks") can understand life and relationships only via a hetero-normative paradigm. In one scene in *Sunset Park* (1996), Butter and Drano sit and study in the locker room. As part of an attempt to help Butter maintain his athletic eligibility, Coach Saroka has assigned Drano to assist Butter with his algebra. As they begin to study, Drano asks, "Okay, if two 'x' equals 42, what does three 'x' plus five equal?" Butter replies, "That's what gets me. How a letter gonna equal a number? It don't make no sense." Drano pauses to think how he could explain this to Butter in terms that he will understand. Drano says, "I got it. Check this out. Say you got two honeys, right? And you got to buy both of them a chicken, right? Now you gonna buy these two chickens, and for two chickens it cost 42 dollars, right? So, what is three chickens plus five dollars?"[2] Butter asks, "Well, what's the five dollars for?" "The hotel," Drano quickly replies. "Riiiiight," the two players say in unison as they slap hands, and miraculously, Butter is able to solve the equation with no problem.

Similarly, one of the final scenes in *Wildcats* also reinforces hetero-normativity, albeit in a different way, providing an example of what Curry (1991: 196) classifies as "doing gender through homophobic talk." The scene begins with the players in the locker room at half time of the city championship game. At this point, the Wildcats are grumbling about the fact that they are two touchdowns behind, and some infighting and "finger pointing" begins. One of the players, Krushinski, interjects: "Hey look, it's nobody's fault. They're champions, and we're a bunch of dildos." In other words, we (the Wildcats) are losing. We are losers. By implication, we lack the "real" phallic power and so must be satisfied with being imitators—like women, like lesbians, and even like gay men, who, despite having a phallus, fail to use it in the "right" (i.e., heterosexual) way.

The sexual rhetoric of the locker rooms of *Sunset Park* (1996) and *Wildcats* (1986) provides evidence that the presence of female authority did little to disrupt misogynist and homophobic talk. Also worthy of note is the way these films deal with any sort of effort by the women themselves to disrupt the misogyny and sexism they face. In one scene of *Sunset Park* (1996), Coach Saroka enters the locker room after the team's first victory, full of team spirit and enthusiasm. "You guys were fantabulous!" she exclaims. When her enthusiasm goes unmet she looks around and asks the team, "What is the matter with you guys? You look like you've seen a ghost."

Shorty reminds Coach Saroka of the fact that the team won their first game last year and then proceeded to lose the next 15 games. Even after her attempt to brush off their concerns with a brief "That was last year" speech, the team still looks less than enthused. She sarcastically addresses what she sees as the team's concern: "Oh, well, what do I know; I'm a *girl*. Why don't you *guys* tell me—what does it take to make a winner?" When no one responds, she assigns the team homework: they must come to the next practice prepared to tell her what it takes to make a winner. Following her rant, she turns to leave the locker room, tossing an adolescently cheery "See you on the bus, Gus" to the team as she departs. Although she calls the team out on their perceived sexism, any attempt for a serious disruption of hegemonic locker room practices and attitudes goes unchallenged when Coach Saroka is infantilized immediately after the spectators see her angry and frustrated.

Wildcats (1986) handles Coach McGrath's charge of sexism in a similar style. In this case, however, she is not calling out sexism displayed by the members of her team, but of the colleagues who have refused to offer her a coaching position within her own school, instead sending her to the "rough" part of the town to work with the Wildcats. "You think a woman can't be tough enough?" Coach McGrath challenges the three men who sit around her. "Well, I'll show you tough; Watch me!" she exclaims, storming out of the office. The three men look around at each other, a bit taken aback. Coach McGrath returns a few seconds later, strides into the room and quickly grabs her handbag off the chair as she whispers, "I forgot my purse." This action calls attention to McGrath's gender and how ill-fitting it is within the world of football, perhaps suggesting that football has no need for purses *or* women.

CONCLUSIONS

The importance of examining these two films must be underscored. Contrary to Goldie Hawn's sentiment that "*Wildcats* is not the kind of film you can critique. You have to go to a theater, see people laughing and say, 'This movie is fun'" (Shapiro, 1998: 136), by highlighting the denigration of women that takes place via misogynist and homophobic locker room rhetoric, this analysis makes salient the sexism and struggles that women coaching men's teams must face on a daily basis in addition to the institutional barriers they must surmount (see Staurowsky, 1990).

As this study suggests, the infusion of women as coaches of men's teams failed to significantly challenge the routine performances of masculinity common in the locker room setting. Furthermore, these media messages tended to reinforce the status quo of a patriarchal society and patriarchal institutions, instead of offering up new paradigms in which women as coaches might be accepted and respected. This suggests that an effort to break the cycle of misogynist and homophobic rhetoric must begin with the male players and male coaches of men's teams (Longman, 2002). Then, as Auriemma suggests, "What happens on the men's side is irrelevant" (Corley, 2002) and coaches will, indeed, be welcomed and selected based on their merit.

NOTES

1. Punani, in this case, is used as a slang term for vagina. Within this scene, it can be taken more generally to mean engaging in sexual relations and/or intercourse with women.
2. Earlier locker room conversation had Butter discussing a trip to the south with his teammates, where, according to Butter, it is customary to buy a woman a chicken before "getting any punani."

REFERENCES

Araton, H. (2004, November 21). Chauvinism lives in the locker room. *New York Times*: S9.

Corley, C. (2002, March 27). Report. *Morning Edition*. National Public Radio.

Curry, T. (1991). Fraternal bonding in the locker room: A pro-feminist analysis of talk about competition and women. In Kimmel, M. S. and Messner, M. A. (Eds.), *Men's lives*. 5th ed., 188–201. Boston, MA: Allyn and Bacon.

Disch, L. and Kane, M. J. (1996). When a looker is really a bitch: Lisa Olson, sport and the heterosexual matrix. In Joeres, R. B. and Laslett, B. (Eds.), *The second Signs reader: Feminist scholarship, 1983–1996*, 326–356. Chicago, IL: University of Chicago Press.

Fornoff, S. (1993). *Lady in the locker room.* Champaign, IL: Sagamore.

Fuller, L. K. (1992). Reporters' rights to the locker room. *Feminist Issues* (Volume 12, Number 1) Spring: 39–45.

Kobrin, S. (2008, February 13). Cable news' locker-room mentality really stinks. Women's eNews. Available: (http://www.womensenews.org/article.cfm/dyn/aid/3492).

Longman, J. (2002, March 29). Debating the male coach's role. *New York Times*: C15.

Miracle, A. and Ress, R. (1994). *Lessons of the locker room: The myth of school sports.* Amherst, NJ: Prometheus Books.

Murray, S. (2002, April 23). Posting up in the pink ghetto. Available: (http://www.feminist.org/sports/wsf_feature.asp).

Pearson, D. (2001). The depiction and characterization of women in sport film. *Women in Sport & Physical Activity Journal* (Volume 10, Number 1). Spring: 103–124.

Shapiro, M. (1998) *Pure Goldie: The life and career of Goldie Hawn.* Secaucus, NJ: Carol.

Staurowsky, E. (1990). Women coaching male athletes. In Messner, M. A. and Sabo, D. F. (Eds.) *Sport, men and the gender order: Critical feminist perspectives*, 163–170. Champaign, IL: Human Kinetics Books.

Sunset Park. Director Steve Gomer. TriStar, 1996.

Wildcats. Director Michael Ritchie. Warner Bros., 1986.

CHAPTER THIRTEEN

Foul Language: A Feminist Perspective ON (American) Football Film Rhetoric

LINDA K. FULLER

> Words are very low on the list of things men like to say. They speak in codes, terms, euphemisms, diagrams, epigrams, and clichés, but rarely do they make clear, simple statements in comprehensible language. The terminology of football demonstrates that, left to themselves, without women around to force them to elaborate, men would all end up talking to each other via signal lamps and X's and O's.
>
> —SALLY JENKINS, *MEN WILL BE BOYS* (1996), P. 82.

In 1925, Harold Lloyd starred in a silent movie called *The Freshman*, an uproarious caper where he serves as "blocking dummy" on the football team. Today, the foul language featured in football films serves as a barometer of our relationship with the sporting world. Content analysis of the more than 100 such motion pictures, situated within various historical, political, racial, ethnic, socioeconomic, and gendered issues, provides a fascinating framework for better understanding the role that sports play in media and social violence.

THE LANGUAGE OF FOOTBALL

Going All the Way

Strategically, the goal of American football seems pretty basic: eleven players on each team, *offense* or *defense*, try to reach *end zones* where they can *score*. The team with the most points wins.

The ball, sometimes (erroneously) referred to as a *pigskin*, is handled by a *ballcarrier*, who hopes to keep it away from ball hawks. So, there might be *body blocking, butt-blocking, chop blocking, power blocking, roughing a kicker or passer, ball-stripping, zone blocking, flea-flicking, spiking, encroaching*, or *eating the ball*. A player might be a *headhunter, a heavy hitter, a scrimmage kicker, a sledgehammer, a jumper, a monster, a punishing runner*, or a *punter*. Opponents are always on the lookout for weak sides. He might deliberately spear a fellow player's helmet, make a *sucker play, sack, or shank the ball, make a plunge, tackle,* even *head-butt*.

There are even some ghoulish terms, a *coffin corner* being one of the four places where sidelines and goal lines intersect, a *dead ball* is one out of play, and *dead-man* (or *sleeper*) play refers to an illegal pretense for passing. Actually, there are a number of illegal terms: formation, block, crackback, shift, motion, substitution, return, use of hands, arms, or body by offense, even illegal equipment. A *dying quail*, when a toss lacks speed and power, can also be called a duck ball. *Skull sessions*, also known as chalk talk, review and predict plays. At the other extreme, how does one explain that football lingo also includes "Hail Mary," a low-percentage desperation pass that appeals to a higher power for completion. It may not surprise you that there can be *intentional grounding, intercepts, slashing, "unsportsmanlike conduct,"* and a *disabled list*. Or that *possession* is of prime importance.

My analyses of the language of sport (1999) began with a sportscast of the Super Bowl during the Persian Gulf War, in response to learning that instances of domestic violence in the United States escalated during celebration of the country's largest annual television event (Sachs and Chu, 2000); since then, I have examined how "Super Sunday" has become a highly hyped ratings leader, an unofficial national holiday, our second-largest day of food consumption, after Thanksgiving, an excuse for some 7.5 million parties, a "testosterone-driven male event," and how, in 2009, some $8.5 billion went into betting and a 30-second ad cost $3 million (Duncan and Aycock, 2008; Kanner, 2007; St. John, 2009; Weiss and Day, 2003).

For those of us interested in the sportscaster language of Super Bowl (Fuller, 2008), we are alert to terms such as *bombs and bomb squads, offense/defense, flanks, victories and defeats, casualties, chucking, cleating, killing, hitting, holding, hooking, ammunition, weapons, taking aim, fighting, detonating, squeezing the trigger*, and *dominating*. Other phrases might be noted, such as "blockading the way," "ground and air attacks," "fighting and dying on the frontlines," and "battling in the trenches." Strategies and tactics might include *offenses, a game plan*, "two-minute drills," *kamikaze squads*, the "two-platoon system," or "minefields," sometimes being reduced to employing "unnecessary roughness." Feminists react to jargon such as "going all the way," *pinching, squeezing, pumping*, "deep penetration," "grinding it out," "clutch plays," "bump and run" stratagem, "gang-tackling," "naked reverses," and "belly-backing" techniques. Sometimes there are *fumbles, muffs, huddles, hurry-up offenses, quick hits or releases*, or even "fakes." *Kicking* can be key.

As noted in my Introduction to this volume, militaristic and sexist terms are inherent in football talk. "The mythology and symbolism of contemporary combat sports such as football are probably meaningful and salient to viewers on a number of levels: patriotism, militarism, and meritocracy are all dominate themes," Michael A. Messner (2007: 103) reminds us. "But it is reasonable to speculate that gender is a salient organizing theme in the construction of meanings around sports violence."

A Brief History of (Violent) Football

American football has its roots in rugby, by way of soccer, an extremely rough sport that dates from 1314 Britain; Eric Dunning (2002) cites a 1601 report by Sir Richard Carew about players "retyring home as from a pitched battaile, with bloody pates, bones broken and out of joynt, and such bruises as serve to shorten their daies." Yale halfback Walter Camp is credited with transforming the game in the 1880s such that it became an intercollegiate and then professional sport. By 1905, 18 fatalities and 159 serious injuries had been reported, *The World* of New York claiming football as "the most brutal, perilous, and unnecessary sport sanctioned by any country in the world" (Considine, 1982: 123). In 2001, the XFL (for "eXtreme Football League") was introduced, six days after the National Football League concluded Super Bowl XXXV; a brainchild of Vince McMahon of the World Wrestling Federation (WWF), its existence was fortunately short-lived.

Sport violence has been encouraged, even elevated, since at least the original Olympic Games (Fuller, 2000). Whether framed as a mirror of society, a result of fan behavior, economic incentives, innate aggression, and/or the consequence of psychological stress, the jury is still out as to how it should be handled. "Football's historical prominence in sport media and folk culture has sustained a hegemonic model of masculinity that prioritizes competitiveness, asceticism, success (winning), aggression, violence, superiority to women, and respect for and compliance with male authority," according to Sabo and Panepinto (1990: 115). Approaching football as cultural text, Michael Oriard (1993: xxii) believes that its example "can suggest more generally how meaning is produced in a mass-mediated society. Popular spectator sports such as football differ in important ways from related cultural representations; in contrast to movies and television dramas, for example, football games are unscripted, their action real.

But...whatever the violence in football means to specific spectators, the issue of violence is inescapable."

Literature Review

Stating that "sports violence may be seen as either reflecting or shaping social norms and values, as either legally punishable 'real' violence or as ritual, symbolic play," Jeffrey Goldstein (1983: 3) outlines the role of both external and internal constraints, determining the importance of historical, social, and psychological contexts. It is a topic that has received recent academic interest (e.g., Messner and Sabo, 1994; Welch, 1997; Benedict and Yeager, 1998; Bridges, 1999; Dunning, 1999; Leizman, 1999; Barry, 2001; Norwood, 2004; Falk, 2005; Freeman, 2004; Paolantonio, 2008). The scholarship of Jeff Benedict (1997, 1998, 2000) has concentrated on violence perpetrated by athletes against women. Jib Fowles (1999: 83) makes this astute observation: "In analyses of sporting events, the word 'violence' is often reserved for aggressive actions that are illegal and reproachable, but it is clear that much of what occurs within the rules is also violent by everyday standards. This is indisputable for football, in which players are maimed on a regular basis, sometimes to a paralyzing, life-threatening extent."

Some books have been written describing or explaining various football terms. For example, as early as 1966, Rote and Winter (1966) produced *The Language of Pro Football*, containing more than 700 terms. Tim Considine's 1982 *The Language of Sport* includes a section on football terminology, and Larry Adler has collected *Football Coach Quotes: The Wit, Wisdom, and Winning Words of Leaders on the Gridiron* (1992).

There are also some books out there suggesting to women the importance of learning about football—expressly, to please their men, and/or to talk their talk. These range from a sappy one by The Learning Annex titled *How to Talk Sports to Men* (1984) to an equally down-speaking one by Suzy Beamer Bohnert called *Game-Day Goddess: Learning Football's Lingo* (2003: 1). "Imagine receiving an invitation to your boss's party to watch a football game," it self-promotes, "...you love your job, and you want to impress your supervisor and colleagues. But what's a touchdown? What are those men knocking each other down and charging about wildly?" Holly Robinson Peete's *Get Your Own Beer, I'm Watching the Game!* (2005) encourages women to enjoy the game for themselves.

Sally Jenkins' more focused *Men Will Be Boys: The Modern Woman Explains Football and Other Amusing Male Rituals* (1996: 3) takes a different approach: "We get it, okay? It doesn't take a genetic imprint. We get the Beauty and the Nuance. We get the Violence and the Ballet. We get the concept of War Without Death and the Lure of the Uniform." And yet another perspective is presented in Mariah

Burton Nelson's *The Stronger Women Get, the More Men Love Football: Sexism and the American Culture of Sports* (1994: 7): "Manly sports are more than a refuge from the reality of women's liberation. By creating a world where masculinity is equated with violence, where male bonding is based on the illusion of male supremacy, and where all of the visible women are cheerleaders, manly sports set the stage for violence against women."

Football and Females

No sport, I have argued, "better exemplifies the nexus of Big Business, big stakes, and big boys than American football" (Fuller, 1999: 165). In a culture that venerates athletes, and in the context of recent news stories about star football players arrested for crimes ranging from assault to sexual battery or even murder, the time is long overdue for an examination of the culture of violence that comes with sports. Questioning the invincibility that comes with multimillion-dollar National Football League and other sports contracts, groups such as the National Coalition Against Violent Athletes have been formed.

Gender, clearly, needs to be factored in. NBC Sports president Dick Ebersol points out that "men want to know the score and women want to know the whole story" (in Jenkins, 1996: 14). Sportswriter and sports commentator Sally Jenkins expands on this notion: "Guys concentrate on specific plays and strategies that result in a final score that will leave them either exuberant or foul-tempered for the remainder of the day. Women see a whole range of behavior, much of it which, frankly, looks dumb to us. So if guys think we ask stupid questions, well, sometimes it's a stupid subject." She cites some of those *stupid* questions (pp. 55–57):

- Why is it called football when they don't use their feet?
- How come when a guy scores, even his own teammates hit him?
- In sudden death, does someone play dead?
- How come the NFL fines players for leaving their shirttails out, but if you hit a guy in the back, it's only a penalty?
- Is there such a thing as the *whole*back, and if not, why not? If a guy is called a *quarter*back, shouldn't there be four of him? Do *tail*backs have tails?
- Why is he called the nose guard when his face is always bleeding?
- How come steroids are against NFL rules, but sexual assaults aren't?

"The key for women translating football language from malespeak to femalespeak is," Jenkins contends, "when in doubt, to think in terms of war and sex metaphors. They are the Rosetta stones of the game" (p. 87).

THE LANGUAGE OF FOOTBALL FILMS

On the field, football, one of the most lucrative sports in the United States, provides its own kind of infotainment; in the movies, the message translates to what a man's world it is after all. What follows is a brief review of the genre, wide-ranging but still unfailingly always about fighting.

Football Films

It has been reported that the first football film caught a contest between teams from Michigan and the University of Chicago in 1904 (*The Michigan Stadium Story*, http://www.umich.edu/~bhl/stadium/stadtext/fbchi04.htm). Produced by the American Kinetograph Company of Orange, New Jersey, a movie production facility owned by Thomas Edison, surviving footage of a seven-minute clip is available online. Since then, starting in the Silent Era, more than 100 football-related films have aired in our movie houses and homes. A select number are listed here in a filmography, including names of director/producers.

They might be funny (e.g., *The Freshman*, 1925; The Marx Brothers' *Horse Feathers*, 1932; George Plimpton's *Paper Lion*, 1986; Robin Williams in *The Best of Times*, 1986; Robert Downey, Jr., in *Johnny Be Good*, 1987; Adam Sandler as *The Waterboy*, 1998; Keanu Reeves and Gene Hackman in *The Replacements*, 2000), musicals, mysteries, dramas (e.g., *The Longest Yard*, 1974; *The Program*, 1993; *Weapons of Mass Destruction*, 1997), or based on real persons and/or events (e.g., Ronald Reagan as *Knute Rockne*, 1940; Burt Lancaster as *Jim Thorpe*, 1951; *Brian's Song*, 1971; *Rudy*, 1993; *We Are Marshall*, 2006; *Leatherheads,* 2008, and a number of made-for-television films, such as *Triumph of the Heart: Rickey Bell*, 1991 or *Gift of Love: Daniel Huffman*, 1999), even films made into a TV series, such as *Friday Night Lights* (2004). Often they are symbolic, such as *The Longest Yard* (1974/2005), which ostensibly might seem like a prison film but it really is about group unity. ESPN's *The Season: Behind Bars* (2004) follows players in maximum security detention—how appropriate.

Football movies are usually fictional, *North Dallas Forty* (1979) being one that is considered by many people as the best football film of all time. We have had our share dealing with terrorism (e.g., *Two Minute Warning*, 1976; *Black Sunday*, 1977), but recent world events might scare off corporate support for more. Maybe they are easiest when reduced to raw material, as in this statement from *The Program* (1993): "The best thing about football is that you don't have to think about anything…just hurting people, and who's hurting you."

Tom Cruise plays a high-schooler depending on football as his ticket to college in *All the Right Moves* (1983), he then takes the role of a slick sports agent in *Jerry Maguire* (1996). Cuba Gooding, Jr., won a Best Supporting Actor Oscar for his "Show me the money!" performance as the pro player in that film; he then showed another side to his talent in the based-on-fact *Radio* (2003), which presents yet another direction for pigskin pictures, sensitizing viewers to "mentally challenged" people.

Girls and women usually have stereotypical roles in football films, an exception being Helen Hunt's part in the coming-of-age film *Quarterback Princess* (1985) that goes against traditional sexism. Goldie Hawn plays a female football coach trying to convince inner-city kids they have the right stuff in *Wildcats* (1986), which also stars Wesley Snipes, Swoosie Kurtz, and Woody Harrelson before they became famous. It introduced the controversy of women in the locker room. *Everybody's All-American* (1988), an adaptation of Frank Deford's novel about a Washington Redskins star (Dennis Quaid), has a classic response by homecoming queen Jessica Lange about her major: "Gavin and me." But the female-bashing in *The Last Boy Scout* (1991) is much more common.

Even if they have bombed with the critics (e.g., *The Program*, 1993; *The Replacements*, 2000), most football films have scored at the home box office, even if few have done very well abroad. Amongst the most recent favorites, *Varsity Blues* (1999) won support from anyone who has ever worked under a hard-assed coach (here, Jon Voight), while *Remember the Titans* (2000) works as a star vehicle for Denzel Washington in an important indictment against racism in the sport. Consider this opening line by twins Alex and Andrew Smith in *The Slaughter Rule* (2002), where Montana men play hard: "My father told me if I was hard enough I'd never break. He lied."

Beginning August 26, 2003, the 24-hour sports television channel ESPN offered an eleven-part series of fictional drama centering around pro football called *Playmakers* (Fuller, 2004) that met with quite a bit of controversy. While it supposedly attempted to mirror reality, focusing on gritty topics such as drug use, domestic violence, hidden homosexuality, injuries, racism, criminal activities, ferocious coaches, and team politics, it was more successful garnering criticism. With a moniker challenging, "If all you see is the athlete, open your eyes," too many advertisers and audience members alike saw it mainly as a male soap opera, and it drew the wrath of the Association for Women in Sports Media (AWSM), who complained about how women in broadcasting are depicted. At the time of writing, its contract has not been renewed.

And so football continues cinematically, albeit formulaically. Yet, of all the football films ever made, none better encapsulates my argument about their combining violence with foul language than the appropriately named *Necessary Roughness* and Oliver Stone's opus: *Any Given Sunday*.

Necessary Roughness

The NFL has a long list of rules, particularly penalties for "unnecessary roughness" (http://www.nfl.com/fans/rules/definitions), which forms the basis for a 1991 comedy about a 34-year-old quarterback's return to college football. Your basic story about underdog losers who have to come together as a team for the classic comeback, *Necessary Roughness* stars Scott Bakula, Hector Elizondo, Robert Loggia, as well as Sinbad and Kathy Ireland; directed by Stan Dragoti, this Paramount Pictures film features the Texas State Armadillos, former football champions who have new rules about recruitment (e.g., one needs to be seriously enrolled in college) and ethics.

There are cameos by quite a cast of celebrities: football pros Dick Butkus, Ben Davidson, Bubba Smith, Earl Campbell, Roger Craid, Tony Dorsett, Ed "Too Tall" Jones, Randy White, Jim Kelly, Jerry Rice, and Herschel Walker, besides boxing champ Evander Holyfield and sportscaster Chris Berman. Nelson (1994: 46) adds the gender element to the team that invites Lucy, a soccer player, to be their place-kicker:

> Team members fear that they'll be the laughingstock of the conference, and they make sexual comments about her body. But Lucy scores the tying kick in the final game. A player from the opposing team, his sense of masculinity dominance clearly threatened, gratuitously and angrily knocks her to the ground, saying, "Welcome to football." Her teammates, by then appreciative of her ability but still ensconced in their mythic man-as-protector role, run toward the guy who had tackled her as if to retaliate. No need. Lucy can take care of herself. She kicks him in the groin, saying, "Welcome to football."

Not to hold you in great suspense, but yes, amazingly, this mélange of misfits pulls it off and wins the big one. Despite the trumped-up plot(s) and cliché-filled conversations, it was received as generally enjoyable. Beyond that, and not to turn anyone off, it turns out that the term "Necessary Roughness" has quite a connotation in the porn world. Although there is no date listed, another movie with the same name is subtitled *Mason's Dirty Trixxx #2*, billed as "Strong enough for a man, But made by a woman! Choking, Spitting, slapping, gagging, swalling, atm, double anal, head dunking, trash talking…And the girls had fun too!" In addition, The Lady of Rage has lyrics to a song released on the Death Row label in 2001 called *Necessary Roughness* that have a running theme of "break(ing) a sucker down to dust."

Any Given Sunday

Subtitled "Life Is a Contact Sport," *Any Given Sunday* is a 2 hours, 45 minutes long, modern-day epic of the battles fought both on and off the field when it comes to professional football—modern-day gladiators, if you will, in a war zone that is as much an all-out assault on our senses as any of Oliver Stone's war movies. Premiering on December 21, 1999, it made more than $70 million even before being released to video stores. Written by Stone and John Logan and distributed by Warner Brothers, it stars Al Pacino, Dennis Quaid, Jamie Foxx, Cameron Diaz, and James Woods. Charlton Heston, portrayed as *Ben Hur* gone gun-crazy, appears in one of many star-studded cameos.

Any Given Sunday, which refers to the day when American football is most often played, begins with a quotation from the famous coach Vince Lombardi exalting those lying "exhausted on the field of battle." Right away, then, we see the players of the imaginary team called the Miami Sharks getting their key lesson about relying on one another for survival. The supercharged plot centers around the old-style, constantly hollering coach (Al Pacino) and a hotshot, rising star (Jamie Foxx—who, by the way, was chosen because of all the actors who tried out, he had the best toss). But the real star is the media, and Stone never lets us forget its role: he filters film through a variety of formats, with split-screen effects, freeze frames, and never-ending montages that dazzle, even dizzy, the viewer. (I know more than one person who claimed feeling seasick after watching it.) Visual is not all, though: Stone also manipulates his audience by incorporating loud thudding sounds, low mutterings from the coach to himself, bone-crunching assaults, and music so thunderous that at times you feel as if you are on the football field rather than in a Dolby-inspired theater. "TV changed everything," the coach bemoans. "The first time they stopped the game to cut away to some fucking commercial, that was the end of it." For the film, Stone made sure he got an "R" rating, enticing viewers with promises of strong language, violence, sexuality, and here even full frontal male nudity.

Early on, two star players get bone-crushingly injured—no surprise, really, as we know how long they have been playing, and how "all out" they have gone for the sport. In fact, they have been playing with earlier injuries never properly healed and yet were encouraged/expected to "go out there and fight." This is what they have been trained to do, and what we as viewers/consumers expect them to do. The instant replay of the quarterback getting injured is played over and over, the sportscasters encouraging it even though, as they point out, "it gives you a sickening feeling in the pit of your stomach," since "the dynasty is in trouble."

Although racism is implicit, sexism is all-pervasive. Men dominate the big money sport of football, which is played exclusively by men, announced by men, coached by men, and watched primarily by men. And who else but male photographers would focus so frequently on nearly naked cheerleaders. A player named Shark snorts a line of cocaine off a woman's breast. Money buys sexual services and allows the team's head doctor to break ethical codes.

Even the advertisements are geared toward men: mostly (Budweiser) beer, but also cars (Mercedes, GMC trucks, Jaguars, Ford Explorers) and computers and WWF programming. In fact, this movie could have been just as easily titled "Any Given Advertisement," it contained so many embedded commercials. While labels were apparent for Polo, Armani, Hugo Boss, Fubu, and Levi's, Reebok ruled; at one point, it fit into the plot whereby L. L. Cool J. played a running back working to break the 2,000-yard rushing record so he could get a multibillion dollar contract from the shoe leader. Motorola's Startek and Nokia vie as the cell phone of choice, while Macanudo cigars were puffed on for celebrations. The cover of *Forbes* was framed, copies of *Sports Illustrated* let lying around, and an issue of *Time* was captured. Queen's "We Will Rock You" resounded. And the football, later eulogized by Tom Hanks as a *Cast Away* (2000), was a Wilson—seen here in at least eleven close-ups. Add Apple, Adidas, Pepsi, IBM, First Union Bank, Bacardi, Excel helmets, Sprint, Sony, Tag, Telex headphones, Toyota, Home Depot, DMX, VO-5, Old Spice, Right Guard, All Sport, Nikon cameras, Lay's chips, Mr. Peanuts, Poland Springs, even a sponsor-cited commercial break for MET-REX. Give *us* a break!

Women in *Any Given Sunday* are either drunks or dominatrixes, epitomized by Cameron Diaz's character—a tough-as-nails owner/inheritor of the team who is constantly reminded what her father would do for the team and her soused mother, ably played by Ann Margaret. A prostitute approaches Al Pacino at a bar, knowing he's an important coach but not knowing much about the game. She hits on him, whispering her fees ("$1,000 for an hour, $5,000 for the night"). We soon realize that the underlying message is that most women can be bought. We see groupies at parties, all over the players, doing anything to get their attention. While some conversations are indecipherable, most are laced with swear words and with sexy statements such as "don't act like a pussy," "fuck us up," "kick some butt," "do for dick," or "be a complete prick." After all, "We win, we penetrate, we win."

Film scholars focus on "the gaze," typically referring to voyeurism relative to women, and more recently to men as well. A classic scene in *Any Given Sunday* has Cameron Diaz walking into the testosterone-loaded shower room, where the naked players are, to yell at the coach. Greeting them, she rubs one's shoulder muscles and whispers, "Don't stiffen up on me," seemingly referring to his muscles, but one cannot help but notice that his genitalia are not covered. In fact, the whole film alternates between exposé and glorified football fandom.

CONSIDERATIONS

Whether in football or in life in general, foul language is hardly ever necessary or effective. It behooves us to be aware of the double-edged nature of the controversies encircling it in the context of media; balancing presumed consumer desires with what the market might bear, we must nevertheless be aware of the effects that may accrue from sports language and sports actions. Once we realize that most sports fouls are formulaic, even if we are encouraged to think that they are spontaneous, even "fun," we begin to own the answers. Once we realize that most sports violence is merely an issue of power, albeit corporate strength so disguised that we often cannot know what corporation is actually sponsoring it, we begin to be critical media consumers. And that means all of us, regardless of educational and socioeconomic status.

Once we understand how sports language and sports action operate within the world of infotainment—when, where, how, and why—our next step as individuals and community members is to operationalize that knowledge. If we are teachers, we can introduce media literacy about the role(s) of entertainment in our lives; if we are policymakers, we can help influence decision-making toward inclusion of diverse, alternative ways of conceptualizing, producing, and distributing (sports) media; if we are concerned citizens, we can form coalitions of persons interested in broadening media choices. And whatever our stance(s), if we care about sports we can keep in mind its essence: celebrating the body, enjoying the empowerment of reaching goals and the thrill of teamwork, playing by the rules, and participating where possible, being spectators when not. But when all is said and done, fairness beats foulness.

The American variation of football has had only about a century of history and filmic images. It may be a metaphor for human existence, dealing as it does with the value of team play, making sacrifices and powerful plays, rolling with the punches, focusing on goals. Yet, like *Necessary Roughness* and *Any Given Sunday*, football magnifies both the glory and the gory of sport.

Football Filmography

Legend: [P] = Producer

Year	Film	Director
1904	*Michigan vs. Chicago*	American Kinetograph Co. [P]
1932	*Horse Feathers*	Norman Z. McLeod
1934	*Gridiron Flash*	Glenn Tryon
1940	*Knute Rockne, All American*	Lloyd Bacon
1951	*Jim Thorpe—All American*	Michael Curtiz
1968	*Paper Lion*	Alex March
1971	*Brian's Song*	Buzz Kulik
1974	*The Longest Yard*	Robert Aldrich (2005: Peter Segal)
1976	*Two Minute Warning*	Larry Peerce
1977	*Black Sunday*	John Frankenheimer

Year	Film	Director
1977	*Semi-Tough*	Michael Ritchie
1978	*Heaven Can Wait*	Buck Henry, Warren Beatty
1979	*North Dallas Forty*	Ted Kotcheff
1983	*All the Right Moves*	Michael Chapman
1983	*Quarterback Princess*	Noel Black
1986	*The Best of Times*	Roger Spottiswoode
1986	*Wildcats*	Michael Ritchie
1988	*Everybody's All-American*	Taylor Hackford
1988	*Johnny Be Good*	Bud S. Smith
1991	*The Last Boy Scout*	Tony Scott
1991	*Necessary Roughness*	Stan Dragoti
1991	*Triumph of the Heart: The Ricky Bell Story*	Richard Michaels
1993	*The Program*	David S. Ward
1993	*Rudy*	David Anspaugh
1994	*Rise and Walk: The Dennis Byrd Story*	Michael Dinner
1996	*Jerry Maguire*	Cameron Crowe
1998	*The Waterboy*	Frank Coraci
1999	*Any Given Sunday*	Oliver Stone
1999	*Fumbleheads*	Mark Lasky
1999	*A Gift of Love: The Daniel Huffman Story*	John Korty
1999	*Varsity Blues*	Brian Robbins
2000	*Remember the Titans*	Boaz Yakin
2000	*The Replacements*	Howard Deutch
2000	*Whatever It Takes*	David Raynr
2001	*Go Tigers!*	Kenneth A. Carlson
2002	*A Hero's Heart*	Mark Bossley
2002	*Hometown Legend*	James Anderson
2002	*Jim Brown: All American*	Spike Lee
2002	*The Junction Boys*	Mike Robe
2002	*Second String*	Robert Lieberman
2003	*Radio*	Michael Tollin
2003	*The Season: Behind Bars*	ESPN [P]
2004	*Death and Texas*	Kevin DiNovis
2004	*Friday Night Lights*	Peter Berg
2004	*Heartland Son*	Jeremy Major
2004	*Walking Tall*	Kevin Bray
2006	*Facing the Giants*	Alex Kendrick
2006	*Gridiron Gang*	Phil Joanou
2006	*Invincible*	Ericson Core
2006	*We Are Marshall*	McG
2007	*The Comebacks*	Tom Brady
2008	*Leatherheads*	George Clooney
2008	*Pittsburgh Passion*	Jennifer Yee
2008	*Six Man, Texas*	Alan Barber
2009	*Down and Distance*	Brian De Palma
2009	*Skiptracers*	Harris Mendheim

REFERENCES

Adler, L. (1992). *Football coach quotes: The wit, wisdom, and winning words of Leaders on the gridiron.* Jefferson, NC: McFarland and Company.

Barry, J. (2001). *Power plays: Politics, football, and other blood sports.* Jackson, MS: University Press of Mississippi.

Benedict, J. (1997). *Public heroes, private felons: Athletes and crimes against women.* Boston, MA: Northeastern University Press.

Benedict, J. (1998). *Athletes and acquaintance rape.* Thousand Oaks, CA: Sage.

Benedict, J. (2000). Out of bounds: Inside the NBA's culture of rape, violence, and crime. Boston, MA: Northeastern University Press.

Benedict, J. and Yeager, D. (1998). *Pros and cons: The criminals who play in the NFL.* New York: Warner Books.

Bohnert, S. B. (2003). *Game-day goddess: Learning football's lingo.* Glen Allen, VA: eNovel.com.

Bridges, J. (1999). *Making violence part of the game.* Commack, NY: Kroshka.

Considine, T. (1982). *The language of sport.* New York: World Almanac.

Duncan, M. C. and Aycock, A. (2008). "I laughed until I hurt": Negative humor in Super Bowl ads. In Wenner, L. and Jackson, S. J. (Eds.), *Sport, beer, and gender: Promotional culture and contemporary social life*, 243–260. Zurich: Peter Lang.

Dunning, E. (1999). *Sport matters: Sociological studies of sport, violence, and civilisation.* London: Routledge.

Dunning, E. (2002). *Civilising soccer.* Available: (http://www.footballculture.net/players/feat_playerviolence.html).

Falk, G. (2005). *Football and American identity.* New York: Routledge.

Fowles, J. (1999). *The case for television violence.* Thousand Oaks, CA: Sage.

Freeman, M. (2004). *Bloody Sundays: Inside the dazzling, rough-and-tumble world of the NFL.* New York; HarperCollins.

Fuller, L. K. (1999). Super Bowl speak: Subtexts of sex and sex talk in America's annual sports extravaganza. In Carstarphen, M. G. and Zavoina, S. C. (Eds.), *Sexual rhetoric: Media perspectives on sexuality, gender, and identity*, 161–173. Westport, CT: Greenwood.

Fuller, L. K. (2000). The culture of violence and the rhetoric of sport violence. Paper presented to the International Association of Media and Communication Research, Singapore.

Fuller, L. K. (2004). Fictionalizing (American) football: A case study of the TV show *Playmakers.* International Association for Media and Communication Research conference, Porto Alegra, Brazil.

Fuller, L. K. (2008). *Sportscasters/sportscasting: Principles and practices.* New York: Routledge.

Goldstein, J. (1983). *Sports violence.* New York: Springer-Verlag.

Jenkins, S. (1996). *Men will be boys: The modern woman explains football and other amusing male rituals.* New York: Doubleday.

Kanner, B. (2007). *The Super Bowl of advertising.* New York: Association of National Advertisers.

Learning Annex (1984). *How to talk sports to men.* New York: Berkeley Books.

Leizman, J. (1999). *Let's kill 'em: Understanding and controlling violence in sports.* Lanham, MD: University Press of America.

Messner, M. A. (2007). *Out of play: Critical essays on gender and sport.* Albany, NY: SUNY Press.

Messner, M. and Sabo, D. F. (1994). *Sex, violence and power in sports.* Freedom, CA: Crossing.

Nelson, M. B. (1994). *The stronger women get, the more men love football: Sexism and the American culture of sports.* Orlando, FL: Harcourt Brace.

Norwood, S. H. (2004). *Real football: Conversations on America's game.* Jackson, MS: University Press of Mississippi.

Oriard, M. (1993). *Reading football: How the popular press created an American spectacle.* Chapel Hill, NC: University of North Carolina Press.

Paolantonio, S. (2008). *How football explains America.* Chicago, IL: Triumph Books.

Peete, H. R. (2005). *Get your own damn beer, I'm watching the game! A woman's guide to loving pro football.* Stamford, CT: Rodale.

Rote, K. and Winter, J. (1966). *The language of pro football.* New York: Random House.

Sabo, D. F. and Panepinto, J. (1990). In Messner, M. and Sabo, D. F. (Eds.), *Sport, men, and the gender order: Critical feminist perspectives,* 115–126. Champaign, IL: Human Kinetics.

Sachs, C. J., and Chu, L. D. (2000). The association between professional football games and domestic violence in Los Angeles county. *Journal of Interpersonal Violence,* Vol. 15: 1192–1201.

St. John, A. (2009). *The billion dollar game: Behind-the-scenes of the greatest day in American sport.* New York: Doubleday.

Weiss, D. with Day, C. (2003). *The making of the Super Bowl: The inside story of the world's greatest sporting event.* New York: McGraw-Hill.

Welch, M. (1997). Violence against women by professional football players: A gender analysis of hypermasculinity, positional status, narcissism, and entitlement. *Journal of Sport and Social Issues* (21): 392–411.

CHAPTER FOURTEEN

Hail TO THE Chiefs: Race, Gender, AND Native American Sports Mascots

C. RICHARD KING

The playing fields of North America have become battlefields, as Native American sports mascots, once celebrated symbols, increasingly foster intense conflicts over history, culture, and identity. Consequently, scholars and commentators have seized upon these struggles to consider the changing articulations of race and power in American culture. Importantly, an expansive literature has offered critical analyses of Native American sports mascots, stressing that they can facilitate the creation of identity, community, and history (Connolly, 2000; Davis, 1993; King, 2001, 2002, 2003; King and Springwood, 2000, 2001a, 2001b; King et al., 2002; Nuessel, 1994; Pewewardy, 1991; Spindel, 2000; Staurowsky, 1998).

A concern for race, especially "Indianness," has anchored these interpretations. And although Eitzen and Zinn (1989, 1993) have rightly highlighted the implications of naming and imaging sports team for women on and off the playing field, gender has received little attention in accounts of pseudo-Indian imagery in sports (for a noteworthy exception, see Davis, 1993). Indeed, most studies of Native American sports mascots have foregrounded race at the expense of gender. Native American political leader Dennis Banks (1993) has even unequivocally rejected the significance of gender in efforts to understand and highlight such icons.

The neglect and dismissal of gender is most unfortunate because it has obscured a full understanding of the complex meanings of Native American sports mascots. More specifically, scholars to date have failed to build on Laurel Davis's (1993) observation that on the one hand the use of pseudo-Indian imagery reinforced dominant notions of masculinity, while on the other hand the controversy over mascots derived in part from efforts to defend traditional formulation of identity in the United States, especially its foundations in race (whiteness), gender (masculinity), nation (American-ness), and history (the myth of the frontier). Consequently, the intense attention to race in the absence of gender has caused scholars to overlook the troubling discourses that sanction racialized team spirits by marshaling dominant ideas about gender.

This chapter seeks to redress this oversight through an examination of the use of sexual rhetoric in arguments defending Native American sports mascots. It focuses on the writings of conservative commentator David Yeagley, especially the ways in which he explicitly and implicitly employs masculinity and femininity in his assessments of cultural ideals; coding of ideological perspectives; and evaluations of race, nation, and politics.

RACE, GENDER, AND SPORTS MASCOTS

Native American sports mascots have much to teach about race; at the same time, they also offer valuable lessons about gender. First and foremost, they underscore that sports, like public culture in general, remain predominantly homo-social, hetero-masculine spaces, centering on men and their exploits and celebrating masculinity or those traits and ideals that define what it means to be a man in American society, such as aggression, independence, and competitiveness. The prevalence of teams named Warriors, Braves, and Red Raiders conforms to this pattern; so too does the previously discussed imagery used to represent such teams and schools.

Significantly, Native American mascots not only reflect and reinforce hegemonic masculinity but also have deep entanglements with struggles over what it means to be a man. Laurel Davis (1993) has argued convincingly that the usage of such symbols emerged in response to a crisis in white masculinity during the late 19th century in association with efforts to reformulate what it meant to be a man through (misleading) ideas about the American West—namely, the myth of the Frontier. The idealized connection between masculinity and the West, often cast in terms of Indianness, remained hegemonic for much of the 20th century, until challenged as part of broader social movements, including feminism as well as cultural and political resurgence across Native America. Many Americans, consciously or unconsciously, interpret the critique of pseudo-Indian imagery in athletics as an assault on American values, identities, and traditions, including hegemonic forms of masculinity. Consequently, Davis concludes, struggles over mascots are also struggles to redefine what it means to be a man and, hence, are met with fierce opposition. Clearly, as discussed in the next section of the chapter, this is a central element of the conservative response to mascots, especially their deployment of sexual rhetoric.

Importantly, Native American sports mascots not only clear a space for the perpetuation and performance of hegemonic masculinity but also offer important interpretations of femininity and gender relations, including the image of women; roles open to women; the kind and quality of gender relations; and inequities as well as limitations imposed by the symbols, performances, and narratives at the heart of sport. In fact, the use of pseudo-Indian symbols has resulted in the devaluation, oppression, erasure, sexualization, and disempowerment of women.

Eitzen and Zinn (1989, 1993) suggest that the naming of sports teams is often a sexist practice. They have identified six such practices: (1) taking a non-sexist male team name and adding lady (Lady Indians); (2) double gender marking (Lady Chocs when the men are Choctaws); (3) male name with female modifier (Lady Braves); (4) paired polarity (Warriors/Squaws); (5) use of feminine suffix for women's teams (among others, Bonner Springs High School (KS) and Flathead High School (MT) both call their boys teams the Braves and the girls teams the Bravettes); and (6) the use of physical markers emphasizing femininity. Clearly, these practices extend to teams with Native American sports mascots. Such practices suggest that women are secondary, supplemental, dependent, lesser. Men are the central actors: The norm. They literally degrade women and, importantly, demarcate the kinds of roles to which they might aspire. The use of racialized words, most notably "squaw," can intensify the injuries associated with team names, precisely because they simultaneously inscribe ethnic stereotypes and gender norms.

Native American sports mascots also erase women. The University of Illinois has a long history of Playing Indian at half-time, centering around a figure known as Chief Illiniwek, a white male student who performs in Indian regalia. Each performer has had his name recorded for posterity. During World War II, an Indian Princess replaced Chief Illiniwek. Dressed in a short skirt, a female student cheered the teams to victory. After the war, when Chief Illiniwek made his triumphant return, subsequent chiefs literally effaced the names of the young women who had performed in their absence, scratching individual names from the ceremonial placard.

In addition to the manner in which they position women as supplemental, marginal, and invisible, Native American sports mascots allow for individuals and institutions to fashion images of women as well. For several decades, the sports teams of the Arkansas State University have represented themselves at home games not through a solitary dancing Indian, but through an ensemble cast known as "the family." A chief, a maiden, and a brave constitute the family, but this is more than a domestic unit: while bellicosity characterizes the portrayal of the male figures, sexuality (suggestive dress and flirtation) defines the maiden (Landreth, 2001).

Arkansas State University has not been alone in its usage of Native American sexuality. Many secondary schools, colleges, universities, and professional sports teams use pseudo-Indian imagery to clothe their cheerleaders as well as their athletes. The Stanford University Dollies and the Washington Redskinettes are but two of many examples that might be cited. Wherever they appear, young women in short skirts and/or revealing tops, often reminiscent of indigenous regalia, sometimes with feathers or face paint, jump about, dance, and perform routines, using their objectified bodies to delight, titillate, and excite the crowd. More disturbing, perhaps for their explicitness rather than their effect, are tee-shirts worn by supporters of North Dakota State University (home of the Bison), the in-state rivals of the University of North Dakota Fighting Sioux. One bears the phrase "Buck the Bison," accompanied by an image of an obese Indian copulating with a buffalo from behind. Another shows a Native American on his knees with mouth open, beneath a larger, fiercer buffalo, the caption completing the message: "Blow us. We saw, they sucked, we came." From the normalized display of the female body as an object for male pleasure to more obscene visions of bestiality, sexualization is fundamental to what pseudo-Indian imagery means in sporting contexts and to what ends institutions and individual can put it.

Oddly, Native American sports mascots have not simply reproduced gender hierarchies, as they have on occasion opened spaces within which EuroAmerican women lay claim to power and equality. When Saint Bonaventure University became a coeducational institution in the 1960s, the new women's teams needed a symbol and mascot. To complement the Brown Indian, the Brown Squaw was chosen. Many women at the time were pleased with the moniker. One commented, "We were so proud to be Squaws... I'm ashamed of it now, but it was part of my identity—it made us feel equal to the men" (quoted in Staurowsky, 2000: 382).

Pseudo-Indian imagery obviously has facilitated engagements with gender in changing social worlds (from crises in masculinity to quests for equality for women) that have accentuated, elaborated, and occasionally interrogated the contours of masculinity and femininity in American culture. Significantly, gender also centers on how some talk about Native American sports mascots, directing attention to the prominence of sexual rhetoric in the controversy of such symbols.

SEXUAL RHETORIC AND THE DEFENSE OF NATIVE AMERICAN SPORTS MASCOTS

Increasingly, supporters of Native American sports mascots incorporate sexual rhetoric into their arguments. Importantly, as will be suggested here, this discourse entangles race and gender to secure its effects. That is, to defend mascots it conjoins assertions about gender with implicit and explicit statements about racial difference.

In the work of David Yeagley, a conservative Comanche commentator, this discourse finds its fullest expression. Yeagley has been a prolific and vocal defender of pseudo-Indian sports symbols, authoring numerous opinion pieces for David Horowitz's online forum, *Frontpage Magazine*, delivering dozens of lectures on college campuses and to community groups, regularly appearing on newstalk programs, and offering expert testimony in newspaper articles. Along with Shiflett, Poe, and many others, he believes not only that Native American sports mascots honor indigenous peoples, particularly men, but also that attacks against them expose more fundamental ruptures within (Native) American society. His views on society, gender, and race provide an important foundation for more fully understanding his interpretations of mascots.

For Yeagley, Native American men are best understood and appreciated as warriors; for him, mascots reflect and respect the heritage and ideals of indigenous communities, offering rare occasions to value Native American men and to educate a broader public. Sadly, according to the Comanche commentator, the native warrior has fallen and the remaining imagery rightly celebrating has come under siege by feminists and Leftists. Even renowned leaders come under suspicion. He criticizes Lakota Russell Means, a Native American political leader best known for his work with the American Indian Movement, for, amongst other things, his rejection of the ideals of the warrior, particularly aggression; he claims, "I cannot follow a man who denies the warrior tradition of my Comanche people" (2002b). In this time of crisis, he, echoing the views of fundamentalist groups such as the Promise Keepers, asserts that many of the problems in Indian Country derive not from racism (which he reads as an "excuse") or sociohistorical structures of power and oppression, but from the weakness of men: "When men fail to be men, everyone suffers" (2002a). In turn, he continues, change, betterment, or salvation is attainable only through the actions of men: "We Indian men must finally face our worst enemy: our own irresponsibility" (Ibid.). Yeagley not only accepts that (Native) American society rises and falls on the actions and characters of men, for good and for ill, but (as discussed momentarily) endorses a corollary position as well: Images of men, namely the warrior mascot, hold the promise of saving the nation in its time of need, as it fights wars on terror.

Native American women, in contrast, threaten tradition, society, and men. Yeagley has grave concerns about the number of American Indian women marrying non-Indians, which he sees both as a sign of the weaknesses of Native American men and as an indication of Native American women's lack of dedication to their people. In fact, he questions the Indianness, integrity, and intention of Elise Meeks, member of the United States Commission on Civil Rights and key proponent of their collective statement against mascots, noting that she married a white man (something Yeagley's own mother did as well): "While she had every right to do, her choice does indicate a less than passionate commitment to the preservation of Indian heritage and bloodlines" (2001a). And although miscegenation troubles Yeagley, he writes, "Some [Native American women] find other, more inventive, ways of humiliating, punishing, emasculating, and otherwise rejecting Indian men" (2002a). Here, he specifically seeks to condemn the efforts of an all-female drumming group to participate in a pow-wow in Minnesota, claiming that it runs counter to tradition and works to dissolve one of the few remaining sources of strengths and power for Native American men. In this context, it is important to note that Yeagley understands the movement against mascots to be "the latest campaign to emasculate society's last remaining symbols of strength, the Indian warrior mascot" (2002g), and that women, sometimes referred to as "socialist women," have often taken a leading role in this destructive project.

Whereas women trouble Yeagley, threatening his vision of the social order, Leftists alarm him, intent as they seem to be to dismantle what he sees as the virtues of modern society and his beloved warrior imagery. He does not view them as political rivals or adversaries but as enemies: enemies of common sense and decency, enemies of the American way, enemies of the state, enemies of the warrior tradition. In his writings, he repeatedly castigates as Leftists (always capitalized) those with whom he disagrees and those working against mascots. Most commonly, he links those whom he labels as Leftists with women in general, and with socialist women, liberal female and minority professors, and feminists in particular. In effect, Yeagley feminizes the perspectives of individuals concerned about pseudo-Indian imagery and its effects. This rhetorical move is meant to delegitimate social criticism through gender.

Yeagley's thoughts about race are no less troubling. To date, he has spoken only about whiteness, blackness, and Indianness. His comments are revealing. Not surprisingly, he has great praise for indigenous traditions, especially the warrior heritage of the Comanche. He regularly defends conventions and the past in the face of "degradation" that for him tend to come from Leftists and feminists. In a piece titled "Leftists Rape Indian Barbie Doll" (2002d), he interprets Patricia A. MacCormack's critique of Native American Barbie as an example of Leftists trying to "humiliate Indians." Elsewhere, he asserts that Leftists are "making Indian images a crime" (2002c). And he speaks of the struggle against Native American sports mascots as ethnic cleansing. While defending Indianness, he also strategically deploys his heritage to advance his position, regularly noting that he is Comanche. In essence, he implies that his ethnicity legitimates his arguments. At the same time, he uses Indianness to delegitimate the claims of other Native Americans; to offer but one example, "My sources tell me that the Indian students and faculty who oppose the mascot are almost all Ojibwa and Arikara. Not Sioux" (2001g). Whereas his Indianness grants him legitimacy in broader discussions, particularly when the warrior (as image and ideal) demands an advocate, other Native Americans do not have the same possibility or privilege to speak for themselves or on behalf of other indigenous peoples.

If Native Americans are worthy and honorable, yet under attack, African Americans are pitiful at best. Yeagley describes them as contemptuous, pathetic, and weak. He finds that "superior beauty is in the white race…In the darker races, everything is always the same, dark brown and black a beastly bore" (2002f). More than this though, he fears that Native Americans have begun to walk "the Black man's path," that is, "the familiar strategy of black civil rights leaders, who bait, belittle, provoke, and bully white people, then run for cover, screaming 'racist' when their white victims react" (2001d). Yeagley reads social justice movements as efforts to transform people who were once proud of themselves into victims; victimization, to him, in turn suggests weakness and a lack of dignity. By association, he imagines African Americans as weak, undignified, victims, the antithesis of the warrior. This is something he makes clear in "It's a Warrior Thing. You Wouldn't Understand" (2001e), an essay in which he chastises an African American who questioned his failure to recognize the irony of mascots and the decimation of indigenous peoples during the colonization of North America. He claims that while Euro-Americans "took [my land] like a warrior fair and square…treated my people harshly…he never denied their bravery, never besmirched their memory as warriors. You did." Again, African Americans are depicted in the media as weak complainers. Their attention to race and racism strips them of dignity, according to Yeagley; their claims of harm make them weak.

While Yeagley expresses contempt for African Americans, he celebrates Euro-Americans. That is, he accords the white warrior great respect, implicitly legitimating the conquest of Native America. In large part this derives from his sense that Euro-Americans are like Native Americans: They are warriors. He admires them for defeating the Comanche and for doing what the Comanche would have done to their foes (2001e). In fact, he believes that "the white man won the Indian warrior's image with his own blood" (2002e). Thus, Euro-Americans won the right to use pseudo-Indian imagery by besting indigenous people on the battlefield. Might makes right. Yeagley regularly expresses admiration for Euro-Americans. More implicitly, he accepts Euro-Americans as superior—aesthetically (as noted above), militaristically, and perhaps even culturally—precisely because of their triumphs and conquests.

Against this background, Yeagley's take on mascots becomes clearer. Native American sports mascots, for him, are all about race and gender: Pseudo-Indian imagery, he asserts, honors Native Americans, particular their warrior ancestors. Speaking specifically about the mascot controversy at the University of North Dakota, he suggests that the Fighting Sioux moniker "shows admiration for the courage and manliness fir the Sioux warrior, who laid the so many whites in their graces just a few generations ago" (2001d). Those who want to change the school spirit betray and disrespect Lakota warriors as they display their disinterest in masculine virtues and the indigenous people who so boldly brought them to life. Not surprisingly, for Yeagley, "mascots provide an opportunity to re-educate America, as well as Indians, on the virtues of being man" (2002g). In fact, the warrior is not simply an antiquated ideal, but the foundation for the future: " I'm looking to the future. It seems to me that modern American Indians have very little imagery to deal with. We have pre-reservation imagery of the warrior, the brave, the man that's courageous, the man that lives for his people, the man that will sacrifice his life for his people. This side of the war days our imagery is quite different. We have the Indian alcoholic, the Indian suicidal," and so on (2001c).

Nostalgic, Yeagley continually joins race with gender to sanction the warrior. In fact, during the recent debate in the Californian legislature over a bill intent to remove Native mascots from the state (Boisen, 2009), he insisted that the legislation was the work of socialists and man-haters, suggesting it would "fell both the Indian and the white man" simultaneously (2002e). For Yeagley, and for many other conservatives, Native American sports mascots honor indigenous peoples precisely because they code Indianness in terms of hegemonic masculinity.

Yeagley's rhetoric quickened after the events of September 11, 2001. He let out a war cry, inflected with race and gender. Not content with the administration's action, he called for a stronger response: "We've heard glorified condemnations before. We're tired of hackneyed adjectives, and effeminate, poetic dramatizations...We want action" (2001b). He casts Bush as feminine, promoting a more bellicose reaction to the attacks. Oddly, symbols center Yeagley's call to arms; in particular, he sees the post-9/11 world as one primed for the proliferation of Native American sports mascots:

> Where are the warriors? Since February [2001], I've argued that the warrior images of American Indian mascots should remain forever in American schools and universities. If ever there was a time warriors were needed, it's now!...Keep every mascot there is! Make more of them! Educate the country about warrior-hood. Let the people know what the great Indian warrior did for their people. If Americans really want to use Indian images on army badges, helicopters, police cars, and sports teams, then let's remind them all what Indians really can be. (2001b, 2001f)

In sum, David Yeagley elaborates a multilayered argument in favor of Native American sports mascots, anchored in sexual and racial rhetoric. His uses and understandings of gender allow him to simultaneously celebrate masculinity, the warrior, and mascots, while questioning the fidelity of women, dismissing his opponents, and calling for a renewal of masculinity, imagery, and nation in the wake of colossal tragedy. Connecting gender to race, in common with Poe and Shiflett, he uses sexual rhetoric to devalue and feminize African Americans, movements for social justice, and critics of pseudo-Indian imagery.

CONCLUSIONS

Clearly, gender has everything to do with Native American sports mascots and the ongoing controversy over them. As a rhetorical toolkit, gender affords authors a set of strategies to ground their perspectives, attack their opponents, and craft a vision of the world. The entanglements of race and gender make the use of sexual rhetoric to defend pseudo-Indian imagery all the more powerful.

Dave Shiflett, Richard Poe, and David Yeagley reflect a more general trend in the ongoing mascot controversy. On the one hand, they celebrate hegemonic masculinity, particularly as embodied by Native American sports mascots, protecting white male privilege as they defend antiquated, stereotypical renderings of indigenous peoples. On the other hand, they feminize others (blacks, critics, Leftists, liberals) in an effort to devalue them and dismiss their perspectives. Sexual rhetoric is so central to this discourse precisely because what is at stake in the mascot controversy is not just the names of sports teams or the imagery used at athletic events, but also the meanings of gender and race in contemporary United States. In fact, the defense of mascots, as the authors discussed in this chapter reveal, is in many ways a defense of masculinity, a response to a crisis in what it means to be a citizen, a subject, a man.

Recognizing the prominence of sexual rhetoric in debates over pseudo-Indian imagery and the sociohistorical conditions animating them should encourage scholars to rethink the mascot controversy. Gender must be placed at the center of future analyses to gain the fullest appreciation of the history and significance of such symbols and spectacles. At the same time, individuals working against mascots must commit themselves to discerning the ways in which gender intersects with race. Such an understanding entails grasping the gendered meanings of mascots no less than the sexual rhetoric employed by supporters, in turn devising strategies to effectively counter them.

REFERENCES

Banks, D. (1993). Tribal names and mascots in sports. *Journal of Sport and Social Issues, 17* (1): 5–8.

Boisen, J. P. (2009, February 25). Grassroots movement pursuing ban on Native American mascots, logos. *Native American Legal Update*. Available: (http://www.nativelegalupdate.com/2009/02/articles/tribal-law-and-justice/grassroots-movement-pursuing-ban-on-native-american-mascots-logos/print.html).

Connolly, M. R. (2000). What in a name? A historical look at Native American related nicknames and symbols at three U.S. universities. *Journal of Higher Education 71*(5): 515–547.

Davis, L. (1993). Protest against the use of Native American mascots: A challenge to traditional, American identity. *Journal of Sport and Social Issues, 17* (1): 9–22.

Eitzen, D. S. and Zinn, M. B. (1989). The de-athleticization of women: The naming and gender marking of college sport teams. *Sociology of Sport Journal* (7): 362–369.

Eitzen, D. S. and Zinn, M. B. (1993). The sexist naming of collegiate athletic teams and resistance to change. *Journal of Sport and Social Issues, 17* (1), 34–41.

King, C. R. (2001). Uneasy Indians: Creating and contesting Native American mascots at Marquette University. In C. R. King and C. F. Springwood (Eds.), *Team spirits: Essays on the history and significance of Native American mascots* (281–303). Lincoln, NE: University of Nebraska Press.

King, C. R. (2002). Defensive dialogues: Native American mascots, anti-Indianism, and educational institutions. *Studies in Media & Information Literacy Education, 2* (1). Available: (http://www.utpress.utoronto.ca/journal/ejournals/simile).

King, C. R. (2003). Arguing over images: Native American mascots and race. In R. A. Lind (Ed.), *Race/gender/media: Considering diversity across audiences, content, and producers*. Boston: AB-Longman.

King, C. R. and Springwood, C. F. (2000). Choreographing colonialism: Athletic mascots, (dis) embodied Indians, and Euro-American subjectivities. *Cultural studies: A research annual* (5): 191–221.

King, C. R. and Springwood, C. F. (2001a). *Beyond the cheers: Race as spectacle in college sports*. Albany, NY: State University of New York Press.

King, C. R. and Springwood, C. F. (Eds.) (2001b). *Team spirits: Essays on the history and significance of Native American mascots*. Lincoln, NE: University of Nebraska.

King, C. R., Staurowsky, E. J., Baca, L., Davis, L. R. and Pewewardy, C. (2002). Of polls and race prejudice: *Sports Illustrated*'s errant "Indian Wars." *Journal of Sport and Social Issues* (26): 382–403.

Landreth, M. (2001). Becoming the Indians: Fashioning Arkansas State University's Indians. In C. R. King and C. F. Springwood (Eds.), *Team spirits: Essays on the history and significance of Native American mascots* (46–63). Lincoln, NE: University of Nebraska Press.

Nuessel, F. (1994). Objectionable sports team designations. *Names: A Journal of* Onomastics (42): 101–119.

Pewewardy, C. D. (1991). Native American mascots and imagery: The struggle of unlearning Indian stereotypes. *Journal of Navaho Education, 9* (1): 19–23.

Spindel, C. (2000). *Dancing at halftime: Sports and the controversy over American Indian mascots.* New York: New York University Press.

Staurowsky, E. J. (1998). An act of honor or exploitation? The Cleveland Indians' use of the Louis Francis Sockalexis story. *Sociology of Sport Journal,* 15 (4): 299–316.

Staurowsky, E. J. (2000). The Cleveland Indians: A case study of American Indian cultural dispossession. *Sociology of Sport Journal,* 17 (4): 307–330.

Yeagley, D. (2001a). Can a 'breed' lead? *FrontpageMagazine.com* (17 December). Available: (http://www.frontpagemagazine.com/Articles/Printable.asp?ID=280).

Yeagley, D. (2001b). Comanch war cry. *FrontpageMagazine.com* (14 September). Available: (http://www.frontpagemagazine.com/Articles/Printable.asp?ID=1692).

Yeagley, D. (2001c). David Yeagley vs. Russell Means. *FrontpageMagazine.com* (2 April). Available: (http://www.frontpagemagazine.com/Articles/Printable.asp?ID=1271).

Yeagley, D. (2001d). Don't walk the black man's path. *FrontpageMagazine.com* (13 February). Available: (http://www.frontpagemagazine.com/Articles/Printable.asp?ID=1952).

Yeagley, D. (2001e). It's a warrior thing. You wouldn't understand. *FrontpageMagazine.com* (7 March). Available: (http://www.frontpagemagazine.com/Articles/Printable.asp?ID=1950).

Yeagley, D. (2001f). Make more Indian warrior images. Available: (http://www.geocities.com/americashauntedpast.htm).

Yeagley, D. (2001g). Who is more Indian than whom? *FrontpageMagazine.com* (26 December). Available: (http://www.frontpagemagazine.com/Articles/Printable.asp?ID=1951).

Yeagley, D. (2002a). The failure of Indian men. *FrontpageMagazine.com* (20 February). Available: (http://www.frontpagemagazine.com/Articles/Printable.asp?ID=274).

Yeagley, D. (2002b). I'm more Indian than Russell Means. *FrontpageMagazine.com* (11 February) Available: (http://www.badeagle.com/html/indian_mascot.html).

Yeagley, D. (2002c). An Indian mascot wins again. Available: (http://www.badeagle.com/html/indian_masot.html).

Yeagley, D. (2002d). Leftists rape Indian Barbie doll. *FrontpageMagazine.com* (18 March). Available: (http://www.frontpagemagazine.com/Articles/Printable.asp?ID=270).

Yeagley, D. (2002e). The new Indian killer. Available: (http://www.theamericanenterprise.org/hotflash020523.htm).

Yeagley, D. (2002f). What's up with dark men? *FrontpageMagazine.com* (26 February). Available: (http://www.frontpagemagazine.com/Articles/Printable.asp?ID=273).

Yeagley, D. (2002g). Where were the Fighting Whites? *FrontpageMagazine.com* (1 May). Available: (http://www.frontpagemagazine.com/Articles/Printable.asp?ID=265).

CHAPTER FIFTEEN

Powerful OR Pornographic? Photographs OF Female Bodybuilders IN *Muscle & Fitness* Magazine

DEBRA MERSKIN

Janet Jackson's six-pack abs, Linda Hamilton's buff biceps, and Madonna's defined deltoid muscles have attracted considerable media attention. While many fans look upon their favorite stars with admiration and awe, others find the flexing freakish. Consider the following: at the 2002 Grammy Awards, more attention was paid to Jackson's abdominal muscles than to her singing or dancing. Her physicality didn't set well with everyone. "Janet Jackson pushed the envelope—it's too much," commented David Kirsch, owner of Madison Square Club, a New York gym, adding, "Guys are meant to look like guys, and girls are meant to look like girls" (cited in Sims, 2002). Even coming from a gym owner it is clear that traditional ideas and ideals prevail of what men and women should look like and what is *normal*. A fan pointed out that "Michelle Kwan has a great body but is still sexy and feminine, but Madonna looked like a guy during her last tour" (Ibid.). World Wrestling Federation competitor and bodybuilder Chyna experienced challenges to her "womanliness" in light of her powerful physique, stating, "I've been called ugly, been called a man, and told I would never be able to do this or that because of the way I look" (cited in Chamberlain, 2000).

Opinions about physically fit women vary widely. Bodily accomplishments of hyper-muscular female bodybuilders can be viewed not only as statements about women's athletic capabilities, but also as challenges to dominant definitions of femininity. However, since the mid-1990s, portrayals of female bodybuilders in mainstream bodybuilding magazines became highly sexualized, undermining athletic accomplishments (Heywood, 1998; Steiner, 2000). This chapter is about the pornographication of women in mainstream American bodybuilding magazines—bodybuilding here describing athletic participation in weightlifting competitions. An examination of advertisements and covers of *Muscle & Fitness* (*M&F*)—with the largest circulation of bodybuilding magazines—offers the opportunity to explore the relationship between presentations of women's bodies and the social construction of gender differences, bodybuilding being an activity based on the deliberate construction of bodies. These images become "the pornography of everyday life" (Caputi, 2004: 74) with the capacity to do visual violence to women through contribution to a public political discourse that minimizes abilities and imagination.

Perhaps more than any other female athletes, female bodybuilders challenge traditional gender boundaries whereas representations of male bodybuilders in mainstream bodybuilding magazines often portray a large, hard-bodied man with a feminized adjunct (Bell, 2008). Bodybuilding is a distinctive subculture that, at first glance, might not seem to have much to do with society as a whole. Yet the sociocultural meanings attached to definitions of appropriateness in terms of appearance and behavior transcend this activity. Gyms and bodybuilding competitions are the locus for the literal construction of bodies, a veritable microcosm of sex and gender role reinforcement and redefinitions. Here, "sex" as a noun means biological differences/divisions between men and women; "sexual" as an adjective and "sexuality" are defined as "involving the sexes" (*Webster's*, 1990: 538), "gender" as a noun refers to "culturally established correlates of sex" and to the social construction of what is considered to be masculine and feminine differences (Goffman, 1976: 1). Gyms and bodybuilding competitions are gendered spaces where, although both men and women are present, traditional sex roles are reinforced as women are evaluated on a two-tier system of muscularity and femininity. Regardless of physical accomplishments, a female bodybuilder must remain "feminine."

The focus of this chapter is not on women's *participation* in sport or bodybuilding; rather, it is about *representations* of them. A feminist-centered approach is used to analyze several illustrative images based on Kuhn's (1985) iconography and conventions of pornography to identify gendered codes in mass-marketed pornography (bits and pieces, caught unawares, and invitation). The following sections explore how femininity is defined in Western society, the representation of women in sports in general, and in bodybuilding in particular, followed by an analysis of representations of women in *M&F*. The following is the research question guiding this study: Are images of female bodybuilders in *M&F* magazine pornographic—wherein the "female image is seen through the lens of male sexual fantasy" (Steele, 1991: 92)?

WHAT IS FEMININITY?

What is feminine is as elusive as what is masculine, and yet we know viscerally whether or not someone is either gender when we see or hear him or her. As the binary to masculinity, femininity is as much about what it is as what it is not. How someone walks, talks, is shaped, what s/he wears (or doesn't), and other characteristics are signifiers of gender in many societies. Conceived of as an "aesthetic of limitation," femininity "requires women to be slender, fragile, and to refrain from occupying any more space than necessary" (Bell, 2008: 43). In America, sex roles are clearly defined and gender is socially constructed. Differences are articulated around voice, skin, hair, body, movement, emotion, and ambition. Goffman (1976: 7) writes, "One of the most deeply seated traits of man, it is felt, is gender; femininity and masculinity are in a sense the prototypes of essential expression—something that strikes at the most basic characteristics of the individual." Bodybuilder Heather Tristany has pointed out several prescriptions for proper female behavior, including the following: "Keep your body covered. Don't swear. Don't spit. Look sexy at all times" (cited in Heywood, 1998: 95).

Cultural ideology tells women that "they will not be desirable to, or loved by, men unless they are physically perfect" (Cortese, 1999: 53). This includes framing and control of female sexuality. In Lacan's (2000) view, these traits indicate a lack, which, for women, is articulated in the need to make her more beautiful, more attractive, more desirable. By carefully confining and defining sex roles, femininity "serves to reassure men that women need them and care about them enormously" (Brownmiller, 1984: 17). Representations of the body, both male and female, are "central to society's construction not only of norms of sexual behavior, but of power relationships in general" (Pultz, 1995: 7). Female identity in mediated imagery is almost exclusively defined in terms of female sexuality and *lack* of social power.

By constructing what is "feminine," the media define gender differences bearing the dominant ideology of male dominance. Through repetition, representations appear to reflect reality and follow a kind of logic, making whatever is going on in the text seem natural and normal (Saco, 1992: 25). Thus, sexualized images of women in posters, pinups, and "cheesecake" photographs suggest they are interesting because of their body parts. Schroeder and Borgerson (1998: 168) suggest, "Women are objectified in many ways, each suggesting and reinforcing the perspective that women are objects to be viewed voyeuristically, fantasized about, and possessed." It is curious how these images have become unremarkable by virtue of the fact that they are so commonplace. Photographs say, "Look at this, this body is there for you to look at, and you will enjoy looking at it. The formal arrangement of the body... solicits the spectator's gaze" (Kuhn, 1995: 275), communicating availability. Images in the media depend heavily on the use of symbols, colors, and allusions to create parallels with the viewer's world, presenting them in ways that are plausible, seemingly natural. Hall (1977) calls the reification process *articulation,* the process of making meaning out of the images we see, drawing on context and tradition to generate what appear to be new meanings or *re-presentations.* For example, "fashion magazines not only arbitrate but also police gender" (Frueh, 1999: 35). It is interesting to consider that many of these images of women are created for women. By "transmuting the 'male gaze' into a 'mirrored gaze,' female readers become simultaneously the spectator and owner of the desired appearance" (Goldman, 1992: 11). The eye, therefore, becomes an erogenous zone for looking and being looked at.

WOMEN AND REPRESENTATION IN SPORT

Sport is a site for determining power relations, sexism, racism, classism, and heterosexism by reflecting "rituals and values of the societies within which they are developed" (Creedon, 1994: 4). It is a "system of social practices based on two symbolic assumptions": (1) "The body is gendered and serves as a tool of power" and (2) "The social construction of the human body is gendered" (Blinde, Greendorfer, and Shanker, 1991: 109). Thus, sports provide a mechanism by which power over women can be demonstrated in ways that seem normal and natural. Most popular sports (meaning those that receive the most media coverage) are designed to highlight men's dominance over women because they are "organized around the most extreme potentialities of the male body" (Messner, 1988: 206).

Since social acceptance is often represented by inclusion in mainstream media, scholars have investigated coverage of women in sport and found it to be lacking (Bryant, 1980; Creedon, 1994; Kane, 1988; Miller, 1975). Studies of television coverage (Blinde et al., 1991; Duncan and Hasbrook, 1988; Duncan, Messner, and Williams, 1991), magazine coverage (Hilliard, 1984; Kane and Greendorfer, 1994; Lumpkin and Williams, 1991), and newspaper stories (Miller, 1975; Theberge, 1991; Wann, Schrader, and Allison, 1998) consistently show that female athletes are either underrepresented or misrepresented. Many of these studies point to male-controlled and male-biased practices in sports such as calling male athletes by last name, female by their first (Duncan and Messner, 1998; Kane, 1988; Knight and Giuliano, 2003).

A key institution for reinforcement of social mores, media participates in the construction of gender difference in ways that appear as reflections of reality supporting the existing power structure by relegating women to the position of the *Other*. By emphasizing supposed "natural" differences between men and women, mass media contribute to ideological hegemony of male superiority (Messner, 1988; Donnelly, 1987; Duncan and Hasbrook, 1988; Birrell, 1990; Duncan, 1990; Greendorfer, 1990; Blinde et al., 1991; Kane and Parks, 1990; Creedon, 1994; Kane and Greendorfer, 1994). In fact, sports now serve as a "primary institutional means for bolstering a challenged and faltering ideology of male superiority in the 20th century" (Messner, 1988: 197). Heywood (1998: 98) points out that the media, through text and photographs, frame women as "special athletes who are depicted primarily as women—genderized—while men are depicted as brave, successful, tough, admirable human beings."

Although interest in female sports increased during and after the 1990s, it was a "superficial social change because deep-seated ideological change [had] not occurred" (Kane and Greendorfer, 1994: 40). While 1996, for example, was declared to be the "Year of the Woman" by *Life, TV Guide,* and the *New York Times*, "A wave of interest and optimism arose around the idea that all female athletes—traditionally 'feminine' or not, mother or childless, heterosexual or lesbian/bisexual—would finally receive full societal acceptance and unwavering appreciation for their *athletic* accomplishments rather than merely for their 'sex appeal'" (Fink and Kensicki, 2002: 318). Yet, reality proved to be quite different.

Women's tennis is an example of a sport in which, as women gained credibility and visibility, image and affirmation of heterosexuality became the focus of media attention. In 2002, tennis professional Anna Kournikova was voted "the world's sexiest woman" by British Men's magazine *FHM* (Roberts, 2002: D1); in the same year, Venus and Serena William were shown wearing slinky evening wear, one "lifting her skirt while grabbing her own bare bottom. There are player tips on buying diamonds, moisturizers, and salt scrubs but no tips on shot selection, no discussions on strategy" (Ibid.). In track, media representations of Olympian Florence Griffith Joyner (FloJo) "emphasized her femininity and sexuality, not her athleticism" (Kane and Greendorfer, 1994: 30) by focusing on her "long tresses, lavish makeup, and racy-one legged running suits that emphasize sexual difference," her fingernails an "external adornment" shouting "femininity—and otherness" (Duncan, 1990: 28).

While feminist research has explored the role of the body in the social construction of gender, and the female body in sport, women's bodybuilding has gone largely unexplored. According to Hall (1996: 50), "Feminists have rarely paid attention to female *sporting* bodies, nor have they always seen the relevance of physicality or empowerment through physical activity to feminist politics."

WOMEN AND BODYBUILDING

For men, bodybuilding has long been considered an activity reinforcing what masculinity is all about: Big muscles, a powerful presence, aggression, and competitiveness. It is about creating a body that is "hard, impenetrable, pure muscle" (Grosz, 1994: 224). Whereas muscles on men are regarded as natural, on women they are thought of quite differently. Physically and sociopolitically, muscles on women are dangerous and disruptive (Johnston, 1996). This constructed body confuses and confounds traditional notions of "femininity." The International Federation of Bodybuilders (IFBB) has long insisted that female competitors "not look hypermuscular, since women would not be attracted to the sport if it made them appear unfeminine" (Steiner, 2000). In the 1984 film *Pumping Iron II: The Women*, a judge stated, "We don't want to turn people off, we want to turn them on" (Ibid.). Heywood (1998: 97) adds that bodybuilding magazines and *Pumping Iron* "are careful to present the women as women before women as athletes." Derogatory terms such as *self-absorbed*, *men in bikini tops*, *dykes*, *Amazons*, *offensive*, and *gross* have all been used to describe the body of a muscled woman (Heywood, 1998). According to Schulze (1990: 69), "Female bodybuilding, like carnival, resists the laws of social control ('women are not supposed to look like that') and inverts the conventions of the gendered body. It also interrogates patriarchy at the level of one of its essentialist foundations, patriarchy's old alibi, the 'natural' physical supremacy of the male."

Public images of bodybuilding are drawn simultaneously around repulsion and attraction. Although many people view female bodybuilders as grotesque, others find them motivating, intriguing, and erotic. According to one male fan, "Women can't overdo it when it comes to building muscle. There's just something intriguing about a woman who looks like she could kill you" (cited in Sims, 2002). While men still outnumber women in the sport, women are "disproportionately represented to the public because they are favorites of the media and intensely intriguing to the public" (Klein, 1994: 8). Bodybuilding behemoth (now California governor) Arnold Schwarzenegger has stated, "There was no such thing as bodybuilding for women when I was first introduced to the sport. When women eventually began competing in the 1970s, a lot of people didn't like it. They didn't approve of women building muscle and they professed not to like the way these women looked" (cited in Dobbins, 1994: 7).

Women's competitive bodybuilding did not become an officially recognized sport until 1985 (Klein, 1994: 77), but obstacles to their participation remained. Women faced not only competition from other women, but also a "hostile and male-dominated institution" (Klein, 1994: 77), where their efforts at bodybuilding were viewed as their "toying with weights by mirroring male behavior" (Klein,

1993: 81). In addition, judging criteria for women adhered to a different standard than that for men and the criteria were always changing (Ian, 1991: 591). In the first "serious" female bodybuilding contest, in 1979, contestants had to wear high heels as part of their posing requirements (Merryman, 1994: 306). Women were not officially allowed into the IFBB bodybuilding competitions until 1980, when the first Ms. Olympia contest took place (Dobbins, 1994: 26), and not until 1993 did the IFBB lift its ban on "big muscles" for women (Dowling, 2000: 195).

While men were and are judged solely on the basis of definition, muscle, proportionality, overall symmetry, style, skill, and fluidity of posing, women were judged on the undefined characteristic of "femininity" (Ian, 1991). Dobbins (1994) points out that "all sports are played according to rules, and knowing the rules is critical to maintaining competitiveness in any type of athletic contest." Women's bodybuilding contests have often been judged by rules that seem to change unexpectedly and arbitrarily, leaving many women in the dark as to what is expected of them. Even after judging criteria stabilized, female bodybuilders are required to don traditional accoutrement of femininity, such as jewelry, makeup, and, in particular, stylized hair. Frueh (1999: 46) has noted,

> Countering an image of the big, hard female body as manly and bellicose, as brute force, many female bodybuilders feminize themselves: by dying their hair blonde, they employ a sign of vulnerability and innocence; by painting their fingernails and curling, ornamenting, or upsweeping their hair, they utilize decorative grooming; by undergoing breast implant surgery, they emphasize by fetishized part of female bodies; and by wearing corsets or other lingerie for photo shoots, they court conventional sexual fantasy. (p. 46)

Female bodybuilding both blurs and demarcates the lines between femininity and masculinity, rendering female muscle subversive and sexy, thus enhancing and undermining self-esteem. The sport requires competitors to have masculine attributes of being muscular, lean, and hard and yet appear feminine, attractive, and "soft," suggesting that the female bodybuilder must be both athlete and woman. The double bind of being built and being feminine requires a great deal of body maintenance (Johnston, 1996). Not only do female competitive bodybuilders devote tremendous amounts of time and effort into thinking about their diets, but also many turn to cosmetic surgery to replace what "dieting down" takes away—breasts. Both men and women diet away as much "subcutaneous and even intra-muscular body fat as possible when preparing for a competition" in order to appear ripped (Ian, 1991: 591). Considering that most female bodybuilder's have less than 10 percent body fat (slowing and sometimes preventing menstruation), and that breasts are composed primarily of fat, the ultimate symbol of femininity must be artificially replaced. Thus, many female bodybuilders choose breast implants "to try and salvage the 'femininity' they lost in the eyes of their beholders as they gained in muscularity" (Ibid.: 3).

Johnston (1996: 331–336) suggests three readings of female built bodies: (1) Docile, (2), Transgressive, and (3) Abject. Consequently, the gym functions as a "sociopolitical space" that confirms and "reworks bodies in the feminine/masculine binary," confirming "some of the most blatant feminine and masculine body stereotypes" (p. 328). It is a space where "muscular women are accepted as long as they are not *too* muscular; maintain their 'femininity,' care about their hair, makeup, and general appearance, and are clearly heterosexual (have a relationship with a male partner or at least suggest an interest in the opposite sex)" (Shea, 2001: 43).

EVERYDAY PORNOGRAPHY

In the 1990s, mainstream bodybuilding and fitness magazines shifted their focus from women as athletes to women as sex objects (Shea, 2001). Pictures of high-heeled, stylized female bodybuilders wearing "leather bras, high heels, fishnet stockings, and lace gloves assured readers (and voyeurs) that sensual appeal is their goal in body building" (Heywood, 1998: 34).

Female bodybuilders in books and magazines as wells as on videos and websites are presented as sexually available through particular poses and positions that emphasize particular body parts (not biceps or quadriceps). Photography "is the primary mode of representation for bodybuilders... [it] remains the primary means through which a woman's physical progress is documented and her body is presented to an audience outside of the gym" (Ibid.: 91). Thus, a photographer's sense of light, line, and angle, along with the use of props of femininity and sexuality such as "veils, high heels, leather and lace," besides expressive inputs from the woman being photographed, come together to create an image of how a female bodybuilder should look (Ibid.: 98). The result is framing strong women as sexual beings first and athletes second.

These gender displays are not only enacted in what is commonly called pornography but also occur on and between the covers of *M&F*. To explore whether Kuhn's (1985) typology of pornography and representations of female bodybuilders' bodies in *M&F* (photographs on the covers, attached to editorials, and as part of advertisements) qualify as everyday pornography, I analyzed ten randomly selected issues between 1997 and 2002. A starting point of visual analysis is *description*, a method supported by semiotics (Barthes, 1983/1990; Williamson, 1978), art history, and cultural criticism (Stokstad, 1995; Schroeder and Borgerson, 1998). In the tradition of Goffman (1976), a selection of non-mutually exclusive, illustrative images are described and interpreted next according to Kuhn's (1985) codes (invitation, bits and pieces, and caught unawares), with the addition of violence—a fourth category that appeared during my analysis.

Invitation

Seven of the ten covers are examples of this presentation. In each case, a woman is adjunct to a man, whose prominent physique is above and behind her. She appears in short shorts or bikini as a flirtatious adornment. One cover shows a leopard-print bikini-clad woman for the "Sex and Exercise" issue, and, for their 60th anniversary issue, six-time *Ms. Olympia* Cory Everson is posed below the magazine's founder Joe Weider.

On the January 2002 cover, an African American couple is presented. She stands behind and above him, with long soft curly hair and a V-neck swimsuit from which her large breasts are partially revealed. The focus of the man is his muscularity—she lifts his tank top, revealing his deeply cut six-pack. The April 2002 cover shows a woman playfully posed next to an equally fit man. She has long, tousled blonde hair, is smiling with lips gently parted, and wears a black swimsuit reminiscent of S&M attire—thin black straps held to each side of the garment by silver metal rings made of black material held together across the chest and at the hips. Long manicured fingernails reach down to hold a swim flipper. Her body is curved partly toward him and partly toward the camera, and his hand is placed on her inward angled thigh, revealing the curvature of her buttocks.

Bits and Pieces

Representing women only as parts, emphasizing particular body parts for the viewer's gaze, is a mainstay of advertising photography (Goffman, 1976). In what is also referred to as objectification, often a model's head is missing and her body is angled toward the camera to offer maximum display. Body parts such as breasts, buttocks, and lips are fetishized. An example is *M&F*'s July 1999 issue featuring in a centerfold equivalent the image of bodybuilder Julie (D.J.) Wallis, who, we learn, is pursuing a Ph.D. The opening photograph features Ms. Wallis' image blown up to fill half the facing pages. Her body extends from the left-hand page angled to the lower right, where here legs run off the page at her knees. She wears a metallic silver G-string bikini, the bottoms of which she pulls up tightly. The eye naturally goes between her legs where the fabric strains to cover her. As the feature continues, Ms. Wallis is shown kneeling in what appears to be a hairdresser's chair, her derrière pointing outward, her back arched—revealing the muscles of her upper thigh and buttock.

Caught Unawares

Here a woman enjoys her own body, often pleasuring herself; unaware that she is being watched, she is transported by her pleasure. Her eyes are often closed, she faces away from the camera, her body is open, her genitals concealed. She often appears surprised at the moment the photograph is shot. The April 2002 issue features "Our most revealing swimsuit issue ever." Comparable to *Sport's Illustrated* swimsuit issues, where photographs of women have little to do with swimwear, this issue differs in that the swimsuits are not real but are *painted* on. The introductory description announces, "Four beautiful women, a pool and the hottest new bikini fashions—the 2002 *M&F* Swimsuit Edition has everything you'd expect. Or did we forget something? Take a closer look at our tribute to the 'art' of the female form" (p. 147). The spread features women who know they are being observed and like it. An example is a photograph of model Denise Paglia-Cole, enjoying her own body and transported by her pleasure: "Two staples of soft-core porn" (Kuhn, 1985: 30). Paglia-Cole's body is available for viewing; she faces the viewer, who she seems to be aware of even though she has been caught in the act of her own passions—what Kuhn (1985: 30) calls "lawless seeing." The hierarchy of male (viewer subject) power over female (object) power is evident by her vulnerability and the appeal to voyeurism.

Violence

This hardcore crossover uses visual violence in ways that combine elements in the other categories to present situations in which the woman is clearly not in control—or, if she is, she aggressively dominates the viewer or other people in the photograph. Once again, *M&F* covers provide excellent examples of this type. The November 1999 cover shows a jungle-print bikini- clad woman sitting on her right hip, leaning toward the camera, looking directly at the viewer. Her long brown hair is fluffed up, her lipstick is dark and shiny—framing her slightly parted lips. The floor around her is scattered with flower petals and blossoms. Behind her we see the neck, upper torso, and shorts of a male figure. He looms in the background, his six-pack abs lined up with her body. She is clearly seated in a vulnerable position below him and does not appear to know he is there. A September 1999 cover shows a young woman "sparing" with a male counterpart. His veiny, ripped torso is at an angle to her busty yellow bikini-clad body. His right arm is pulled back, fist clenched in a yellow glove, as if he is going to hit her in the stomach. She is smiling, her dark brown hair flowing in a backward-brushed mane. Her upper body is angled toward the camera while the viewer gets a side view of her left buttock, peeking out from her bikini bottom. A headline right below the exposed cheek says, "Tighter waist with this simple movement."

CONCLUSIONS

This chapter has discussed the double-bind of female bodybuilders: In order to succeed, they must not only work on their bodies as athletes but also conform to mainstream ideas of what a "normal" woman looks like. Are images of female bodybuilders in *M&F* pornographic? Yes, they are. Photographs of female bodybuilders in the magazine clearly fit Kuhn's Conventions of Pornography (1985, 1995). There are at least two implications.

First, these portrayals contribute to a message that women in general, and female bodybuilders in particular, have very little value other than being decorative—as compared to their male counterparts. This is consistent with Lambiase's (2007: 111) "repetitive cover formula" in magazines (in this case, *Maxim*). These portrayals trivialize the gains in strength and visibility of women in sport by highlighting their "feminine" rather than athletic qualities, reinforcing traditional gender roles. When depicted only as sex symbols rather than as accomplished athletes, these both symbolically and factually powerful women ultimately support the ideological hegemony of male superiority. Women can play, but they still must be sexy and alluring.

Second, the sexualization of female bodybuilders in photography says something important about the (dis)regard for women in society as a whole. What is important is not just the sexual nature of representations that objectify women and show them as submissive and less powerful than men, but also the *meaning* these bodies make as everyday pornography projects. Bodybuilding photography of women sexualizes them in ways that "effectively subverts any disruptive potential of this new version of the feminine form" (Heywood, 1998: 113). These limiting representations are presented in a context that clearly demarcates differences between men and women, thereby undermining the literal and symbolic strength of women's bodies. The results conflate female fitness and photography into a unified whole, normalizing the viewing of women as only sexual and the displaying of girls as sexually stimulating and available, and violence as the next logical level.

REFERENCES

Barthes, R. (1983/1990). *The fashion system.* M. Ward and R. Howard (trans.). Berkeley: University of California Press.

Birrell, S. (1990). Women of color, critical autobiography and sport. In Messner, M. A. and Sabo, D. F. (Eds.), *Sport, men and the gender order,* 185–199. Champaign, IL: Human Kinetics.

Blinde, E., Greendorfer, S., and Shanker, R. (1991). Differential media coverage of men's and women's intercollegiate basketball: Reflection of gender ideology. *Journal of Sport & Social Issues* (*15*, 2): 98–114.

Brownmiller, S. (1984). *Femininity*. New York: Fawcett Columbine.

Bryant, J. (1980). A two-year selective investigation of the female athlete in sport as reported in the paper media. *Arena Review* (4): 32–44.

Caputi, J. (2004). *Goddesses and monsters*. New York: Popular.

Chamberlain, T. (2000, December). Chyna's dynasty. *Wrestling Digest*. Available: (http://findarticles.com/p/articles/mi_m0FCO/is_4_2/ai_67872115).

Cortese, A. J. (1999). *Provocateur: Images of women and minorities in advertising*. Lanham, MD: Rowman & Littlefield.

Creedon, P. J. (1994). *Women, media & sport: Challenging gender values*. Thousand Oaks, CA: Sage.

Dobbins, B. (1994). *The Women: Photographs of the top female bodybuilders*. New York: Artisan.

Donnelly, P. (1987). Sport as a site for "popular" resistance. In Gruneau, R. (Ed.), *Popular cultures and political practice*, 69–81. Toronto: Garamond.

Dowling, C. (2000). *The frailty myth*. New York: Random House.

Duncan, M. C., and C. A. Hasbrook (1988). Denial of power in televised women's sports. *Sociology of Sport Journal* (5): 1–21.

Duncan, M. C. (1990). Sports photographs and sexual difference: Images of women and men in the 1984 and 1988 Olympic Games, *Sociology of Sport Journal* (7): 22–43.

Duncan, M. C., and Messner, M. A. (1998). The media image of sport and gender. In Wenner, L. (Ed.), *Mediasport*, 170–185. New York: Routledge.

Duncan, M. C., Messner, M. A., and Williams, L. (1991). *Coverage of women's sports in four daily newspapers*. Los Angeles: Los Angeles Athletic Foundation.

Fink, J. S. and Kensicki, L. J. (2002). An imperceptible difference: Visual and contextual constructions of femininity in *Sports Illustrated* and *Sports Illustrated for Women*. *Mass communication & society*, 5 (3): 317–339.

Frueh, J. (1999). The real nude. In Frueh, J., Fierstein, L., and Stein, J. (Eds.). *The modern amazon*, 34–43. New York: Rizzoli.

Goffman, E. (1976). *Gender advertisements*. Cambridge: Harvard University Press.

Goldman, R. (1992). *Reading ads socially*. New York: Routledge.

Greendorfer, S. L. (1990, August). *Media reinforcement of stereotypic ideology of women in sport*. Paper presented at the Institute for International Sport Seminary. University of Rhode Island, Kingston, RI.

Grosz, E. (1994). *Volatile bodies: Toward a corporeal feminism*. St. Leonards, NSW: Allen & Unwin.

Hall, M. A. (1996). *Feminism and sporting bodies: Essays on theory and practice*. Champaign, IL: Human Kinetics.

Hall, S. (1977). Culture, media, and the "ideological effect." In Curran, J., Gurevitch, M., and Woollacott, J. (Eds.). *Mass communication and society*, 315–348. London: Sage.

Heywood, L. (1998). *Bodymakers: A cultural anatomy of women's bodybuilding*. New Brunswick, NJ: Rutgers University Press.

Hilliard, D. C. (1984). Media images of male and female professional athletes: An interpretive analysis of magazine articles. *Sociology of Sport Journal* (1): 251–262.

Ian, M. (1991). From abject to object: Women's bodybuilding. *Postmodern Culture* (1, 3): 591. Available: (http://muse.jhu.edu/login?uri=/journals/postmodern_culture/v001/1.3ian.html).

Johnston, L. (1996). Flexing femininity: Female bodybuilders refiguring "the body." *Gender, Place, and Culture: A Journal of Feminist Geography* (*3*): 327–341.

Kane, M. J. (1988). Media coverage of the female athlete before, during, and after Title IX: *Sports Illustrated* revisited. *Journal of Sport Management* (*2*): 87–99.

Kane, M. J., and Greendorfer, S. L. (1994). The media's role in accommodating and resisting stereotyped images of women in sport. In Creedon, P. J. (Ed.), *Women, media & sport: Challenging gender values*, 28–44. Thousand Oaks, CA: Sage.

Kane, M. J., and Parks, J. (1990). Mass media images as a reflector of historical and social change: The portrayal of female athletes before, during, and after Title IX. *Psychology & Sociology of Sport* (2): 21–30.

Klein, A. M. (1993). *Little big man: Hustling, gender narcissism, and body building subculture.* Albany, NY: SUNY Press.

Klein, A. M. (1994). The cultural anatomy of competitive women's bodybuilding. In Sault, N., *Many Mirrors,* 76–104. New Brunswick, NJ: Rutgers University Press.

Knight, J. L., and Giuliano, T. A. (2003). Blood, sweat, and jeers: The impact of the media's heterosexist portrayals on perceptions of male and female athletes. *Journal of Sports Behavior* (26, 3): 272–284.

Kuhn, A. (1985). *The power of the image: Essays on representation and sexuality.* London: Routledge.

Kuhn, A. (1995). Lawless seeing. In G. Dines, G. and Humez, J. M. (Eds.), *Gender, race, and class in media*, 271–278. Thousand Oaks, CA: Sage.

Lacan, J. (2000). In Leader, D. and Groves, J. (2000). *Introducing Lacan.* St. Leonards, NSW: Allen & Unwin.

Lambiase, J. (2007). Promoting sexy images: Case study scrutinizes *Maxim's* cover formula for building quick circulation and challenging competitors. *Journal of Promotion Management* (13, 1/2): 111–125.

Lumpkin, A. and Williams, L. D. (1991). An analysis of *Sport Illustrated* feature articles, 1954–1987. *Sociology of Sport Journal*, (8): 1–15.

Merryman, M. (1994). The active female archetype in popular film. In Creedon, P. J. (Ed.). *Women, media & sport: Challenging gender values*, 300–313. Thousand Oaks, CA: Sage.

Messner, M. A. (1988). Sports and male domination: The female athlete as contested ideological terrain. *Sociology of Sport Journal* (5): 197–211.

Miller, S. H. (1975). The content of news photos: Women's and men's roles. *Journalism Quarterly* (52): 70–75.

Pultz, J. (1995). *The body and the lens: The role of photojournalism in mediating reality.* Thousand Oaks, CA: Sage.

Roberts, S. (2002, July 1). They're young: They're sexy. They're targets. *New York Times*: D1.

Saco, D. (1992). Masculinity as signs. In Craig, S. (Ed.), *Men, masculinity, and the media*, 23–29. Thousand Oaks, CA: Sage.

Schroeder, J. E. and Borgerson, J. L. (1998). Marketing images of gender: A visual analysis. *Consumption, market and culture* (2, 2): 161–201.

Schulze, L. (1990). On the muscle. In Gaines, J. and Herzog, C. (Eds.), *Fabrication, costume, and the female body*, 59–78. New York: Routledge.

Shea, C. (2001). The paradox of pumping iron: Female bodybuilding as resistance and compliance. *Women and Language* (24, 2): 42–46.

Sims, A. C. (2002 March 13). Female celebs flex more than star power. *Fox News.com.* Available: (http://www.foxnews.com/story/0,2933,47772,00.html).

Steele, V. (1991). Erotic allure. In Wilkes, A. (Ed.), *The idealizing vision: The art of fashion photography*, 81–96. New York: Aperture.

Steiner, W. (2000, May 15). Lost in Amazonia. *The Nation*. Available: (http://past.thenation.com/cgi-bin/framizer.cgi?url=http://past.thenation.com/issue/000515/0515steiner.shtml

Stokstad, M. (1995). *Art history*. New York: H. N. Abrams.

Theberge, N. (1991). Toward a feminist alternative to sport as a male preserve. *Quest* (10): 193–202.

Wann, D. L., Schrader, M. P., Allison, J. A., and McGeorge, K. K. (1998). The inequitable newspaper coverage of men's and women's athletics at small, medium, and large universities. *Journal of Sport and Social Issues*, 22 (1): 79–87.

Webster's New College Dictionary, 3rd ed.. (2008). New York: Houghton Mifflin Harcourt.

Williamson, J. (1978). *Decoding advertisements: Ideology and meaning in advertising*. New York: Boyars Book.

PART VI

CLASSIC CASE STUDIES

CHAPTER SIXTEEN

Off His Rocker: Masculinity AND THE Rhetoric OF Violence IN America's Favorite Pastime

JOHN P. ELIA, JON B. MARTIN, AND GUST A. YEP

> Clearly, both sports and media contexts are fertile ground for not only constructing and maintaining masculinity, but are also critical contexts for reproducing hegemonic masculinity as well.
>
> —B. DANA KIVEL AND COREY W. JOHNSON (2009, P. 130)

INTRODUCTION

From the historical legacy of baseball to its current vast media coverage, it is clear that baseball is billed as North America's national pastime, epitomizing what it means to be "All-American"; Walt Whitman wrote, "I see great things in baseball; it's our game, the American game." While it is sometimes easy to get swept up in nationalism and all of the glory that symbolizes the alleged greatness of the United States, the particular case of how professional baseball player John Rocker was (mis)handled when he acted out in 1999 illustrates quite clearly that the homophobia, racism, and sexism Rocker exhibited were clearly forms of rhetorical violence. This infamous yet telling episode was brought to light in a *Sports Illustrated* interview with Rocker by reporter Jeff Pearlman in December 1999.

The proverbial stadium lights have been fixed on this case for years, making it not just possible, but also necessary, to do a critical analysis of the meanings and implications it has for sports rhetoric and the accompanying violence that is inextricably linked to such actions. To demonstrate the seriousness of Rocker's actions and how his case is an example of a systemic problem in terms of how hyper-masculinity produces hateful and damaging rhetorical violence, we turn to descriptions and analyses of (1) The historical significance of American baseball and how it has been linked to our national identity and psyche; (2) Constructions and representations of masculinity; (3) The John Rocker case; and (4) Implications that the Rocker case has for sexual sports rhetoric.

A HISTORY OF AMERICAN BASEBALL AS A NATIONAL IDENTITY

While baseball has roots extending to the 1740s on the continent of North America (McCulloch, 1995), professionalization of the sport occurred in the middle of the nineteenth century, evolving as the Industrial Revolution occurred in the United States. According to historian Jules Tygiel (2000: 11), "The men who shaped baseball in the 1850s and 1860s fashioned it in their own image... the originators of the game embraced the modern, rational, scientific worldview that had grown prevalent in mid-nineteenth-century America." In many ways, baseball has mirrored the development of U.S. society; in fact, it has been referred to as the nation's barometer and soul (Skolnik, 1994). It is also interesting to note, as many baseball historians claim, that writing about baseball goes well beyond a chronicling of the game and, in many ways, tells our history.

By the early twentieth century, baseball became a permanent fixture of American culture, an institution matched by virtually no other institution (Spalding, 1911). It was ubiquitous: Nearly every town and city witnessed boys playing in sandlots or ball fields, learning the rudiments of the game. Spalding (Ibid.: 4–5) wrote a lengthy disquisition on how baseball is synonymous with America and what it stands for, emphasizing,

> I claim that Base Ball [*sic*] owes its prestige as our National Game to the fact that as no other form of sport it is the exponent of American Courage, Confidence, Combativeness; American Dash, Discipline, Determination; American Energy, Eagerness, Enthusiasm; American Pluck, Persistency, Performance; American Spirit, Sagacity, Success; American Vim, Vigor, Virility. Base Ball [*sic*] is the American Game *par excellence,* because its playing demands Brain and Brawn, and American manhood supplies these ingredients in quantity sufficient to spread over the entire continent.

Spalding identifies many of the attributes that baseball brings out in players, correctly identifying it as a male sport involving combativeness and brawn. It is also interesting that professional baseball sprang up during the Industrial period—associated with the capitalism of J. P. Morgan, John D. Rockefeller, Andrew Carnegie, and other Big Business tycoons.

With its history of racially segregated leagues, baseball's past was one of white dominance and privilege; despite the success of players from various races today, it is still part of a system of white dominance. One way to see this is through the lens of whiteness.

Relief pitcher John Rocker is clearly one who benefits from this system of white privilege, as will be seen here. Sports are socially constructed, "A core component of American culture" (Schrack-Walters, O'Donnell, and Wardlow, 2009: 81). Presented by the media as if they exist outside of other social relations and meanings, sports still are "products of human social and political construction" (Clarke and Clarke, 1982: 63)—meaning they are both informed by and reinforce key aspects of dominant American ideology, including matters of race, economics, and gender. Cultural hegemony is both a result and a foundation of sport ideology in our postmodern society (Rail, 1998), so baseball must be seen as a product and an agent of a white male-dominated society. As such, athletes are expected to perform gender as scripted by hegemonic masculinity, perpetuating dominant ideas concerning how gender should and should not be performed.

Media coverage of sports is selective, determining which sports make the most desirable viewing, and which aspects of particular sports are the most important (Clarke and Clarke, 1982). Hence, media present male sports as the only serious, *real* sports to consider—no wonder men's sports receive 90 percent of all sports coverage (Graydon, 1983; Messner, 1988). Coverage of women's sports focuses on those emphasizing grace and aesthetic appeal, often placing more emphasis on appearance than athletic abilities, and frequently demeaning female athletes by referring to them as "girls" or "ladies" (Coakley, 2008). There have been social and political efforts to level the playing field, according to Messner (1988: 202): "With women's rapid postwar movement into the labor force and a revived feminist movement, what had been an easily ignorable undercurrent swelled into a torrent of female sports participation—and demands for equity. In the U.S., Title IX became the legal benchmark for women's push for equity with males." To date, however, such equity has not been achieved; in fact, the athletic world in general has not followed "feminist, postmodern, or poststructural ideologies" and continues to embody masculinity (Schrack-Walters, O'Donnell, and Wardlow, 2009: 82). In sports, it remains a man's world.

CONSTRUCTIONS AND REPRESENTATIONS OF MASCULINITY

The study of masculinity as a field of scholarly inquiry and academic discourse is growing rapidly (Alsop, Fitzsimons, and Lennon, 2002; Brod and Kaufman, 1994;

Whitehead and Barrett, 2001a), and research has revealed connections between athletics and the social construction of masculinity (Anderson, 2005; Kivel and Johnson, 2009). Approaches to masculinity and masculinities range from essentialist conceptions of gender as universal, trans-historical, apolitical, and/or "natural" to constructionist notions of gender as fluid, historic-specific, political, and cultural creations (Alsop et al., 2002). Although such approaches appear to exist side by side in contemporary culture, the social construction of masculinity has become increasingly useful as a lens through which to theorize, understand, unpack, and interrogate current popular conceptions of masculinity in our cultural landscape (e.g., Berger, Wallis, and Watson, 1995; Connell, 1987, 1995; Kimmel, 1994; Messner, 1992; Whitehead, 2002; Whitehead and Barrett, 2001b). Historically, Kimmel (1994) has noted that two models of manhood prevailed in the late eighteenth and early nineteenth centuries in the United States. The first, the genteel patriarch, acquires his identity from land ownership. A model of manhood was manifested through his supervision of family and estate: He was a refined and elegant man, and a loving and dutiful father. The second model, the heroic artisan, derived identity from physical strength and civic virtue. He was financially independent, hardworking, and committed to his family and community. These two models coexisted until the early part of the nineteenth century, when a new vision of masculinity emerged in the 1830s; calling it "marketplace manhood," Kimmel (1994: 123) observed that this new form focused on a man's success in the marketplace. Wealth, power, and status became the markers and indicators of the new masculinity:

> Marketplace masculinity describes the *normative definition of American masculinity* [today]. It describes his characteristics—aggression, competition, anxiety—and the arena in which those characteristics are deployed—the public sphere, the marketplace. If the marketplace is the arena in which manhood is tested and proved, it is a gendered arena, in which tensions between women and men and tensions among different groups of men are weighted with meaning. These tensions suggest that cultural definitions of gender are played out in a contested terrain and are themselves power relations. (p. 124, italics ours)

Put another way, marketplace manhood has become hegemonic in our culture (Connell, 1995; Kimmel, 1994), marked by hegemonic masculinity (Alsop et al., 2002; Connell, 1987). In *Newsweek*, Tony Dokoupil (2009: 50) claims that "the fundamentals of American manhood have gone remarkably unchanged over the last century." According to Kimmel (1994), this hegemonic masculinity is characterized by four fundamental features: (1) Masculinity as the flight from the feminine, (2) Masculinity as a homosocial enactment, (3) Masculinity as homophobia, and (4) Homophobia as a cause of sexism, heterosexism, and racism. Characterized by its repudiation of femininity (Kivel and Johnson, 2009), masculinity's defining feature is its affirmation by negation; as such, masculine gender identity is fundamentally tenuous and fragile, in constant need of affirmation and validation. Adolescent boys, for example, often shore up, secure, and reinforce such masculinity in their peers (Oransky and Marecek, 2009). The never-ending cycle of "proving" one's manhood requires learning to suppress and banish "feminine" qualities such as nurturance, compassion, and tenderness. Within this heterosexual matrix, Butler (1995: 26) explains,

> The desire for the feminine is marked by that repudiation: he wants the woman he would never be; indeed, he would not be caught dead being her; thus, he wants her. She is at once his repudiated identification (a repudiation he sustains as identification and as the object of his desire). One of the most anxious aims of his desire will be to elaborate the difference between him and her, and he will seek to discover and install that proof. This will be a wanting haunted by a dread of being what it wants, a wanting that will also always be a kind of dread; and precisely because what is repudiated and hence lost is preserved as a repudiated identification, this desire will be an attempt to overcome an identification that can never be complete.

Because the process of overcoming such a repudiated identification is never fully satisfactory or complete, a man may be trapped in an incessant cycle of need to "prove" and (re)establish his manhood. Hegemonic masculinity is a homosocial enactment. Since women's perspectives are devalued in society, manhood is demonstrated and enacted for other men's approval. The male gaze scrutinizes and evaluates a man's performance of masculinity. Kimmel (1994: 129) elaborates, "Think of how men boast to one another of their accomplishments—from their latest sexual conquest to the size of the fish they caught—and how [they] constantly parade the markers of manhood—wealth, power, status, sexy women—in front of other men, desperate for their approval."

However, this process of homosocial enactment can be fraught with anxiety and danger and feelings of intense competition. Although enactment of manhood might have been met with other men's approval this time, the prospect of failure and ridicule by other men is ever present. Hegemonic masculinity tends to be characterized by intense homophobia—an overriding organizing principle of the cultural definition of manhood (Alsop et al., 2002). The terror over homosexual desire is one of no longer being a "proper" man, but being a "failed" man, of being a figure of monstrosity or abjection (Butler, 1995). But homophobia is not just terror over desire for other men, as Michael Kimmel (1994: 131) has observed: "Homophobia is more than the irrational fear of gay men, more than the fear that we might be perceived as gay.... Homophobia is the fear that other men will unmask us, emasculate us, reveal to us and the world that we do not measure up, that we are not real men."

This fear affects nearly everything a man does—what he wears, how he talks, what he eats, how he conducts himself. Fear of humiliation makes him ashamed to be afraid, and shame can lead to silence, and silence perpetuates the current system of hegemonic masculinity (Ibid.). Homophobia is intricately connected with sexism and racism; Kimmel (1994) argues that fear of being perceived as homosexual can propel men to exaggerate behaviors to "prove" their manhood—such as denigrating, devaluing, disparaging, and excluding the "other" (women, non-white men, non-native-born men, homosexual men). The "other" is the screen against which hegemonic masculinity was developed and maintained (Alsop et al., 2002; Kimmel, 1994; Messerschmidt, 1998). In sum, hegemonic masculinity creates and perpetuates a set of standards to which all men are measured.

An arena where such standards are played out is sport, which is fundamentally a male-dominated (McLaughlin, 2004; Schrack-Walters, O'Donnell, and Wardlow, 2009) and sexist institution (Messner, 1992). Sport culture is a symbolic representation of a masculinist system, a male-gender dominated social order (Burstyn, 1999; Messner, 1992), offering ideal types and behavioral standards for men. Sport divides people against themselves by separating people as individuals or teams in the name of competition. In the United States, sports tend to be commodified spectacles that are packaged and produced in a capitalist economy, and the sport-media complex has been largely responsible for the maintenance and perpetuation of hegemonic conceptions of masculinity in contemporary American culture.

HEGEMONIC MASCULINITY AND THE CASE OF JOHN ROCKER

In the December 1999 issue of *Sports Illustrated*, Atlanta Braves' pitcher John Rocker was interviewed by reporter Jeff Pearlman in which he made numerous homophobic (heterosexist), racist, sexist, and xenophobic remarks. The story began by painting a vivid picture of a man who was disturbed, angry, and emotionally out of control, the reporter recounting that Rocker, while driving down Atlanta's Route 400, became irritated because a woman just ahead of him was driving too slowly. He called her a "stupid bitch" and ultimately, angrily "flipped her off." Continuing on his journey, commenting about how drivers are incompetent in Atlanta, he said, "Look! Look at this idiot! I guarantee you she's a Japanese woman." As reporter Jeff Pearlman spent more time with Rocker, interviewing him, the more outrageous he found the baseball player's comments. He made comments about not liking New York because of its foreigners and claimed he was not "a big fan of foreigners."

When asked if he would ever play for a New York team, Rocker replied, "I would retire first. It's the most hectic, nerve-racking city. Imagine having to take the [Number] 7 train to the ballpark, you're looking like you're [riding through] Beirut next to some kid with purple hair next to some queer with AIDS right next to some dude who just got out of jail for the fourth time right next to some 20-year-old mom with four kids. It's depressing" (cited in Pearlman, 1999: 5). Rocker also referred to an overweight African American teammate as "a fat monkey." These are only some of the egregious things Rocker has said and done.

As a result of the published interview, Baseball Commissioner Bud Selig ordered John Rocker to undergo a psychological evaluation, commenting how concerned he was about his remarks and behavior. Braves' president Stan Kasten agreed that punishment was in order for Rocker but then "watered down" his concern by saying, "But we at least need to give the man an opportunity to demonstrate his heartfelt remorse and correct the problem" (cited in CNN *Sports Illustrated*, 2000: 1). Although several groups such as Atlanta's City Council, Atlanta's AIDS Survival Project, and others called for Rocker's resignation, no such thing happened.

Ultimately, Commissioner Selig ordered that Rocker be fined $20,000 and suspended from the league for the first month of the regular season, but an arbiter later reduced the penalties and Rocker was fined a mere $500 and suspended for only two weeks, besides being forced to undergo sensitivity training. Many of Rocker's teammates were embarrassed by his behavior, and he was a much talked about figure both within and outside of baseball circles.

Although it would be hyperbolic, and even erroneous, to claim that all professional baseball players'—or, for that matter, all professional male athletes'—behavior manifest in this type of rhetorical violence through hegemonic masculinity, it is clear that professional baseball supports such hyper-masculinity. Using this case as a point of analysis, such a claim can be readily supported. First, it is clear that John Rocker enjoys heterosexual privilege; he happens to be a big (6'4," 200+ pound) white guy. He is a brawny, strapping hunk, even the All-American guy that Al Spalding characterized as the embodiment of a fine professional baseball player. Would an athlete of color likely get away with such heinous behavior? Second, this is a celebrated case, and Rocker was merely "slapped on the wrist" for verbal violence that included references to gender, sexuality, race, and class. His comments ultimately were not taken too seriously; it might even be said that such a superficial admonishment supported his hateful comments. Third, articles that have been published since the case as well as media representations of it either hyped the case or were dismissive of it. This is, in some ways, a classic double-edged sword or double bind: On the one hand, to play down such a case allows the behavior to go unexamined and unchallenged; on the other hand, if such an incident receives a lot of attention it can increase celebrity status and reinforce the ubiquitous hegemonic masculinity that is so much a part of the Western male expectation and experience. Rocker continues to enjoy an elevated status as an outstanding former professional baseball player and was no doubt protected as such. To admonish him more severely would threaten the type of hegemonic masculinity that professional male sports promotes, and to which most men in the United States aspire, as indicated earlier.

In an online poll about Rocker's behavior, writer Jay Croft (2002) of *The Atlanta Journal-Constitution* reported that, of 7,961 people polled, 4,889 (61 percent) indicated that John Rocker's behavior was "Totally Acceptable: Go, John." Fewer than one-third (29 percent) said that his behavior was "Reprehensible." Even though the merits of this poll may be questionable regarding the research design and methods, these data, even if remotely representative of how the general public viewed Rocker's remarks, are disturbing. It is likely that the hegemonic masculinity expected of males—particularly of male professional athletes—is fully at work here. It is the norm, unquestionably expected.

Even given numerous vociferous outcries by various civic groups demanding John Rocker's resignation as a professional baseball player by such groups as United Youth-Adult Conference and Atlanta's AIDS Survival Project, he remains a prominent figure in America's favorite pastime. Again, we see in full view the reification and reproduction of hegemonic white male privilege complete with all of the trappings of hegemonic masculinity that no doubt continues to negatively impact many people, including women, queers, people of color, persons living with HIV/AIDS, and any combination of individuals herein.

IMPLICATIONS FOR SEXUAL SPORTS RHETORIC

It is abundantly clear that John Rocker serves as an exemplar of what we will tolerate of professional baseball players. We have already mentioned that he received a mere "slap on the wrist" for his vicious homophobic, racist, sexist, and xenophobic comments. The fact that he went relatively unscathed for his actions is telling. What message does this send to our young people? The cultural hegemony of hyper-masculinity is ubiquitous and rarely, if ever, gets challenged.

Despite the stranglehold of hegemonic masculinity in baseball, there have been cases of alternative masculine performances and ways of reading the sport. Consider Mark McGwire: Although his masculine performance is largely traditional, several features are notable in both his personal life as well as in his professional work—as a leader among his teammates, he has been described as responsible, nonviolent, nonracist, and humble (Marantz and Knisley, 1998). He is a conscientious and loving father; he even had a clause in his contract that assured a seat for his son on the team's chartered flights (Ibid.). He has spoken openly about being in psychotherapy, and he even cried at a press conference announcing his pledge to donate $1 million a year to combat the sexual abuse of children (Ibid.)—examples contradicting the stereotypical notion that "boy's don't cry." While McGwire's masculine performance is encouraging, it should be noted that he was in a unique position to express himself thus: He was one of the most successful baseball players in history. He is white, heterosexual, attractive, physically powerful, and intelligent. From the intersections of these identifications, he has been well positioned to deviate from the hegemonic script without significant penalty or loss of privilege.

An interesting way to confront hegemonic masculinity in baseball is through alternative readings, or decodings, of the sport. As an audience member, one can decode media messages from a variety of positions (Hall, 1990/1999; Martin and Yep, 2004; Slagle, 2003). For example, one might view the performance of hegemonic masculinity in baseball as "normal" and "natural," representing what Hall (1990/1999) refers to as a *dominant hegemonic* decoding. It is a reading of the sport that implies an acceptance of the dominant ideology. Another viewer might recognize the gender inequality in professional sports but fail to recognize the many ways in which hegemonic masculinity is oppressive to both women and men. This would be an example of a *negotiated* decoding, when the dominant ideology is challenged somewhat, but not thoroughly opposed. Finally, a viewer could also perform an *oppositional* decoding, thoroughly rejecting dominant ideology—which has been one of our goals in this project. According to Hall (1990/1999), an audience member may fully comprehend the preferred, dominant hegemonic messages embedded in the coverage of professional sports but, based on his/her own experiences, political beliefs, and particular insights, choose to decode the messages according to alternative frames or points of reference. The possibility of creating oppositional readings points out the agency and creativity individual viewers can exercise when faced with oppressive, normalizing dominant hegemonic messages.

Readers perform different decodings based on their complex social locations. Consciously performing variously informed readings of baseball can produce many insights and point to many possibilities for addressing privilege and oppression in society. For example, a feminist reading of baseball might point out how hegemonic masculinity is not only limiting and oppressive to women but, ultimately, also oppressive to men trapped in its system. A decoding informed by whiteness studies, such as the examples discussed earlier, might seek to illustrate how professional baseball has been and still is, a product of a white supremacist system, and how it limits the access and full participation of nonwhite players.

Another such oppositional decoding would be a queer reading of baseball. The potential homoeroticism of all-male baseball teams makes a queer theory reading both possible and fruitful. Queer readings of popular media seek, among other things, to challenge notions of "natural" and "fixed" categories of sexual identity and gender, pointing out their fluid and unstable nature. Such readings also present a challenge to hetero-normativity by re/negotiating dominant meanings and understandings of the sport and its players, thereby opening up cultural space for the expression of queer identities. For example, a queer decoding of baseball might recognize the potentially symbolic interaction of the players and the phallic baseball bat. Knowing that several formerly closeted professional athletes have "come out" as gay after their retirement points to the possibility that any player at any time could secretly or potentially be queer-identified, a realization suggesting very different understandings of the congratulatory "pat on the ass" and the steamy after-game shower. Such a reading would reveal how hidden, and yet, omnipresent, sexuality is in baseball and serve as a challenge to hegemonic gender performance and sexuality.

CONCLUSIONS

It is clear from our point of view that John Rocker's behavior was truly reprehensible. We also believe that, although this case was "celebrated" and received much attention in the media, it is extremely representative of a well-entrenched cultural practice of hegemonic masculinity, the brand that hurts others much in the same ways that Rocker's comments were injurious to scores of individuals. This is a systemic cultural problem in desperate need of critical attention. People are being harmed every day as a result of hegemonic masculinity. Sexual sports rhetoric deserves much more scholarly attention from critical cultural studies' perspectives to begin to erode some of the taken-for-granted rhetoric that has been historically and inextricably linked to the athletic experience.

REFERENCES

Alsop, P., Fitzsimons, A., and Lennon, K. (2002). *Theorizing gender: An introduction.* Hoboken, NJ: Wiley.

Anderson, E. (2005). Orthodox and inclusive masculinity: Competing masculinities among heterosexual men in a feminized terrain. *Sociological Perspectives,* 48 (3): 337–355.

Berger, M., Wallis, B., and Watson, S. (Eds.) (1995). *Constructing masculinity.* New York: Routledge.

Brod, H., and Kaufman, M. (1994). Introduction. In Brod, H., and Kaufman, M. (Eds.), *Theorizing masculinities,* 1–10. Thousand Oaks, CA: Sage.

Burstyn, V. (1999). *The rites of men: Manhood, politics, and the culture of sport.* Toronto: University of Toronto Press.

Butler, J. (1995). Melancholy gender/refused identification. In Berger, M., Wallis, B., and Watson, S. (Eds.), *Constructing masculinity*, 21–36. New York: Routledge.

Clarke, A., and Clarke, J. (1982). "Highlights and action replays"—Ideology, sport and the media. In Hargreaves, J. (Ed.), *Sport, culture, and ideology*, 62–87. Boston, MA: Routledge & Keagan Paul.

Coakley, J. J. (2008). *Sport and society: Issues and controversies*, 9th edition. New York: McGraw Hill.

Connell, R. W. (1987). *Gender and power*. Cambridge, UK: Polity.

Connell, R. W. (1995). *Masculinities*. Berkeley, CA: University of California Press.

Croft, J. (2002, August 6). John Rocker again? People can't we just move on, please? *The Atlanta Journal-Constitution* (November 16).

Dokoupil, T. (2009, March 2). Men will be men. *Newsweek*, 153 (9): 50.

Graydon, J. (1983). "But it's more than a game. It's an institution": Feminist perspectives on sport. *Feminist Review*, (13): 5–16.

Hall, S. (1990/1999). Encoding, decoding. In During, S. (Ed.), *The cultural studies reader*, 2nd ed., 507–517. London: Routledge.

Kimmel, M. S. (1994). Masculinity as homophobia: Fear, shame, and silence in the construction of gender identity. In Brod, H., and Kaufman, M. (Eds.), *Theorizing masculinities*, 119–141. Thousand Oaks, CA: Sage.

Kivel, B. D., and Johnson, C. W. (2009). Consuming media, making men: Using collective memory work to understand leisure and the construction of masculinity. *Journal of Leisure Research*, 41 (1): 109–133.

Marantz, S., and Knisley, M. (1998). American hero. *Sporting News*, 222 (38): 12–22.

Martin, J., and Yep, G. (2004). Eminem in mainstream public discourse: Whiteness and the appropriation of black masculinity. In Lind, R. A. (Ed.), *Race/gender/media: Considering diversity across audiences, content, and producers*, 228–235. New York: Longman.

McCulloch, R. (1995). How baseball began: The long overlooked truth about the birth of baseball. Los Angeles, CA: Warwick.

McLaughlin, T. (2004). Man to man: Basketball, movement, and the practice of masculinity. *The South Atlantic Quarterly*, 103 (1): 169–191.

Messerschmidt, J. W. (1998). Men victimizing men: The case of lynching, 1865–1900. In Bowker, L. H. (Ed.), *Masculinities and violence*, 125–151. Thousand Oaks, CA: Sage.

Messner, M. A. (1988). Sports and male domination: The female athlete as contested ideological terrain. *Sociology of Sport Journal*, (5): 197–211.

Messner, M. A. (1992). *Power at play: Sports and the problem of masculinity*. Boston, MA: Beacon.

Oransky, M., and Marecek, J. (2009). I'm not going to be a girl: Masculinity and emotions in boys' friendships and peer groups. *Journal of Adolescent Research*, 24 (2): 218–241.

Pearlman, J. (1999, December 23). At full blast. *Sports Illustrated Online*. Available: (www.cnnsi.com).

Rail, G. (1998). Seismography of the postmodern condition: Three theses on the implosion of sport. In Rail, G. (Ed.), *Sport and postmodern times*, 143–161. Albany, NY: State University of New York Press.

Schrack-Walters, A., O'Donnell, K., and Wardlow, D. L. (2009). Deconstructing the myth of the monolithic male athlete: A qualitative study of men's participation in athletics. *Sex Roles*, (60): 81–89.

Skolnik, R. (1994). *Baseball and pursuit of innocence: A fresh look at the old ball game*. College Station, TX: Texas A&M University Press.

Slagle, R. A. (2003). Queer criticism and sexual normativity: The case of Pee-Wee Herman. In G. A. Yep, K. E. Lovaas, and J. P. Elia (Eds.). *Queer theory and communication: From disciplining queers to queering the discipline(s)*, 129–146. New York: Harrington Park.

Spalding, A. G. (1911). *America's national game*. Lincoln, NE: University of Nebraska Press.

Tygiel, J. (2000). *Past time: Baseball as history*. Oxford: Oxford University Press.

Whitehead, S. M. (2002). *Men and masculinities: Key themes and new directions*. Cambridge, UK: Polity.

Whitehead, S. M. (2002). *Men and masculinities: Key themes and directions*. Cambridge, UK: Polity.

Whitehead, S. M., and Barrett, F. J. (2001a). The sociology of masculinity. In Whitehead, S. M., and Barrett, F. J. (Eds.), *The masculinities reader*, 1–26. Cambridge, UK: Polity.

Whitehead, S. M., and Barrett, F. J. (Eds.). (2001b). *The masculinities reader*. Cambridge, UK: Polity.

CHAPTER SEVENTEEN

Wham! Bam! Thank You, Ma'am!: The Rhetoric Surrounding Female Professional Boxers

SHURA ALEXANDRA GAT

INTRODUCTION

There is nothing subtle about the connection between female professional boxing and sexuality. Perception of boxing as a purely masculine endeavor makes women's combat sexually titillating for male observers, and professional boxing's unique blend of spectacle and sport contributes narratives alternately framing female boxers as unfeminine/sexy/lesbian and/or all of the these. By examining what language is used by boxers and members of the media to describe female pugilists, this chapter portrays how the experience of being a female boxer in the 21st century is profoundly shaped by popular ideas about gender and gender-appropriate behavior.

A recurring element in representations of female boxers centers on notions about them as heterosexual, with traditionally feminine interests. This (presumably) largely unconscious effort serves dual functions of de-stigmatizing athletes who compete in a sport stereotypically considered lesbian and reassuring the general population that, although these women fight adeptly, outside the ring they do not challenge established gender roles.

GENDERED SPORT/BOXING

As the discipline of critical cultural studies has theorized, sport's role in culture is far more than just a game; rather it is "a cultural form that is embedded in and constituent of sociopolitical forces of culture" and, as such, "serves as a site for the creation and maintenance of societal forces and institutional forms" (Theberge and Birrell, 1994: 326). In other words, through sport, ideas about the world in which we live are affirmed, challenged, and sometimes modified. One function of sport is maintaining and reproducing dominant ideologies within a culture—most notably, ideas about gender and gender-appropriate behaviors (Katz, 1996; Messner, 1994).

The Manly Art

Frequently described as "The Manly Art," boxing is laden with a masculine identity like no other sport—except perhaps American football. Professional boxers step into the ring wearing body protection: groin cup for men, breast protection for women; a mouth guard; and boxing gloves on hands wrapped in gauze. In a bout controlled by a referee and scored by judges, the combatants—their faces smeared with Vaseline to mitigate the effect of punches—hit each other in the face and torso for a series of three-minute (two for women) rounds. Fights are scheduled to last from as few as four to as many as fifteen rounds, each round followed by a one-minute rest period. Victory is realized by knocking out an opponent or a "win on points" according judges' decisions.

With bloodied faces, unconsciousness, brain damage, and death as potentially part and parcel of the game, boxing is hardly a sport for the faint-hearted. The boxing ring has long been seen as the ultimate arena in which masculinity is showcased and tested. "Boxing is a purely masculine activity and it inhabits a purely masculine world," Joyce Carol Oates (1987: 70) has famously declared. "Prizefighting has been characterized by some as a true test of skill, courage, intelligence and manhood" (Sammons, 1988: 71). The heavyweight champion is considered to be the most impressive and "butchest" of men and, as Oates (1987: 70) cites, "A fairy tale proposition: the heavyweight champion is the most dangerous man on earth: the most feared, the most manly. His proper mate is the fairy-tale princess whom the mirrors declare the fairest woman on earth."

Oates's claim captures the established role of woman within the so-called "squared circle": nonexistent. Within popular conception, to men, females exist as mates or sexual partners, certainly not as boxers; in fact, women's most visible role in the ring, until recently, has been as "ring-card girl." To the cheers and applause of the mostly male crowd, these scantily clad, voluptuous women step into the ring, through ropes held chivalrously open for them, then parade once around the perimeter holding up a placard announcing the number of the upcoming round.

Most assuredly, what boxing is not about—or at any rate has not been about—is women, womanhood, or femininity. Boxing is the antithesis of what has traditionally been considered feminine—sugar, spice, everything nice. However, in recent years women have been entering the sport at amateur and professional levels in relative droves, and both popular and sporting cultures are being forced to contend with this change.

Women's Boxing, Yesterday and Today

Considering the aggressively masculine reputation of boxing, it may be a surprise to learn that women's participation in prizefighting and boxing is documented as far back as the 18th century (Toulmin, 1999; Halbert, 1997; Hargreaves, 1996). Since then, the sport has gone through cycles of slight popularity, women fighting on fairgrounds in Britain and later in the United States in the 18th and 19th centuries. Through each decade of the 20th century, women's boxing persisted, albeit in a small way, until the mid-1990s when a shift occurred. By the beginning of the 21st century, several women boxers have come to be well known; it has been the subject of literary efforts and films; and the Women's World Boxing Championship is held annually.

The dramatic growth of the sport was kick-started when the New York Golden Gloves amateur competition first allowed women to compete in 1995. Then, when Laila Ali, daughter of boxing legend Muhammad Ali, came on the scene in a storm of media hype in 1999, public awareness of women's professional boxing took off. Promoter Don King introduced Christy "The Coal Miner's Daughter" Martin, Mia St. John (a former taekwondo competitor and sometime *Playboy* cover girl) joined the young Ali, and the popularity of the sport began to grow significantly—the first Women's World Boxing Championship of 2001 featuring 115 competitors from 30 nations. First held in the United States, it has since been staged in Turkey, Russia, India, and China.

Women's boxing has introduced the subject into popular culture. *Shadow Boxers*, Katya Bankowsky's superb 1999 award-winning documentary, highlights World Champion Lucia Rijker's professional boxing career. *Girlfight*, Karyn Kusama's 2000 fictional representation of a Latina fighter in Brooklyn won awards at both the Cannes and the Sundance film festivals. Clint Eastwood's 2004 *Million Dollar Baby* takes on not only the legitimacy of women's boxing but also euthanasia and was rewarded four Oscars. Most recently, Jonathan Dillion's *Rigged* (2008) deals with a con man working with a strong woman fighter whose scam gets them into dangerously high stakes. Books such as Kate Sekules' *The Boxer's Heart: How I Fell in Love with the Ring* (2000), Mischa Merz's *Bruising: A Journey through Gender* (2000), Lynn Snowden Picket's

Looking for a Fight (2000), Leah Hager Cohen's *Without Apology: Girls, Women, and the Desire to Fight* (2005), and Louise Walsh's novel *Fighting Pretty* (2008), about a female boxer in the U.K., all skillfully tackle the subject of what it means to be female and a boxer. Further, Delilah Montoya's *Women Boxers: The New Warriors* (2006) is a fascinating collection of photos and essays about women's boxing.

Hit Like a Girl

While cultural perceptions about female boxing slowly change, there is no question that women who choose to box in contemporary United States run the risk of censure. Some critics resent women's entrance into the masculine realm of boxing and deny their capacity to fight, while others fret that a woman who chooses to fight is compromising her femininity or boldly indicating lesbian inclinations. In 1987, Joyce Carol Oates expressed the brutal opinion that "the female boxer...cannot be taken seriously—she is parody, she is cartoon, she is monstrous." Excepting Lucia Rijker, boxing promoter Bob Arum dismissed female boxers: "A lot of these women who are fighting have no talent, or very little" (cited in Bankowsky, 1999). And promoter Frank Warren has observed that "women could never excel at boxing because they are not built for it and from a business point of view, it's a loser" (cited in Lindsay, 2001).

British champion boxer Henry Cooper declared, "Girls' fighting is not 'nice.' And parents would not want their daughters coming home with broken noses and black eyes" (cited in Choi, 2000: 25). Whether or not parents would want their sons coming home with broken noses and black eyes, boxing, in fact, exemplifies much of how according to traditional ideology a girl or woman should not act; they are expected to be kind, generous, heterosexual, pretty, maternal, and not athletic (Lenskyj, 1986; Krane, 2001; Hargreaves, 1994; McCaughey, 1997; Dowling, 2000).

But boxing requires aggression, a comfort with experiencing and inflicting pain, and a tremendous amount of strength and agility generated through a powerful, muscular body. Women's self-defense scholar Martha McCaughey (1997: 7) has noted, "When women train to fight back, they defy gender norms. It's manly, but not womanly, to protect and fight." With so much at stake within an athletic career, plus the influence of social messages encouraging femininity that are encoded in media, advertisements, and social interactions, many boxers work hard to create a "feminine," heterosexual image. Yet, at the same time, if a woman is too successful in asserting her femininity, she risks losing her perceived legitimacy as a capable athlete and can, instead, become a sex object, trivialized and sexualized.

Ring-card Girls, Lesbians, Victims and Doms

Female boxers face an additional burden to those shouldered by most other female athletes—namely, the deeply entrenched idea framing female combat as a sexual show. Kate Sekules (2000: 20) speculates that (mostly) men perceive women fighting to be erotic because "battle is the antithesis of female sexuality, whereas male sexuality is fused to it. Girl fights are a male turn-on because of the abandon, the passion they see displayed. It reminds them of women caught in flagrante delicto." When discussing women's boxing from the turn of the century through the mid-1960s (taking place mostly within brothels and carnivals), Jennifer Hargreaves (1996: 127) had a different interpretation of the turn-on credited to boxing's "explicit sexualization through bare breasts and the ripping of clothes, the scope for male fantasies, and potential as a surrogate for male brutality against the 'weaker' sex."

Some simply find the showcasing of female power and muscularity erotic. Thomas Gramstead (2002), founder of The Amazon Connection, an Internet site for female wrestling and boxing fans, has explained, "Amazons are the real thing—women as they might be and ought to be. Amazons are actualizing the full potential of the female form." And for Brame, Brame, and Jacobs (1996: 465), "Erotic wrestling enthusiasts are aroused by the sight of women who push the body's limits and vie for primacy." Other forms of erotic combat coexist with professional boxing in contemporary culture, such as the so-called cat-fighting; hot oil, mud, or jello-wrestling; and Foxy Boxing, where bikini-clad women hit each other with big foam gloves.

Watching women fight may give some viewers sadistic pleasure, for others there might be the appeal of domination. In *The Boxer's Heart*, Kate Sekules (2000) wrote of her discovery that one of her male sparring partners got pleasure from being hit by women and thus was an eager volunteer. So while women who are competing in professional boxing are likely focusing on the athletic aspects of their endeavors, live audiences or those at home could well be interpreting the action as erotic or sexual. Female boxers are in a culturally interesting situation: They are part of a society discouraging women from participation in aggressive, violent activities while trying to improve their abilities in the face of skeptics who either think that women aren't capable of skillful fighting or who find it a sexual turn-on.

ON BOXING

The Players

Profiled here are the four female boxers in the United States who have gained the most media attention. Christy Martin is known as the pioneer of contemporary women's boxing since her undercard fight in 1996 with Ireland's Deirdre Gogarty, earning her the respect of many fight fans. Her bloodied face on the cover of *Sports Illustrated* catapulted women's boxing into public consciousness; since then, she has compiled an impressive record of 47 wins, 5 losses, and 3 draws with 31 knockouts. Lucia Rijker, the focus of *Shadow Boxers*, is a Dutch fighter who reigned as a champion kickboxer for ten years in Europe before moving to the United States and becoming a professional boxer; in addition to documenting her undefeated 37-wins record as a kickboxer, her boxing record stands at 17 wins and no losses, 14 by knockouts. At the other end of the skill spectrum from the talented Rijker lies Mia St. John, principally recognized as the boxer who appeared nude in a 1999 issue of *Playboy*—dressed in skimpy, skintight "boxing-style" trunks with her bare breasts partially covered by boxing gloves. Her record of 44 wins and 9 losses, with 18 knockouts, was compiled in a series of four-round fights against opponents who are considered incompetent and inexperienced by boxing cognoscenti. But the name most recognized in women's boxing today belongs to Laila Ali, the newest entrant into the sport, who demonstrates boxing skills that may be worthy of all the media coverage she receives as a matter of course.

"Old-fashioned Guys Resistant to Women Pummeling Each Other"

The idea of women boxing has not been, to put it mildly, uniformly accepted. Some critics suggest that women are incapable of boxing well, while others indicate that it is not an appropriate activity for a woman to want to take part in:

> "I support them because I have to support them...But I don't feel they should be in there [fighting]...It's a man's sport and no matter how you want to look at it, it's a violent sport. I just don't think I want to look at a woman with a busted nose and a cut over her eye."
>
> Sunny Marson, Northern California president of U.S.A. Boxing (cited in Hoffman, 1996).

> "I have nothing against women boxing and nothing against men stripping at Chippendales, I just don't want to see it."
>
> Bert Sugar, boxing historian (cited in Murphy, 2001: 18)

> "It troubles me...I'm one of those old-fashioned guys resistant to women pummeling each other and damaging their bodies."
>
> *Philadelphia Daily News* columnist Stan Hochman (cited in Murphy, 2001: 18)

An interesting corollary to the disbelief expressed that women could or should box is that the ultimate praise for a female boxer is the accolade that she "fights like a man." In doing so, she apparently transcends her gender as if, as indicated by the condemning phrase "to hit like a girl," the idea of femaleness cannot reasonably be linked with excellent boxing.

"Can't nobody beat the lady," a veteran male fighter observed about Lucia Rijker. "She the best in the world. She the man" (cited in Wright, 2002). "Boxing aficionados, most of them men, give [Rijker] the male boxing world's highest compliment... she fights like a man" (cited in Fellner, 2002). Christy Martin has also received similar compliments from fellow boxers: "She punches like a man, a 130-pound man," said a trainer at the famous Gleason's Gym in Brooklyn (cited in Hirsch, 1996).

Title Fight

The titles of the many articles about women's boxing and female boxers fall into several different categories, most of which reflect cultural norms about women and gender-appropriate behavior. Relatively few approach the subject as simply sport, instead treating the occurrence of a woman fighting in a boxing ring as a social issue. Some trivialize the sport and the athletes, while others create a discourse of gender around the subject by using terms generally associated with traditional femininity. A third category implies that the world is a bit "off" if women are boxing, and a fourth tries to fit women into established phrases about the sport. Predominantly, though, article titles about the sport are chosen to emphasize the appearance of the athletes.

The least remarkable group of titles appears respectful of the athletes and their fistic abilities or simply informs the reader about results: *Woman Warrior* (Plummer and Grant, 1996), *Rijker's Island* (Dunn, 2000), *Tough Girl* (Dundas, 2002), or *Girl Fighters* (Mott, 2001). Many titles trivialize female boxers and their efforts, such as an article about Ali in *Seventeen* entitled "Boxing Babe" (Sansing, 2000).

Some associate the boxers with objects that are typically perceived as feminine, effectively undermining their physical power—examples being "With This Ring: Women Fall for Boxing" (Winzelberg, 1999); "Diamonds in the Ring" (Barovick, 2000); "A Battle of Sexes without Kid Gloves" (Saraceno 1999); or "Hard Hitter Has a Soft Touch" (Hirsch, 1996). "For these women, a heavy right is more powerful than sisterhood," Robert Lipsyte (1995) has written, seemingly implying that the natural course of things is for women to be united. "Boxing: The Socking Sisterhood" (Lindsey, 1996) trivializes and mocks women's efforts. One article simply turns the common adage about a woman's place being in the home into "A Woman's Place Is in the Ring. Or Is It?" (Hoffman, 1996).

One of the most predominant ways female boxers were introduced was through reference to their (attractive) appearance, title-writers finding the double meaning of the word "knockout" particularly irresistible. Also are articles about Christy Martin as *Femme Fatale* (Burton, 1998), or those claiming that Ali *Looks like a butterfly* (Verdi, 1996).

A Nice Girl, Really!

This is not to say that the sexuality of female boxers is a nonissue for the boxers themselves as well as for those who write about them. When Christy Martin appeared on *Sports Illustrated* after her fight with Deirdre Gogarty and first drew attention to women's boxing, a discourse was immediately launched seeking to create a dichotomy between pretty, feminine fighters and butchy, "mannish" fighters. Both the boxers themselves and the media colluded (unintentionally, no doubt) to reassure and soothe the general public about female boxers. Despite venturing out into the masculine territory of boxing, the women who were succeeding were those who didn't challenge the status quo; they were heterosexually attractive and wouldn't raise a feminist stink. Coverage of boxers then emphasized their heterosexual relationships, the support they received from their families, their appearances, and their interests in stereotypically feminine things—thus working hard to portray the athletes as feminine according to hegemonic ideals.

Life Magazine (Bush, 1997) ran an article entitled "Raging Belle" featuring the boxers on an all-women's fight card in Las Vegas, employing the so-called feminine apologetic to reassure they were socially acceptable. The photo captions chose to focus on elements of the women's lives that had little to do with their fighting abilities:

> Christine Dupree…is one of the few fighters who wear makeup in the ring. (p. 75)
>
> Wildcat Collins likes to find a neutral corner and chill with tunes and fiancé Frankie Globuschutz. (Ibid.)
>
> "Pow, right in the kisser: Women get down. We're hungry. We're passionate," says Baby Doll Riley who was a flight attendant and a stuntwoman before she took up pro boxing. (p. 80)
>
> Family ties: Byrd soars after winning the lightweight title while her mother proudly looks on. (Ibid.)
>
> Riccio-Major's husband, Billy, is always in her corner—he's her trainer. Their kid, Evander Ali—named after guess who, and guess who likes to share Mom's moment in the spotlight. (Ibid.)

As well as contextualizing the boxers within their families and femininity, texts place undue emphasis on appearance, for example, "Bantamweight and single mother Yvonne Trevino... [has] dark hair cinched in a Pebbles ponytail, lips painted bubble-gum pink, Trevino looks more like kid sister than Kid Kayo" (p. 74). The journalist observed that, after a workout session, Kathy Collins' "face is beet-red and her clothes are drenched in sweat," as if this were even mildly notable in an athlete (p. 79). And the reader is treated to other similar comments: "At the weigh-in, the variety of outfits—sport, sexy, posh, baby, scary make the women look like tougher Spice Girls," and "Six hours before the event kicks off, Suzanne Riccio-Major is playing toy trucks in the hotel room with son Evander Ali and husband-trainer Billy" (p. 81).

THE FIGHT FOR FEMININITY

It seems that the bugaboo of women's boxing is largely perceived to be its lesbian reputation, a label from which most fighters are quick to disassociate themselves. "A lot of people think we're a bunch of tough lesbians but I'm an extremely feminine woman who loves boxing for the competition," asserts one boxer (cited in Mott, 2001). An out-lesbian and veteran boxer in San Francisco does not agree, however: "[Gina] Guidi does not believe women's boxing faces the same type of stigma women's golf had endured for so many years. 'I do not think that is the problem for women in the boxing world'" (cited in Warren, 2002). Christy Halbert (1997: 7) observed that "the lesbian label, in fact, seems to be the most popular stereotype of female prizefighters. In fact, women pugilists pose a dichotomy to those who stereotype them as either lesbian (non-heterosexual and not attractive to men) or Foxy boxer (heterosexual and attractive to men)."

Because a lesbian identity is perceived as negative and could, in turn, negatively impact career opportunities, many female boxers often work hard to avoid the label and may use it as a weapon against opponents—boxers Ann-Marie Saccurato and Angel Bovee being exceptions. Christy Martin has worked aggressively to create a heterosexual, "feminine" image. "I'm a woman and proud of it," she has said (cited in Verdi, 1996). "That's why I wear pink. That's why I wear makeup when I fight. That's why I look forward to the day when I can have a family. I'm not a woman's libber" (see also, Martin, 2000). Lucia Rijker, while not quoted as engaging in the battle for femininity, critiques her fellow boxers because they use sex or their fathers' names to succeed in the sport. Articles featuring her tend to focus on her awesome talent and experience, describing her as "the best hitter around" (Lyndsey, 2001), "the world's most talented woman boxer" (Mott, 2001), "the top female boxer in the world," (Kimball, 2002), "the world's most dangerous woman" (Fellner, 2002), and "the best fighter among women" (Iole, 2000). By emphasizing Rijker's beauty and her attractiveness to men, the media successfully frames her as heterosexual and, therefore, acceptable:

> In *Shadow Boxers* we see Rijker, who is as strikingly attractive as she is committed [to boxing]. (Gordon, 2000)
>
> The European girl with enigmatic eyes and full sensual lips. (Estrada, 2001)
>
> A Dutch born beauty...with her looks and devotion [to acting] seems like a natural outlet. (Gordon, 2000)
>
> Her face is striking: full lips, high cheekbones, wiry bronze hair. (Bernhard, 1998)
>
> Lucia Rijker's stellar combination of good looks, boxing skill, charm and charisma has earned her the informal title of "Lady Ali." (Fellner, 2002)
>
> She appears beautiful, relaxed charming and articulate. Like many other L.A. women, she chants and meditates, polishes her toenails, waxes her bikini line. (Fellner, 2002)

When it comes to a discourse about sexual rhetoric and women's boxing, there is not much to finesse about Mia St. John, who unabashedly uses her looks as a marketing tool. She doesn't see a conflict between her choice to pose nude for media and the impact that choice might have on women's boxing. "Mia St. John...[is] making a mockery of women's boxing, making it harder for someone...who wants to be taken seriously," one boxer has declared (in Dundas, 2002). St. John also enters unreservedly and uncritically into the discourse regarding the value of a feminine appearance, saying, "All I'm trying to do is to bring attention to the sport and for people to acknowledge us and to know that we don't have to look like men to fight...I want people to know that I'm a feminine woman. And I'm proud of that" (cited in Gerbasi, 2000).

Of all female boxers, Laila Ali has commanded the most face time in newspapers, magazines, and on television since her entrance into the sport—the initial interest entirely out of proportion to her skill and experience as a boxer. Articles featuring Ali in the mainstream press cover her in ways similar to how Christy Martin was covered in the mid-1990s, emphasizing family, heterosexuality, and appearance. Not only is her famous father always discussed, the reader is usually also told that she is married to her trainer (former boxer Johnny "Yahya" McClain), that she is beautiful, and that she used to run a nail salon. This material is often covered in lieu of any reporting on her fight record or training regimen, reflecting the fact that although the sport of women's boxing has developed tremendously in the intervening decade, popular conceptions about gender, womanhood, and appropriate behavior do not change so quickly.

Titles about Ali continue to juxtapose boxing with traditional ideas about women and ultimately are less about sport and more about the social phenomenon of having a woman box: *Sports Illustrated*'s "Sting Like a Beautician" (Cook, 1999), *People Weekly*'s "What a Knockout," about her wedding (Smolowe and Lacher, 2000), "Muhammad Ali's daughter talks about girl power, being pretty—and slugging it out in China" (Hesse, 2000), or "Laila Ali talks about love, Muhammad Ali and women in the ring" (Collier, 2001). Like Lucia Rijker, Laila Ali too receives media coverage wherein there is no shortage of comments about striking appearance:

> Now I'll tell you one thing, your dad said he was The Prettiest but you're prettier than him. (Sirota, 2000)

> Laila is as ferocious as a pit bull in the ring, but she has gentle elegant features. (Collier, 2001)

> Laila Ali, 23 and as beautiful as a model. (Murphy, 2001: 16)

In contrast to the previous generation of boxers such as Martin and St. John now in their late-thirties, 32-year-old Ali doesn't seem to feel that she needs to compensate in some way for her interest in boxing by emphasizing her femininity and beauty. Nor is she quoted drawing attention to another boxer's perceived lack of femininity; instead, she expresses some frustration with the focus on her appearance:

> "I'm always hearing, you're so pretty. Why do you box? When you think about it, boxing has nothing to do with looks. If I were ugly, would people feel more comfortable with it? The bottom line is, I box because I want to box. That's it! I don't think about my looks. Looks run out anyway." (cited in Collier, 2001)

> "Do I have to look ugly because I want to box? Would they [dare] say that to my opponent?... That really has nothing to do with fighting. A fight is a fight. It doesn't matter what you look like." (cited in Hesse, 2000)

Ali has no intention of marketing her looks beyond perhaps endorsing products such as antiperspirant that any athlete might endorse. Unlike Christy Martin, who proudly announces that she wears makeup and values her feminine appearance in the ring, for Ali, once she steps in the ring, all attention to appearance ceases. She has stated,

> "You don't see me taking my clothes off and half-naked. That's what most people do when they have the body and they have the looks... [If] people think I'm pretty, people think I'm sexy in my regular fight clothes, that's fine. But I don't try to market

my looks.... It's like I'm a role model and I'm a woman. I like to look good. But when it's fight time, it's fight time." (cited in Thompson, 2001)

CONCLUSIONS

Within our contemporary culture, the act of a woman's entering a boxing ring and hitting an opponent still remains quite radical. Despite the long history of female pugilism, according to common understanding, what women are capable of and what they "should" enjoy is far gentler and involves less strength of will and body than boxing necessitates. Since the mid-1990s, when female professional boxing became part of national discourse, debates have raged about the sport, its safety, and women's participation in it. Less evident, however, has been the parallel debate about the redefinition of femininity and womanhood that excellent female boxers necessitate.

It is no longer possible to stereotype all women as incapable of fighting well. Nor is it possible to dismiss the practitioners by painting them all with the same brush of lesbian stereotype. The powerful image of talented female boxers is beginning to overshadow the long-standing idea that any physical fight between women is an insubstantial "cat fight" or an erotic mud-wrestling event. Beginning with the representation of Christy Martin, as the sport gains popularity, the media and the boxing world have begun to struggle through a period of redefinition. Although the same trends that were set in 1996 still continue, such as emphasizing the heterosexuality of the female boxer, it is still possible for women's boxing events to be described simply as sporting events rather than requiring social commentary.

REFERENCES

Bankowsky, Katya (2000). *Shadow Boxers.* New York: Swerve Films.

Barovick, H. (2000, May 1). Diamonds in the ring. *Time* (155): 66–67.

Bernhard, B. (1998). Looking for a fight: Lucia Rijker and the changing face of women's boxing. *LA Weekly* (September 18–24): 2.

Brame, G. B., Brame, W. D. and Jacobs, J. (1996). *Different loving: The world of sexual dominance and submission.* New York: Villard.

Burton, T. (1998, April 16). Femme fatale. digitalstoryteller.com.

Bush, V. (1997, November). Raging belle. *Life* (20): 74–82.

Choi, P. Y. L (2000). Femininity and the physically active woman. NY: Routledge.

Collier, A. (2001, October). Laila Ali talks about love, Muhammad Ali and women in the ring. *Ebony*: 164.

Cook, K. (1999, November 22). Sting like a beautician. *Sports Illustrated* (91): 36.

Dowling, C. (2000). *The frailty myth: Women approaching physical equality.* New York: Random House.

Dundas, Z. (2002, January 9). Tough girl. *Willamette Week* (28): 16–18, 20, 23.

Dunn, K. (2000, February 27). Rijker's island. *The New York Times*: 6.42.

Estrada, J. (2001, Feb 22, 2001). *En riñas de hembras bravas.* (Female brawls in sports.) Available: (http://www.BoxinginLasVegas.com).

Fellner, T. (2002). *The Zen of boxing: Lucia Rijker, The most dangerous woman on earth.* Available: (wholelifetimes.com).

Gerbasi, T. (2000, January). *Defending Mia.* Available: (cyberboxingzone.com).

Gordon, S. (2000). Killer talent on display in shadow boxers. Available: (interfacelife.com).

Gramstead, T. (2002). *The Amazon Connection.* Available: (http://folk.uio.no/thomas/lists/amazon-connection.html).

Halbert, C. (1997). Tough enough and woman enough: Stereotypes, discrimination, and impression management among women professional boxers. *Journal of Sport and Social Issues*, 21 (1), 7–36.

Hargreaves, J. (1994). *Sporting females: Critical issues in the history and sociology of women's sports.* New York: Routledge.

Hargreaves, J. (1996). Bruising peg to boxerobics: Gendered boxing—images and meanings. In Chandler, D. (Ed.), *Boxer: An anthology of writing on boxing and visual culture*, 121–131. London: MIT Press.

Hesse, K. (2000, May 1). Muhammad Ali's daughter talks about girl power, being pretty-and slugging it out in China. *Newsweek*, International Edition: 71.

Hirsch, S. (1996, April 24). Hard-hitter has a soft touch, too. *The Record*: 1.

Hoffman, B. (1996, September 22). A woman's place is in the ring: Or is it? *The San Francisco Chronicle.*

Iole, K. (2000, February 29). Top female boxers brawl in Los Angeles. *Las Vegas Review.*

Katz, J. (1996). Masculinity and sports culture. In Lapchick, R. E. (Ed.), *Sport in society*, 101–109. Thousand Oaks, CA: Sage.

Kimball, G. (2002, March 3). Women fighting uphill battle. *Irish Times*, pp. 23.

Krane, V. (2001). We can be athletic and feminine, but do we want to? Challenging hegemonic femininity in women's sports. Quest. Bowling Green, OH.

Lenskyj, H. (1986). *Out of bounds: Women, sport and sexuality.* Toronto, Ontario: Women's Press.

Lindsay, E. (2001, June 16). Women fight for a fair deal. *The Times of London*, 33.

Lindsey, E. (1996, November 24). Boxing: The socking sisterhood. *The Observer.*

Lipsyte, R. (1995, April 21). For these women, a heavy right is more powerful than sisterhood. *New York Times*: B13.

Lyndsey, E. (2001, April 19). The girls fighting to prove they're no [*sic*]. *The Express.*

Martin, C. (2000). *A fighter's perspective.* Available: (secondsout.com).

McCaughey, M. (1997). *Real knockouts: The physical feminism of women's self-defense.* New York: New York University Press.

Messner, M. (1994). Sports and male domination: The female athlete as contested ideological terrain. In Birrell, S. and Cole, C. L. (Eds.), Women, sport and culture, 65–80. Champaign, IL: Human Kinetics.

Mott, S. (2001, October 3). Girl fighters: Special Report. *The Daily Telegraph.*

Murphy, M. (2001, June 2). Power-punch girls. *TV Guide*, 49 No. 22: 14–18.

Oates, J. C. (1987). *On boxing.* Garden City, New York: Dolphin/Doubleday.

Plummer W. and Grant, M. (1996, June 24). Woman warrior: Boxer Christy Martin crushes opponents—and stereotypes. *People*, 45: 101.

Sammons, J. (1988). *Beyond the ring: The role of boxing in American society*. Urbana, IL: University of Illinois Press.

Sansing, D. (2000, May). Boxing babe. *Seventeen* (59): 98–101.

Saraceno, J. (1999, October 1). A battle of the sexes without kid gloves. *USA Today*.

Sekules, K. (2000). *The boxer's heart*. New York: Villard.

Sirota, H. (2000, April 29). Interview with Laila Ali at Madison Square Garden. Available: (boxingranks.com).

Smolowe, J. and Lacher, I. (2000, September 11). What a knockout. *People Weekly*, (54): 81–82.

Theberge, N. and Birrell, S. (1994). The sociological study of women and sport. In Costa, D. M. and Guthrie, S. R. (Eds.), *Women and sport: Interdisciplinary perspectives*, 323–330. Champaign, IL: Human Kinetics.

Thompson, P. (2001). Gimmick? "Don't believe that hype." Available: (http://www.blackvoices.com/sports/ali-frazier).

Toulmin, V. (1999). *A fair fight: An illustrated review of boxing on British fairgrounds*. Oldham, Lancashire: World's Fair.

Verdi, B. (1996, September 7). Looks like a butterfly... but Martin out to prove women boxers belong in the fight ring. *Austin American-Statesman*: D8.

Walsh, L. (2008). *Fighting pretty*. Brigend, Wales: Seren.

Warren, N. L. (2002, August 29). With this ring: Gina Guidi. *Curve*.

Winzelberg, D. (1999, January 24). With this ring; Women fall for boxing. *New York Times*: 1.

Wright, E. (2002, August 18). Lucia Rijker. *Rolling Stone*.

FILMOGRAPHY

Katya Bankowsky's *Shadow Boxers* (2000)
Leah Hager Cohen's *Without Apology: Girls, Women, and the Desire to Fight* (2005)
Jonathan Dillion's *Rigged* (2008)
Clint Eastwood's *Million Dollar Baby* (2004)
Karyn Kusama's *Girlfight* (2000)
Mischa Merz's *Bruising: A Journey through Gender* (2000)
Delilah Montoya's *Women Boxers: The New Warriors* (2006)
Lynn Snowden Picket's *Looking for a Fight* (2000)
Kate Sekules' *The Boxer's Heart: How I Fell in Love with the Ring* (2000)

AWN ISSUES

AWN, September 3, 1990
AWN, October 14, 1991
AWN, June 22, 1992
AWN, September 13, 1993
AWN, February 21, 1994,
AWN, November 7, 1997
AWN, June/July, 1999
AWN, May 4, 2000

CHAPTER EIGHTEEN

Women Playing Rugby: Rejection OF "The Girly" BY Girls

JESSICA HUDSON

This research is based on a participant observation of women rugby players at Cambridge University in England and on focus groups involving them. Dealing with the challenges and transitions in traditional patterns of gendered behavior, lifestyle, and leisure that women playing rugby are creating, it discusses how culture is constructed and changed through the interaction of men and women who make, resist, and transform the meanings, values, and rules of behavior. In order to do this, it explores representations of identity through the key themes of strength and power, violence and injuries, femininity and the body—making visible the extent to which women playing rugby are engaged in projects relating to masculinity and femininity.

As a female rugby player, I realized I was part of a personal and cultural struggle in which processes of socialization, social representations, and identity management were highly tangible through the lens of social psychologists and social constructivists. Given rugby's masculine representation, why do women play it, and what are they doing by playing it? An in-depth analysis of women playing sports traditionally defined as masculine might uncover the continued significance of gendered structures of power. This research explores women's participation in a sport that is among the least accessible to them. How, then, do they construct and change this accessibility, and what meanings and values does rugby hold for them? What significance do they attach to being able to play rugby? This chapter discusses the disruption of gendering cultural codes through the contradictions of women playing rugby, building muscle, becoming bruised and injured, and demonstrating hostility and aggression on and off the pitch as violent assailants and as sexual predators.

THE SOCIOLOGY OF RUGBY

In *Making Men: Rugby and Masculine Identity*, Nauright and Chandler (1996: 2) claim that "in any list of gendered activities, rugby and other codes of football must come near the top." Robert Morrell (1996: 92) describes rugby in South Africa as providing "a place where men could define appropriate male behaviour…also a place where misogynistic and homophobic language and emotion was given full reign." And Steven Schacht (1997: 338) studies what he claims is the "overtly misogynist setting of the rugby pitch" and the "gendered nature of rugby and the misogynistic attitudes and actions of players," observing "rigid gendered expectations" which are revealed in actions "rejecting anything seen as feminine." He reports on the "sexist derogatory comments" which are frequently made, such as "F**k you, you pussy," "Just shut the f**k up or I'll bend you over and f**k you like a bitch," and "What are you a faggot/pussy?"

Rugby's cultural and political significance far exceeds that of being "just a game." Men dominate many sports, but few actually express an idea of masculinity. That is, attributes of "masculinity" are not usually a part of the sport itself; yet, as a contact sport, rugby conflates powerful muscularity with violent masculinity. Interestingly, off the pitch there is a strong rugby culture, which can be understood through its institutions, language, values, and "rituals" (Schacht, 1996). Jock Phillips (1996: 70) explains that "the purest expression of the stereotype [masculinity] has been found in rugby football and the rituals which surround the game."

Mariah Burton Nelson (1996: 88) suggests that "nowhere are masculinity and misogyny so entwined as on the rugby field. Rape is depicted as a joke." The following evidence demonstrates the culture as it lives and breathes. Schacht (1997: 338) describes some post-match celebrations where the rugby players sing their version of the song "Alouette"—which involves "serenading" a woman, who is planted on a table where all the men turn to face her. The chorus starts, "Alouette, gentille Alouette, Alouette gentille plumeri." I witnessed this song myself at the post-match celebrations at an international men's fixture. The leader of the song began with "How we love her furrowed brow," to which the crowd replied, "Her furrowed brow." The song labels parts of the woman's anatomy in derogatory ways, such as "her greasy skin," "her rotten teeth," "her big fat tum," and crescendos with the most sexual parts of her anatomy: "Her swinging tits," "her shaven muff," "her stinking chuff." There were very few other females in the audience. It made me feel uncomfortable, exposed. The female being serenaded was not visibly upset, as in Schacht's experience, where she ran away crying, but one could not imagine her enjoying what they were saying. In fact, as this song came to a close, a male in the crowd shouted at me a few times and eventually sexually assaulted me. In my research diary I reported that I felt "like the situation brought it on... all in all a horribly restricting, embarrassing experience."

RUGBY SONGS

Songs are a strong part of rugby culture for men as well as a key activity for women. The men's songs refer to the female body as a sexual object, many about getting women pregnant. Nearly all of the sexual songs term sexual intercourse as a triumph, often as a violent act; for instance, one song goes, "Took her to a place where no-one would find her, To a place he could really grind her, Rolled her over onto her front, Shoved his cock right up her c**t." Several songs celebrate intercourse as violent: "F**k all the c**ts till you break them in two," or "Glory, glory Hallelujah, he's gonna shove his prick right through yuh." Here are two complete rugby songs exposing the kind of voice or dialogue usually expressed: *The Engineers Song* is sung by men, *Ya-Ho!* by women:

The Engineers Dream.

An engineer told me before he died
And I've no reason to believe he lied
That he knew a maiden with a c**t so wide
That she was never satisfied.
(bum titty bum titty)
So he built a huge great prick of steel
Driven by a bloody great wheel
Two brass balls he filled with cream
And the whole bloody issue was driven by steam
(bum titty bum titty)
Round and round went the bloody great wheel
In and out went the prick of steel
Till at last the maiden cried "Enough enough I'm satisfied".
Up and up went the level of steam
Down and down went the level of cream
Till again the maiden cried "Enough, enough I'm satisfied"
(Bum titty bum titty)

Now we come to the tragic bit
There was no way of stopping it
She was split from arse to tit
And the whole bloody issue was covered in shit.

Ya-ho!

He put his cock into my eye ya ho, ya-ho!
He put his cock into my eye ya ho, ya-ho!
He put his cock into my eye, I said fuck off you're far too high
Get in get out stop fucking about ya-ho ya-ho ya-ho!

He put his cock into my ear ya-ho, ya-ho
He put his cock into my ear ya-ho, ya-ho
He put his cock into my ear, I said fuck off you're nowhere near
Get in get out stop fucking about ya-ho ya-ho ya-ho!

He put his cock into my nose ya-ho, ya-ho
He put his cock into my nose ya-ho, ya-ho
He put his cock into my nose, I said fuck off you're nowhere close
Get in get out stop fucking about ya-ho ya-ho ya-ho!

He put his cock between my thighs ya-ho, ya-ho
He put his cock between my thighs ya-ho, ya-ho
He put his cock between my thighs, I crossed my fingers and closed my eyes
Get in get out stop fucking about ya-ho ya-ho ya-ho!

These songs portray women as demanding sexual intercourse, although in *The Engineer's Dream* the female ultimately gets punished for it. The women's songs do not change the nature of the sexual act but celebrate a stronger sense of females controlling it and of belittling the male contribution. *Ya-Ho!* refers to penetration as the pinnacle of the sexual act, and as an achievement: "I crossed my fingers and closed my eyes." Paradoxically, what could be constructed as an act of violation by the male is symbolically recreated as an exchange where the female is the aggressor: "Get in, get out, stop fucking about." Although women tend to remain the object rather than the subject and are "done to" rather than "doing," it is important to understand that these songs do uphold the female as the manipulator. Although it can easily be read as vindicating the violation of women's bodies, this is *not* the construction of the women who sing it, but it does tend to be the understanding of many academics who have read this. Even though the female is "done to," it is important to consider that power may not reside with the "doer" but with the person who requires the act to be done. It is this exquisite manipulation of gendered power roles that *Ya-Ho* plays upon, and the reason why this song *does* celebrate females as sexual predators.

Mariah Burton Nelson (1996: 91) has protested that she had "never heard [a woman] refer to seducing a man as 'scoring,'" that it is "a uniquely male concept, sex as a triumph, victory." But I have certainly seen the idea of sex as a conquest being part of the rugby culture among men *and* women. Sadly, in both men's and women's rugby songs, sexual relationships are couched in terms of distance, disrespect, objectification, and, at times, abuse.

Clearly, masculinity has been represented over and over again as conflated with strength, power, and violence. In its relational citizenship (Connell, 1995) with the representation of femininity as weak, inferior, and passive ("done to"), the song compositions appear to recreate an unsympathetic dichotomy resembling misogyny. Yet, when women play rugby, they contradict the idea that all females are necessarily feminine; instead, they are strong, active predators. By confusing these gender codes, are they redefining the representation of women? Unfortunately it seems that although they represent their own selves they do not deconstruct the masculine/feminine dichotomy. This remains supported because women playing rugby instead create a new dichotomous representation of females: those who are "girly" and those who are not. The original blueprint remains with women as inferior. Women who play rugby are not breaking the mould; instead they are misfits for it—they are masculine women. Hence, masculinity continues to represent power and strength; by approximating it, women playing rugby only reinforce the idea that it is better than femininity or being a girly girl.

GENDER IDENTITY: HOW DO THESE WOMEN FEEL ABOUT FEMININITY?

As the Cambridge University Women's team were waiting in a car park to leave for a rugby game against another university, Sarah (names have been changed to protect the identity of participants) walked in on a conversation about gender identity and women rugby players, announcing, "I don't have a gender." When asked to explain, she replied, "When I was little... I never did the girl thing y'know, all the dresses and boys and things.... I tried to do the boy thing, y'know football and everything, but it was a bit... them thinking 'you're a girl' and I couldn't do the girl thing coz I didn't want to because they were all a bit girly." One can see clearly that she grew up in a world knowing differences between "the girl thing" and "the boy thing." Boys played football and girls played with dresses. Sarah uses the term "girly" to refer to something she found negative and demeaning, something with which she did not wish to be associated: "I don't get up and put make-up on but I do love going out for a party... putting make-up on and *going* all girly." She continued, "I think that's why I do rugby... it's the chance to go out and roll around in the mud and not be feminine; at the same time I can go back, have a shower and be all girly... so I do both things."

This individual's identity contains what are commonly understood to be both masculine and feminine traits. But since she is a woman, she is living proof that these traits are neither male nor female but are cultural performances around which we move and integrate ourselves in society with others who are also using these constructions to order their own worlds.

It is not that these women want to be men. They are not dismissing their femininity, but attempting to make their personal values consistent with it. Another rugby player, Freya, explains, "I do see myself as very feminine but that's not in any way the stereotypical feminine, I'm not the girly type of woman. It's a different sort of female that I've come to terms with." She adds, "You might say I'm not a pussy I'm not a girly girl." So then, how does she define herself?

RESISTING FEMININITY: HOW DO THESE WOMEN FEEL ABOUT RUGBY?

My teammates were asked why they had started playing rugby. Participants described rugby as requiring "guts" and "strength," and that playing the game is "properly exhilarating." It is also evident that to these women *having* these qualities and *striving to prove it* are together a source of pride and of considerable value. Power and strength are key qualities for rugby players, and I have often observed how teammates would boast about hitting the opposition hard and having the ability to tackle hard and how they would show off their muscles with pride. Kate says, "There's something satisfying about tackling the tall weedy mammas who crumple when you hit them." Clearly, playing rugby provides these women with no insignificant measure of physical empowerment. Annie, for example, reported, "I don't mind doing a flying tackle . . . there's something very liberating about it."

The activity these women were involved in was communicating a very different relationship that they had as women to the image of being "girly." Much chat before and after rugby practice consists of comparing injuries, bruises, and "stud scrapes"—part of why players must wear studded boots. Bruises tend to be talked about with pride: The bigger the better, the bluer and more painful-looking, the more impressive. They represent pain and injury and the ability to receive and "take" this sort of battering; as such, they are evidence of physicality. Kate discussed how she felt about her acts of violence and the bruises she had to prove them: "Anyone that would look, I would show [the bruises]. 'Oh I bosched that bitch the hardest' ['bosched' being slang for hitting a member of the opposition with the force of the whole body, usually causing them not inconsiderable damage], or 'Oh, I made that one bleed' and when they would say 'Oooo' you love it and you feel: 'I'm so hard.'" Sarah spoke about an injury she had, of which she was proud: "Yeh I got a wicked black eye... and it was so cool... when the colours were still there."

Clearly then, representing themselves as strong and powerful was an important activity in these women's lives, one they participated in frequently. This conversation extract reveals how these women rugby players try to manipulate how they are seen by others:

> Poppy: I think a lot of us tend to wander around in dirty kit... I think more than is necessary (smiling)
>
> Annie: Yeah it's like... I can go up to Woollies (UK department store) like this and y'know the little old ladies in the corner just looking at you thinking "oh gosh"

Playing rugby provides some of these women with a platform from which they can communicate their "tough" identity. One teammate described playing the unfeminine sport as "a way of demonstrating self." In a sense, the management of showing off bruises and wearing muddy kit to promote recognition of their rugby-playing activity can be used as what Beth called "a shock tactic." Revealing this kind of "tough" identity can cause people around you to reevaluate the "girly" in front of them.

Many times I personally have experienced differing reactions to the bruises on my body. On the pitch and around my teammates, my bruises were something to show off; at formal dinners or parties, they were reacted to with disgust and horror. People could not comprehend why you would want to do something that results in such "ill" effects. Many women said that onlookers suspected their bruises were the result of an abusive domestic relationship. Again, such suppositions confirm the female as ineffectual and as a victim. It is not easily recognized that women *want* to be physical, and many are even proud to come out bruised. Annie confessed, "I'll have a bruise and it will go really strange colors but you look at it with pride. You know you pat it." When asked why she was so proud of her bruises, she replied, "I suppose it shows that you can play the game and take what comes without flinching... It proves that you're strong that you're not girly."

What we are seeing in rugby culture and what is verbalized in the songs show *both* women and men communicating identities, incorporating what are commonly perceived to be "masculine" attributes of rudeness, crudeness, (sexual) aggression, and independence. It is a false presumption to see these attributes as fundamentally male or female. If they are understood as representations along a masculine–feminine continuum, it can be accessed by both sexes. Unfortunately, it is this choice that is made difficult. There is a tangible sense of disrupting gendering cultural codes. So, what is the result of this disruption?

"YOU'RE LOOKING A BIT BUTCH": RECEIVING RESISTANCE

A key element of my experiences and those of my teammates includes coping with peoples' reactions. It is difficult to stress just how markedly the team experienced being labeled as "deviant." I had friends commenting that I was "un-girly." Some family members supported me and some did not. I would get comments such as "You're looking a bit butch," and reactions ranging from impressed glances and chuckles to comments as disapproving as "It's not right on a woman." Once, I was introduced to a man at a dinner party as a rugby player, and for the rest of the evening he used it as a running joke: "Yes well nowadays we have women rugby players!" A constant source of amusement for him, it was belittling for me.

Jennifer Hargreaves (1994: 171) has suggested that "the implications that athletes may be 'pseudo-men,' 'unfeminine,' gay, masculine, mannish, 'butch,' 'dykes,' or lesbians put pressure on heterosexual sportswomen to play the 'femininity game.'" Participants were asked if they recognized what Hargreaves' called the "femininity game"; in our second focus group, Freya told me, "I often have it forced on me. Why don't I wear dresses and put earrings in, put make-up on, walk like a girl, things like that."

These women continue to play rugby, engaging in an activity that creates frustrating experiences for them in the form of disapproving comments and attitudes. My teammates had many examples of family, friends, and even acquaintances who had all made clear their disapproval. Poppy described an acquaintance who, she said, had "told me I shouldn't be doing that and that I should be having babies instead." Annie told me how she was interrogated: "Why are you doing that? That's for blokes." Both of these comments were from men whom these women hardly knew. They also described their family's reactions:

Poppy: My family disapproves basically. My mother doesn't really mind as long as I don't get cauliflower ears.

Freya: I haven't told [my mother], I just don't want to worry her, she thinks I'm playing football.

Annie: My mum is "I'll never get you married, you'll have terrible legs" and, "As long as you don't ruin your legs or knock your teeth out".

This resistance appears to be plentiful in these women's experiences and has become a part of their experience because they play rugby. There is this constant struggle against the representations people have and what they choose to make quite clear to these women. "Un-girly" is meant to be an insult, to rectify these women's deviance; ironically, however, these women are the very ones who understand "girly" to mean "sissy," pathetic.

CONCLUSIONS

Mariah Burton Nelson (1996: 110) argues that the brutality and violence of rugby reinforces what "being a man" is all about, but for the female rugby players it reinforces what being a tough woman is all about. Weakness and "sissyness" continue to be the pejoratives rugby players use to denigrate "feminine" behavior. "Fucking pussy" becomes an insult that can be used by men or women against men or women, rather than against women only. In reconstructing and reclaiming this insult as one that women can use, there is an attempt to undermine the power of the insult to demean women. However, it fails because although it may undermine the equation "pussy = women," it gets replaced with "pussy = feminine." Hence, the traditional representation of femininity remains unchanged. For the women who rebel, who "resist girl" (Ussher, 1997), their gender identity is subverted, overturning the "feminine" mould. Yet, the authority of the representation of femininity is *not* overthrown; "girly" is *rejected*, but by doing this, these women inadvertently *support* and reify the translation of "girly" as "ineffective."

Hargreaves (1994: 252) argues that "it is inevitable that if men have so much influence they will impose on the women's game their own values and practices and women footballers are being effectively schooled to copy what men do." One player claimed that the promiscuous, crude, and drunken behavior displayed by rugby-playing (male and female) "beer louts" was produced out of a process of "fitting into the mould"—that they "put the hat on" of the "rugby player." In this sense, rugby women are copying what the men do. But Hargreaves exonerates the idea of the passive female only to suppose that she is "schooled" into activity. If we consider other possibilities, we might recognize that not all women are the same. Some women (and men) actually *have* these values and *value* these practices. What is important to recognize is that, in rugby culture, femininity continues to be contaminated with labels of powerlessness and inferiority.

Zemore, Fiske, and Kim (2000: 228) suggest, "As a result of societal devaluation of 'female' characteristics, girls fear being—and not being—feminine." Although the argument highlights the plight of women as being stuck between a rock and a hard place in playing "the femininity game," there has been little suggestion that male gender identity might not actually be a walk in the park either. Indeed, you might understand the women playing rugby as having a go at playing the masculinity game. Women have discovered problems with the macho world of rugby whose "toughing it out" mentality rejects the recognition of real emotional and physical damage when injuries are sustained.

These women do not simply resist femininity; in fact, they are often comfortable with what Sarah and Poppy have both called "doing the girl thing." It is more appropriate to see what they are doing as trying to gain access to other (nonfeminine) behaviors as well: These behaviors and activities reflect their personal identity—not with the intention of excluding feminine aspects of their identity, but to access both masculine and feminine qualities.

My respondents typically insisted that they were not "girly girls." This claim only polarizes and reifies social stereotypes. The problem with this is that without undoing our indoctrination, we continue to project old assumptions into the future and change nothing. The despised "girly girl" label endorses the idea that "girly" is a bad thing to be. It is important to acknowledge the political nature of these social representations of masculinity and femininity. The women studied here express a nonstereotypical personal identity but, arguably, in doing so they breathe life into the very stereotypes and representations they are trying to escape. But they do change some of the representations of individuals around them today, and they may yet change the social representations of gender tomorrow. These women are already convinced that the masculine-feminine continuum is accessible, end-to-end, by males and females alike. In this way, women are no longer synonymous with feminine, and masculine is no longer a quality exclusively available to males. It is convincing others, and thus gaining the freedom to choose how masculine/feminine you want to be, that is the trickier job.

REFERENCES

Connell, R. W. (1995). *Masculinities*. Cambridge: Polity.

Hargreaves, J. (1994). *Sporting females: Critical issues in the history and sociology of women's sports.* London: Routledge.

Morrell, R. (1996). Rugby and white masculinity in Natal. In Nauright, J. and Chandler, J. L. (Eds.) *Making men: Rugby and masculine identity*, 91–120. London: Frank Cass.

Nauright, J. and Chandler, J. L. (Eds.) (1996). *Making men: Rugby and masculine identity.* London: Frank Cass.

Nelson, M. B. (1996). *The stronger women get, the more men love football: Sexism and the culture of sport.* London: Women's Press.

Phillips, J. (1996). The hard man. In Nauright, J. and Chandler, J. L. (Eds.) *Making men: Rugby and masculine identity*, 70–90. London: Frank Cass.

Schacht, S. P. (1996). Misogyny on and off the pitch: The gendered world of male rugby players. *Gender & Society*, 10/5: 550–565.

Schacht, S. P. (1997). Feminist fieldwork in the misogynistic setting of the rugby pitch. *Journal of Contemporary Ethnography*, Vol. 26/3: 338–363.

Ussher, J. M. (1997) *Fantasies of femininity: Reframing the boundaries of sex.* London: Penguin Books.

Zemore, S. E., Fiske, S. T., and Kim, H. (2000). In Eckes, T. and Trautner, H. M. (Eds.) *The developmental social psychology of gender*. London: Lawrence Erlbaum.

CHAPTER NINETEEN

All Bust AND No Balls: Gender, Language, AND Pool

ERIN REILLY

Although pool has traditionally had a predominantly male following, women have also been "chalking up" in poolrooms throughout the history of the game. William Shakespeare provides one of the earliest references to a woman playing pool in Act II, Scene V of *Antony and Cleopatra* (1623), when Cleopatra says, "Let's to billiards...." History tells us here are legends of avid players, such as Elizabeth I and Marie Antoinette. Mary Queen of Scots passed the time playing billiards during her incarceration, and after she was beheaded her doctor reportedly wrapped her body in the cloth from her table (Shamos, 1992). One of the first illustrations depicting a woman at a billiard table is that of the Duchess of Burgundy, playing with a gentleman in 1694, and it is also the first subtle image of flirting during the game (Ibid.).

While upper class women usually played on pool tables in socially approved private billiard parlors, women in the lower classes could occasionally be found playing in taverns and pubs, a situation that was stigmatized by society (Polsky, 1998). In the first decade of the nineteenth century, pool became more popular and more approved for women, and some men were said to be initially pleased with the presence of more women in the pool halls. However, as indicated by the following report from 1900, men may have been more interested in women's enjoyable company than in their playing skills:

> Their presence lends a grace and charm to the pastime; their naïve questions and pretty little blunders have their own particular charm; they inspire the favoured of

> the other sex with an interest in billiards which, however strong it may previously have been, is now increasing to a surprising extent; and in all way the ladies strike a melodious note by lending their patronage to this delightful game (Shamos, 1992: W-8).

The presence of women in poolrooms, then, was largely viewed by males as an opportunity for flirting; a common ruse was to offer lessons as a way to meet women, a ploy that is common even today (Hallinan and Reilly, 1998).

Eventually women became largely unwelcome in pool halls. According to Mike Shamos (1992: W-9), women in poolrooms were at times seen as a "sexual intrusion," and women who frequented public poolrooms "were suspected by both sexes of being hustlers, and I don't mean 9-Ball." Women were often banned from poolrooms in part because of the unsavory masculine characteristics of such places: gambling, spitting, smoking, and the rough language of men (Hallinan and Reilly, 1998; Polsky, 1998; Shamos, 1992).

In addition to flirting over the table, sexuality and the game of pool intertwined in some less subtle ways as well. One of the earliest documented references to billiards in Colonial America came from the diary of William Byrd who, in reference to having made love to his wife wrote, "It is to be observed that the flourish was performed on the billiard table" (cited in Polsky, 1998: 13). Between 1900 and 1930, it was common to see pictures of women depicted in the nude in pornographic magazines, prints, and postcards depicting men wooing women at the pool table; they were popular, often containing puns on billiards terms such as "kiss," "play," and "score" (Shamos, 1992: W-9).

SEXUALIZED POOL ARGOT

There are many contemporary examples of sexual puns, double entendres, and gender-marked pool argot. In Britain, the term "pocket billiards," or "trouser billiards," is slang for a man scratching his genitals or masturbating, and the American equivalent is "pocket pool." Puns on pool equipment, such as balls and the shaft of the cuestick, are common, as are puns on the "rubber" match in league pool—such as nicknaming it "the prophylactic" (Reilly, 2001). According to Shamos, "It is a debated point among players whether a stiff or a flexible shaft is preferable" (1999: 217). Slang terms for the knuckle points, where the cushion tapers toward the pocket, include "tits," "titties," and "nipples" (Billiards Forum, 2008). The British term for spin on the cueball is "screw," which is called "English" in the United States. A recent *Men's Health* article on billiards was entitled "How to Handle Your Balls" (Marion, 2001: 113) and included a section labeled "Hey, Nice Rack."

A "Dolly Parton Break" (all bust and no balls) is a phrase used to describe the lay of the pool table after the break shot, when the balls scatter but none is pocketed, and it involves accusing someone of "breaking like a woman," which carries the same meaning. "Too much testosterone" is a complaint heard after missing a shot because of hitting the ball too forcefully. A player who misses because of shooting too forcefully might also be reminded that "harder isn't always better"—that is, in pool, as opposed to sex, for the intended reference. The side pocket is sometimes referred to as the "virgin pocket," because it can be "hard to penetrate." "Ladies aid" is a slang term for a mechanical bridge, and the term may also be used to tease a male player who has trouble reaching his shot (Billiards Forum, 2008). Gender-marked phrases in pool often reinforce the idea of women being weak, such as characterizing a weak break as "breaking like a woman," and of men being strong—a hard shot being the result of "too much testosterone" (Reilly, 2001).

The authors of a study conducted in an Australian university union bar discussed the reasons why so few women play pool, and what happens to them when they do venture into this traditionally male domain. They found that women were often excluded through verbal harassment and other intimidating behaviors (Broom, Byrne, and Petkovic, 1992). Common phrases heard in the bar when a man was beaten by a woman, according to Broom, Byrne, and Petkovic (1992: 183–184) included the following:

> Where are your balls, mate?Can't you handle being beaten by a skirt?Who's the bird now? You woman! (a man's insult in response to unskillful play by a male partner)
>
> Gees mate...losing to a woman...can I get you a beer?Try my cue sweetheart, it'll guarantee you a good game

Generally, in sports, phrases such as "throwing like a girl" or "playing like a woman" are the ultimate insults, reinforcing the assumption of male supremacy in sport. A woman who is skillful subverts the confirmation of masculinity afforded to men, and "if she can't be beaten, she must be discredited" (Ibid.: 183). As seen in the example above, gender, language, and pool intertwine in social interaction as well as in argot specifically connected with the game and equipment.

SEXUAL LANGUAGE AND POOLROOM SOCIABILITY

Pool is a very social game, where men and women can compete on an equal basis. Alcohol is generally served in pool halls, and pool is one of the few sports in which players can drink during competition. Men and women competing and drinking together in this environment makes for a ripe ground for studying sexual rhetoric in the sociable spaces between actual play.

During league pool matches, most of a player's time is spent watching teammates play and socializing (Mizerak, 1990). Findings from *Gender and Sociability in a Players Pool League* (Reilly, 2001) provides an ethnography focusing on a recreational pool league, indicating that in the setting of the pool hall, sexual language is significant in conversation, in telling jokes and stories, and also in the "joking relationship." Grounded theory methods were used for analyzing data, which consisted of field notes written by a participant observer.

Conversation during pool league nights was used to pass the time and to entertain others with stories, and as a way of getting to know about each other's lives outside the pool hall. Sex talk was common among members of the pool league; Kimberly Kuntz (1996) also found that sex jokes and sexuality as topics were common in a women's bowling league. "Sex talk allows sexual expression, oftentimes repressed at the work site (in clerical sites more than in factory sites) and with family members" (Kuntz, 1996: 23). According to Georg Simmel (1950: 55), "The telling and reception of stories, etc., is not an end in itself, but only a means for the liveliness, harmony, and a common consciousness of the 'party.'" Even though playing or watching pool may be what brought teammates and others together in the setting, side involvements such as conversations sometimes took precedence over the game, especially when the topic was sex.

During a tournament, one player's husband came to watch her play. That night there was a lot of sex talk, and it took attention away from the games. The following discourse emerged in my dissertation research (Reilly, 2001: 132):

> Dave said, "All you guys talk about is sex!" I said, "So what do you want talk about?" He said sports. So we talked about the NBA and hockey for a little bit.

Later, the conversation reverted back to sex, which is what we talked about for the rest of the evening. Dave did not watch his wife play that night, although it had been his reason for coming to the pool hall in the first place.

Most members of the team that I studied were married, and a common topic of conversation was the conventional wisdom that once you get married, you rarely have sex. Male and female teammates debated as to whether this was the fault of husbands or of wives, and other personal aspects of married life were often shared. During a tournament one weekend, a teammate had to leave early and he left his phone number for us to call him if we won.

> On that slip of paper, above the phone number, Walter had penciled in, "For a good time call." Ben came back before we were finished with the match. Walter showed him the paper and said, "Whose number is this? For a good time call?" Ben looked at it and dryly said, "Well, it's obviously not my wife's number." (Ibid.: 174)

Telling sex jokes and joking relationships were other important aspects of poolroom sociability. Being able to tell good jokes gave members social currency in the league, and participating in joking relationships marked members as accepted members of the culture. In the joking relationship, one person could tease or make fun of another person who, it is understood, must take no real offense, since it is not meant to be taken seriously. One of the features of the joking relationship, according to Spradley and Mann (1975: 90) is that "it involves ritual insults and sexual topics." The following excerpt illustrates this relationship between two old friends who were opponents in a Scotch doubles tournament:

> Ned introduced me to our male opponent, a friend of his. He told me that he doesn't get along with Ned, and said, "I hate that son of a bitch!" He also told me his partner's name and said, "She's a sweetheart, but she's an ugly flat-chested woman." He and Ned exchanged some banter back and forth, insulting each other laughingly. The man's sense of humor became even more sharply noticeable when his partner walked up. "See," he said, "there's my ugly flat-chested partner." She was rather well endowed, and nice looking. (Ibid.: 135).

The joking relationship is "restricted to certain participants," and it is also "a public encounter" (Spradley and Mann, 1975: 90). Ned and our opponent did not tease each other's partners in a similar manner, and having an audience for their banter fueled the exchange.

The following sequence of events illustrates an example of sex talk and the impact of a good sex joke among the pool league set, as well as the rite of passage into the joking relationship. On a league night when several team members were exchanging sex jokes, Joe said to me, "Do you know why my brain is bigger than a dog's?" I did not, so he finished with, "Because if it wasn't I'd be humping your leg right now!" Everyone laughed and I felt challenged to tell one in return. I chose Joe to be the fall guy while the others listened to my response:

> "Do you know what the four types of orgasms are?" "No," he replied. I rebutted with, "There is the negative, oh no, oh no; the positive oh yes, oh yes; the religious, oh God, oh God; and the fake, oh Joe, oh Joe!" Everybody laughed, and Joe declared that he heard that every night from his wife. Walter said, "Wow, you have sex every night?" Joe said, "No, I don't know what she was doing... she had her back to me at the time!" Later, when Bob came over, Ann told me to repeat the joke to him. He groaned at the punch line and everybody laughed.

The next week we had to play against the number one–ranked team, and Bob still remembered the joke.

> Bob told me that I should tell the other team the orgasm joke from last week, and use Mike's name. Mike was the captain of the other team, a nice looking man. Bob said

> that the other team "would get a kick out of the joke if I used Mike for it." I noticed the banter between players on the other team did include quite a bit of good-natured ribbing against Mike.

Bob and I used careful strategy to set up a good joke and insult. He picked out a good target, a man whose team particularly enjoyed ritually insulting him, and I waited for the best timing to ensure that the joke would not be rushed, and that there would be a good audience. Here is what happened next:

> Mike, who had just lost, sat back down at the table, and I began to look for an opening to tell my joke. I had to play Pete, and once the game got started I decided to tell the joke while Pete was shooting. He finished shooting just as I was getting started and came over to listen. All of the women were gone from the table at this point, so I found myself standing there facing 11 seated men between the 2 teams. Someone had just finished a joke, and I announced that I had one. I was standing right next to Mike, and I put my hand on his shoulder when I finished the punch line, "Oh Mike, Oh Mike!" All of the men started busting up. My opponent Pete gave me a high five, and someone said, "She must have heard about you!" The players all gave Mike a hard time about his reputation, and I was a big hit. (Reilly, 2001: 142)

The players on that other team were always friendly enough to me when we played against them, but they had never spoken to me much at other times. After my telling that joke, they not only talked and teased me more that night, but also from then on they would make a point of chatting with me and teasing me.

Telling the joke made me an accepted insider to the joking relationship with members of that team. In their study of the social and working world of the cocktail lounge, Spradley and Mann (1975: 92) discussed the importance of waitresses being able to handle the insults of the joking relationship in order to be accepted. They noted,

> The experience of learning to joke is sometimes punctuated by events that seem like a small "rite of passage" and mark a new understanding of the relationship. In a sense, these events confer upon the waitress an additional identity, that of "joking partner."

For me, telling that one joke was in a sense a "rite of passage" with the members of the other team, which made me a "joking partner" with them. Later, when Mike and Pete joined our team for the summer, I had already established a relationship with them. On the first night of summer league, making reference to the joke I had told, Mike commented, "You're not going to dog me now that we're on the same team, are you?" (Reilly, 2001: 143).

CONCLUSIONS

Pool halls have historically been a male domain, and women were at one time frequently excluded, partly because of the rough language of men (Polsky, 1998). However, according to the Billiards Congress of America (http://home.bca-pool.com), as of 2005, approximately 37 percent of pool players in the United States are women. There has been an effort by the billiards industry to clean up the image of poolrooms in order to attract a more suburban clientele, and to attract more women (Polsky, 1998, Krakowka, 1998), recognizing that "women are very influential when it comes to making decisions about couple's activities. If she doesn't want to stay at a billiards center because it's dark and smoky, they probably won't" (Krakowka, 1998: 59).

Although the image of poolrooms has improved, and although there is no longer the stigma once attached to women who frequent such places, alterations such as better lighting and less smoke have not changed the masculine character of the language attached to the game. Insider pool argot is still peppered with gendered and sexualized terms and phrases. For women in the largely male environment of the pool league, it is important for social acceptance to be able to participate in conversations and hold their own telling jokes and participating in the joking relationship, all of which often have a sexual character.

REFERENCES

Billiards Forum (2008). Billiards terms. Available: (http://www.billiardsforum.info/billiard-terms.asp).

Broom, D., Byrne, M., and Petkovic, L. (1992). Off cue: Women who play pool. *Australia and New Zealand Journal of Sociology* (28, 2): 175–191.

Hallinan, C. and Reilly, E. (1998). Symbolic interactions among amateur eight ball pool players. In Alexander, M., Harding, S., Harrison, P., Kendall, G., Skrbis, Z., and Western, J. (Eds.), Refashioning sociology: Responses to a new world order, 504–511. Brisbane: Queensland University of Technology.

Krakowka, L. (1998). Pool parties. *American Demographics* (20, 8): 59.

Kuntz, K. (1996). A league of their own: "Doing gender" in the context of leisure. Unpublished paper, University of Kansas, Lawrence.

Marion, M. (2001). How to handle your balls. *Men's Health* (16, 1): 113.

Mizerak, S. (1990). *Steve Mizerak's complete book of pool.* Chicago, IL: Contemporary Books.

Polsky, N. (1998). *Hustlers, beats, and others.* New York: Lyons Press.

Reilly, E. (2001). Gender and sociability in a players pool league. Unpublished doctoral dissertation, University of Kansas, Lawrence.

Shamos, M. I. (1992). Billiards: A women's history. *Billiards Digest* (14, 4): 41–60.

Shamos, M. I. (1999). *The new illustrated encyclopedia of billiards*. New York: Lyons Press.

Simmel, G. (1950). *The sociology of Georg Simmel.* Wolff, K. H. (Trans.). New York: Free Press.

Spradley, J. P. and Mann, B. J. (1975). *The cocktail waitress: Woman's work in a man's world.* New York: John Wiley and Sons.

CHAPTER TWENTY

Media Grappling WITH Female Success ON THE Mat: Tricia Saunders, Multiple-World Freestyle Wrestling Champion

THERESA A. WALTON

The premiere star of elite women's freestyle wrestling in the 1990s, Tricia Saunders, at 100 pounds, was the first U.S. woman to win a FILA (Fédération Internationale des Luttes Associées) World Championship gold medal, followed with a constant winning presence on the national wrestling scene and more world gold and silver medals to become the most-decorated American female wrestler. Saunders' achievements earned her the distinction of being the first woman inducted into the Wrestling Hall of Fame in Stillwater, Oklahoma, as she never lost—neither at the National Championship nor at the U.S. World Team trials. Ironically, since freestyle wrestling had yet to be offered for women at the Olympic Games until Athens 2004 (Greco-Roman is still closed), Saunders was twice named the United States Olympic Committee's "Woman Athlete of the Month," a distinction earned in 1996 and 1998. Her 1999 gold medal helped lead the U.S. women's freestyle team to win the World Championships.

Her accomplishments indicate success often associated with mediated sport celebrity, yet Saunders is far from a household name, and her wrestling domination garnered little mainstream or wrestling media attention. According to sport scholars Andrews and Jackson (2001: 5), "Celebrities are crafted as contextually sensitive points of cultural negotiation, between those controlling the dominant modes and mechanisms of cultural production, and their perceptions of the audiences' practices of cultural reception." Who gets media attention and becomes a "star," if even fleetingly, offers insight into social boundaries and power relationships. Moreover, when female athletes are the focus, the discourse unfailingly turns toward sexual rhetoric with an emphasis on sexuality and what Batina Fabos (1999) has labeled "beauty capital." This chapter analyzes the mediation of elite wrestler Tricia Saunders to explicate the sexual sports rhetoric surrounding female success in a traditionally male sport. To do so, *Amateur Wrestling News* (*AWN*) and *USA Wrestler*, the two main wrestling periodicals, along with a few mainstream media articles focused on Saunders, were analyzed, considering that sources of information largely determine stories being told.

Having examined mediation of high school girl/boy wrestling, I found stories of female wrestling centering on these themes: female wrestling's not being taken seriously, worries about girls' safety, how to understand female motivations to wrestle, effects of females' wrestling on male participants, as well as issues of the relationship between Title IX and wrestling (Walton, 2005). One of the main underlying concerns of these media representations relates to sport's being a male preserve—particularly sports such as wrestling, which have historically been used for military training and defining masculinity. Sport/legal scholar Sarah Fields (2000: 175) argues that "the most pervasive arguments against co-ed and even female wrestling, particularly in the cultural discourse, has been about sex, power, and domination." Girls' and women's exclusion has had cultural significance in establishing and maintaining a space to create a certain kind of aggressive masculinity to promote the ideology of male superiority. Although women broke barriers to participate in wrestling, how they are understood culturally demonstrates a gendered and sexualized tension of underlying power relations. While elite women and other female wrestlers are generally covered in different sources, there are similar concerns in establishing femininity and heterosexuality. Yet, the wrestling community has concerns differing from mainstream media producers related to female wrestling.

MEDIATION

While girls' wrestling against boys at the high school level has gained some attention in mainstream media (Walton, 2005), elite women's wrestling has received far less; for example, until 2005, only six newspaper articles focused on Saunders. While her success has been covered in wrestling media sources, which offer little coverage of female wrestling, *USA Wrestler* and *AWN* focus on elite women's wrestling in a majority of their uneven coverage. Thus, what little attention it gets in mainstream media goes to high school girls, and what coverage female wrestling gets within wrestling media sources focuses on elites.

Media producers who cover female wrestling often portray them in a way sport scholars have labeled "the apologetic." As Ann Hall (1996: 18) writes, "From the 1960s onward a major focus of gender issues with North American sport sociology and social psychology was to 'prove' that sport competition did not masculinize female participants," arguing that, in the sporting realm, a conflict between gender and culture is understood to exist, especially when women participate in traditionally all-male sports, because sport is "defined by masculine standards" (p. 19). Most sport scholars have moved beyond attempting to "prove" that women can compete in sport and still be "feminine" (and, by extension, heterosexual), instead bringing into question the categories of masculine and feminine and the idea that sport is "naturally" a male domain (Birrell and Cole, 1994; Cahn, 1994; Dowling, 2000; Hall, 1996). Yet, media coverage of female wrestlers is still very concerned with establishing their "femininity."

By granting female wrestlers "special" status, and working to establish their femininity, media representations reinforce stereotypical categories of masculine and feminine, legitimizing wrestling as the natural domain of boys and men. Females who enter that domain are granted honorary male status, while being constructed in traditionally feminine ways away from the mat. As Hall and other feminist sport scholars note, there is cultural inconsistency in expectations for the roles of "woman" and "athlete." Media accounts work to resolve this discrepancy. Despite this, there are significant variations in the mediated coverage of Tricia Saunders within wrestling periodicals; in particular, *USA Wrestler*, the publication of the governing body of amateur U.S. wrestling, offers resistant coverage that goes a long way toward presenting female wrestlers as athletes without conflict over their gender—differing considerably from the other main wrestling magazine, *AWN*.

AWN: WRESTLING, A FAMILY TRADITION

In *AWN*, the self-proclaimed ultimate wrestling resource, women's wrestling receives very little coverage. From 1980 through 2001, in the 228 published issues of 40 to 60 pages each, out of a total of about 10,000 pages, only 79 pages concern women's wrestling, including six feature articles as well as box scores and short mentions within articles about men's wrestling. No female has ever graced the cover, and only 18 photos of women have been included thus far in the publication's 21-year span. *AWN* could not have made it clearer that wrestling is a male domain, symbolically annihilating female wrestlers (Tuchman, 1978). This follows a trend found by sport studies scholars examining the mediation of women in sport (i.e., Duncan and Messner, 2000), the limited coverage of women's wrestling within *AWN* offering particular constructions that serve to allay fears of women's motivation to wrestle while also trivializing and marginalizing them.

While it is difficult to determine how many women wrestle at the elite, never mind lesser levels, it is clear that multiple-world champion Tricia Saunders has figured disproportionately in coverage of women's wrestling in *AWN*. She is mentioned in 28 percent of the text devoted to women's wrestling and is the focus in three of its six feature articles. Four of 18 photos of women are of Saunders. Clearly, her success at the U.S. National and Women's World Championships warrants her coverage as the "ultimate wrestling source." It would seem logical that her tremendous success makes it impossible *not* to cover her. Yet, the first feature article on Saunders in *AWN* occurred before she won any of these medals. An March 1992 article, "The Saunders: Making Wrestling a Family Sport," introduces her to *AWN* readers, Lisa Little informing us, "Wrestling is known for its family traditions—sons following in their fathers' footsteps and brothers tagging along with brothers…Now Townsend and Tricia Saunders aim to add a new type of family tradition to the list—married couple" (p. 12), and reassuring readers of Saunders' heterosexuality. The focus on Saunders' marriage to another wrestler offers "proof" to counter a hidden discourse on homosexuality (Birrell and Theberge, 1994; Griffin, 1998), like the focus on perceived "femininity" within coverage of girls' high school wrestling (Walton, 2005).

Clearly aware of mainstream debates over female wrestling, much of Saunders' coverage focuses on negative perceptions; for example, the first "family" article pokes fun at mainstream misunderstandings of wrestling. As Townsend Saunders says, "If people don't even understand my wrestling, a lot of times they think it's professional wrestling. They say, 'Gee, you're kind of small.' And I say, 'Yeah, my wife wrestles too.' Then they *really* think it's professional wrestling" (cited in Little, 1992: 12, emphasis in original). This harkens back to the idea that women wrestlers must be for the entertainment of male spectators—not for "real" wrestling. He continues, "I usually have to explain that it's not mud wrestling. It's not professional wrestling. She's a freestyle wrestler, Olympic style, just like I wrestle" (Ibid.).

AWN continues building on this "new" family tradition in their coverage of Saunders, even when she does not compete. In 1994, we were informed that "the USA team competed without its star, Tricia Saunders, who could not compete because of pregnancy. She is married to Olympic team member Townsend Saunders" (US women, 1994: 10). Of the eight sentences reporting on the fourth place finish by the 1994 world team, two were devoted to Saunders, who did not even wrestle. In 1998, after Saunders' third world gold medal, we learn that "she is the only U.S. wrestler to have ever won a World Championship, especially interesting since two of those gold medals came after giving birth. Her daughter

Tassia was born in 1994, and her son Townsend was born in 1997. She is married to Olympic Silver Medalist Townsend Saunders" (Little, 1998: 38). This focus on family serves a further purpose in accounting for a woman's motivation to wrestle. Saunders, we are informed, wrestles because her grandfather, father, brothers, and, most importantly, her husband wrestle.

Readers are also assured of Tricia Saunders' lack of feminist motivation to wrestle, as women's intentions when they decide to wrestle are highly suspect. As former University of Iowa coach and wrestling legend Dan Gable notes, "I guess if I had a daughter who loved it, I'd hate to deny her the opportunity if it was for real. If it was for the wrong reasons, I'd definitely be against it" (cited in Little, 1994: 11). Women who wrestle must prove sincere motives for being on the mat—a love of the sport rather than an attempt to demonstrate women's capabilities. According to Saunders, right on the mark in terms of mainstream media,

> A lot of people have said to me that I'm just out here to make a point. If I was just trying to make a point, I'd pick a lot easier way to do it than getting my head beat in every day. All the girls that are out here now, for all the flack they take all the time, you have to know they really love just the sport for its own sake, because there's nothing in it for them. I mean nothing. If they come home a world champion, no one will know. (in Little, 1992: 12)

Yet, even if she is not consciously trying to make a point, Saunders' activities do exactly that. She not only wrestled but also worked 50 hours a week as a microbiologist, another activity outside the traditional norm for women. Thus, she works in an occupation exemplifying why Title IX was brought to the table and passed; further, as we will see in Saunders' coverage in *USA Wrestler*, her activism in promoting women's wrestling has been significant.

Eight months after the first *AWN* article appeared, Saunders won her first World Championships gold medal and was named Outstanding Wrestler of the meet, prompting the women's team coach, Rusty Davidson, to say, "She is a real hero. She trained hard, made sacrifices and got what she went for" (Tricia Saunders wins, 1992: 8). The win garnered a paragraph in *AWN*'s "Wrestling Round-Up" section. Evidently her marriage to Townsend is more newsworthy than winning a gold medal at the World Championships, despite the fact that she was the only woman to do so until 1999. In response to the elimination of men's collegiate wrestling programs and the placing of emphasis on it as a family sport during the late 1980s and early 1990s, wrestling began to undergo an image change. Wade Schalles (1994: 17) asserted,

> Today, too many T-shirts are sold and ads written promoting the aggressive tendencies needed for success in wrestling and the level of brutality required to get one's

> hand raised. Although some of what they expound might be true to some extent, at what cost to wrestling?...Administrators read our ads and realize if they need to drop a sport or cut a budget, wrestling is an easy target because they don't expect a white collar fight from a sport that promotes a blue collar image.

Schalles suggested that wrestling supporters promote the "intellectual and competitive side of wrestling" with such slogans as "Wrestling is a physical chess game and my goal is to be the last king standing!" and "Success in life is learning how to get up after you've been knocked down and nobody knows stand-ups like wrestlers do!" He addressed the potential class issues surrounding wrestling's reputation, urging that "it all starts with promotions, with responsible and creative advertising and the environment of a white collar image" (p. 17).

Along these lines was a shift in advertising away from campaigns emphasizing overaggressive masculinity associated with wrestling. For example, Nike's ads in the late 1980s and early 1990s included these for the Nike Combatant: "Wimps need not apply...If you take your sport seriously, you probably ought to try a pair. Provided you don't belong to a more delicate sport" (*AWN*, October 12, 1987: 27); "Half nelson, half animal...So go get a pair. Because in the world of animals, what do you want to be, predator or prey?" (*AWN*, September 3, 1990: 2); "Two men enter. One man leaves" (*AWN*, October 14, 1991: 23); and, "You know how snugly your forearm fits around your opponent's skull when you have him locked in a vice grip and you're slamming him nose-first into the mat? That's how our shoe fits your foot" (*AWN*, June 22, 1992: 4). There was also this for the Air Reversal, "Off the mat you can jog, jump rope, and lift weights in it. On the mat you can wrench your opponent's appendages until he makes small pathetic whelping noises in it. It's quite versatile this shoe" (*AWN*, September 13, 1993: 27). Not to be left out, Asics also sponsored a similar line of advertisements: "Hostile? Destructive? Prone to violence? Have we got the shoe for you. Asics wrestling shoes are made as tough as the people who wear them" (*AWN*, February 21, 1994, back cover).

Yet, by 1997 Asics ads took a different approach: "Your center of gravity is located in your heart. It is the ultimate desire sport. Wrestling has weight classifications but it has no heart classifications. Two people step out onto the mat to learn lessons about themselves, to make their teammates proud, to go three periods with Destiny" (*AWN*, November 7, 1997, back cover), while Nike disappeared from the wrestling ad scene altogether. Cliff Keen Athletic gear lead the way with new wrestling images in a number of ads promoting it in a way not associated with violence and aggressive working class masculinity, such as, "I do not need a crowd. I do not need cheerleaders. I do not need headlines. I do not need to be on a cereal box. I do not need to explain why I do it. I am a wrestler"

(*AWN*, June/July, 1999: 8) and, "You've shown him the difference between being a tough guy and being tough. Big head. Big mouth. Huge talent. Yet, thanks to the patience and discipline of his coach, he now knows what it takes to win—not just on the mat, but in all the matches he'll face. Wrestling has a history of building character, and we're proud to provide some of the tools" (Ibid., back cover).

By 2001, a new form of working class image was used, celebrating the diversity of wrestling and a Protestant work ethic developed by wrestling, best exemplified by the USA Wrestling ad for the World Championships that were scheduled to be hosted in New York City, during September 26–29, 2001. The print ad featured members of the USA world team dressed as construction workers, including Greco-Roman Olympic star Rulon Gardner, upcoming phenom and women's world team member Toccara Montgomery, and a racially diverse mix from the men's freestyle team (*AWN*, May 4, 2001: 47). Focus on wrestling as a "family" sport had become the norm between 1995 and 2005, and coverage of Tricia Saunders and her wrestling family fit perfectly.

With the Atlanta Olympic Games, from which women's wrestling was absent, came a noticeable lack of coverage of the 1996 Women's World Wrestling Championships. Saunders' World Championship win was not reported directly, although it was mentioned later in a paragraph about her being named United States Olympic Committee Athlete of the month for September 1996. This was an ironic distinction, given that the Olympic Games offered no freestyle wrestling opportunities for women until 2004.

Saunders was lauded in *AWN* not for her championship gold medal, but for bringing recognition to the sport of wrestling from the U.S. Olympic Committee. As will become apparent, Saunders' contributions to the wrestling world include more than her marriage. While *AWN* barely recognizes women's wrestling, *USA Wrestler* offers more extensive and quality coverage, while not reaching nearly as many readers—not being available to readers who are not members of USA Wrestling. Frustratingly, there is only one archived set of *USA Wrestler* issues in the United States—at the USA Wrestling offices in Colorado Springs, Colorado.

USA WRESTLER: WRESTLING FOR ALL

USA Wrestling, the governing body of amateur wrestling that publishes *USA Wrestler*, has been a major supporter of women's wrestling, all USA Wrestling-sanctioned freestyle events offering female divisions comparable to men's. It is the only wrestling publication that has featured women wrestlers on its cover (seven in the 1990s); in its 126 issues from 1980 through 2001, nearly 300 pages were devoted to women's wrestling, with more than 200 photographs—more than half being action shots and 27 feature articles. Yet, although *USA Wrestler* covers women's wrestling more than any other publication, the information does not reach a large or diverse audience, as it is not widely available except for some 131,000 members of USA Wrestling.

Although the magazine does better than other publications, at about 8 percent, it is clear that men's wrestling is the norm. Labeling of events and awards exemplifies this: the "three" main "styles" being freestyle, Greco-Roman, and women's, despite the fact that women too wrestle freestyle. The exclusion of women from Greco-Roman competition for "aesthetic" reasons exemplifies the male "norm."

According to Gary Abbott, communications director at USA Wrestling, in the late 1990s they initiated a campaign to increase wrestling opportunities for women and to educate the wrestling community about them. So far, 21 women wrestlers have been the focus of either feature articles or small spots, the majority of coverage being tournament results—National Championships, World Team Trials, and World Championships, along with major U.S. and International meets.

Not surprisingly, Tricia Saunders plays a prominent role. Given her success, she has been featured more than any other female wrestlers, but her coverage in *USA Wrestler* differs from *AMW*—rather than being defined by her husband or family, Saunders' athletic accomplishments have been highlighted since she became "the first U.S. wrestler to win a gold medal at the Women's World Championships" (Saunders wins Sunkist, 1993: 34). By 1996, when she won her second world title, her dominance on the national scene was secure—described as "competing with power and purpose" (Saunders wins Women's, 1996: 15). Portraying her as a serious, dedicated, and dominant elite athlete, *USA Wrestler* (Saunders named, 1998: 8) reported, "In what has seemed to be automatic, two-time World Champion Tricia Saunders of the Sunkist Kids extended her national record to eight career U.S. Women's National titles."

Focusing on Saunders' work in wrestling away from the mats as an activist for women's wrestling, it is noteworthy that she has been supportive of fellow wrestlers such as Vicki Zummo, Margaret LeGates, and Tina George. When women wrestlers split from USA Wrestling to form the United States Women's Amateur Wrestling Federation (USWAWF) due to lack of financial and tournament support, Tricia Saunders served on the short-lived organization. *USA Today* (White, 1991: C2) stated, "Female wrestlers have declared their independence," but when USA Wrestling received a $35,000 grant from the United States Olympic Committee to help fund women's wrestling, it lured them back (USA wrestling's women's, 1993). This fits the pattern of women's sport organizations being taken over by longer-established men's, best exemplified by the NCAA's take over of the Association for Intercollegiate Athletics for Women (AIAW) in the early 1980s.

The first step was getting Saunders as an ally, electing her to the USA Wrestling Board of Directors, where she served as the chairperson of the USA Wrestling Women's Wrestling Committee. Her lobbying moved them to establish the first National Championships for women in 1992 and the first Pan-American Cup in 1993. Saunders was invited to the Sudafed Women's Sport Dinner, was on the *Joan Rivers Show*, and was awarded USA Wrestling's first Woman of the Year Award as "One of the pioneers in the development of women's wrestling in the nation. She has worked hard to expand opportunities for women" (Saunders named, 1998: 17).

The "pioneer" label caused mixed emotions: Saunders was denied the opportunity to wrestle when she was a youngster. She won a lawsuit to wrestle as an eight-year-old—she placed fourth as a 45-pounder in freestyle and second in Greco-Roman at a national meet—yet when officials would not allow her to wrestle in junior high and high school, her parents decided against more litigation. "I don't think my parents were up for another lawsuit. At 12, I retired and went into gymnastics" (cited Mihoces, 1999: E6). She said,

> People say to me that women's wrestling wouldn't be where it is if it wasn't for me. I was the only one who really had the passion at the time to pursue it. It was a hard decision for me to fight for it. I'm proud of what I've done, but I wish there were more people who would have jumped in and helped me then. It has come a long way. There's a lot more acceptance than before. [But,] girls still have to be much more determined than boys if they want to wrestle. (Saunders named, 1998: 17)

Saunders' support for women's wrestling has been unequivocal. Having faced discrimination, she gets frustrated when blame is placed on women's sport for men's collegiate wrestling programs' being dropped. "I see both sides of it. I don't want to see programs taken away. I have many friends in the college wrestling community that have lost out because of proportionality. But at the same time I don't want those guys who wrestle to say that I don't understand what it feels like. I have felt what it was like to be left out," she has commented (in Witulski, ND). Watching daughter Tassia and son Townsend wrestle, she declared, "Hopefully, they're not going to have doors shut in their faces like I had as a kid" (cited in Mihoces, 1999: E6).

Stories of athletic success often highlight the seemingly insurmountable obstacles that winning athletes sometimes face, the featured female wrestlers in *USA Wrestler* being no exception. These stories not only serve to support the ideology of sport as a meritocracy but also are important to USA Wrestling's campaign to gain greater acceptance for female wrestlers within the male wrestling community. Acceptance by those in control of wrestling opportunities is especially important for increasing women's access, as the main obstacle they face is the cultural belief that girls and women do not belong there. Cultural beliefs, both within the wrestling community and among potential female participants, work as ideological barriers keeping women's participation numbers low.

USA Wrestling has a stake in supporting women's wrestling not only because it is the "right thing to do," as mandated by the Amateur Sports Act, to offer equal opportunities for women, but also because many in wrestling see the growth of women's wrestling as a potential answer to Title IX issues (Walton and Helstein, 2008). Without a "sister" sport, many feel that wrestling is an easy target for athletic directors to cut when faced with budget constraints. Moreover, the collegiate wrestling system is a feeder program for elite USA Wrestling World Teams; thus, for USA Wrestling, it is a win-win situation. By increasing opportunities for women at the collegiate level, the women's World Team would become stronger in the process, while eliminating cuts in men's collegiate programs would benefit the men's World Team.

Unlike coverage of women athletes in popular media sources, women wrestlers in *USA Wrestler* are not sexualized, nor are their accomplishments trivialized. While the nearly exclusive concentration on elite wrestlers itself might be considered problematic, in that it supports a model of sport whereby only the best of the best are worthy of attention, women's wrestling is not represented in a significantly different way than men's in this primarily male magazine. This in itself makes the coverage of women in *USA Wrestler* much different from, and resistant to the norm of, other predominantly male sports magazines, such as *Sports Illustrated*, where women are consistently trivialized and sexualized (i.e., Davis, 1997).

USA Wrestling's campaign to educate the wrestling community about women's wrestling leads to a dual focus: First, coverage of women's wrestling resembles that of men's, establishing the sense that women are "just like" men in terms of their commitment to the sport. The discrimination that female wrestlers face from parents, wrestlers, coaches, and culture in general constitutes the second focus, appealing to the sense of fair play established within the ideology of wrestling as a meritocracy conveyed within mediated wrestling sources.

Some elite, successful wrestlers successfully gained mat skills from judo, rather than wrestling folkstyle in high school. Access that females have to judo, another contact sport, also gets at the cultural work that wrestling does in supporting and constructing hegemonic masculinity, as Tricia Saunders discussed in a 2001 interview with Ted Witulski, the National Coaches Education Program coordinator for USA Wrestling: "Culturally we are different in the U.S. which has held us back. If I talk to a mom and dad and say would you let your daughter take Tae-Kwon-Do or Judo? They would usually say oh yeah, that's no problem. But at the same time if I offered women's wrestling as an alternative they would be fearful of it."

Although there are few essential differences in the physical elements of judo and wrestling, culturally they are worlds apart. Wrestling is associated with blue-collar masculinity, judo with "Asian" customs and beliefs. Even though wrestling seems to have its own particular mental environment, martial arts such as judo are often considered to be disciplines that are as much spiritual and psychological as they are physical. Female acceptance in martial arts is certainly not a universal experience. In Japan, not only are women actively kept out of Sumo wrestling, there is fierce debate over whether or not female government officials will be allowed in the sacred sumo ring. Yet women's acceptance into combat sports such as judo in the United States fits within the positivist dichotomies of male/female and West/East, as oppositional and mutually exclusive.

CONCLUDING REMARKS

Examining mediation of a female wrestling "star" offers a useful site for understanding cultural gender confusion when girls and women step on the wrestling mat. The source of information is the story that is told, or not told, about Tricia Saunders. Wrestling does not garner much media attention in non-Olympic years, so it is not surprising that the women's national freestyle wrestling team is yet to become part of the public consciousness. Yet, the media coverage female wrestling does receive demonstrates a system of boundary maintenance. Coverage of elite wrestler Tricia Saunders highlights cultural tensions over sport and gender, as played out in mediated stories of her life and wrestling career.

In mainstream media and in *AWN*, the highest circulation wrestling periodical, Saunders has received limited coverage, stories about her used to support the family-oriented, inclusive image being constructed by the wrestling community in attempts to reconfigure their image. In contrast, *USA Wrestler*, by the governing body of amateur wrestling, presents female wrestlers who resist dominant ideologies of wrestling as a male domain and women in general as trespassers. Here, Saunders is presented first and foremost as an elite athlete, her activism in support of women's wrestling applauded. She served as one of the women's Olympic coaches in the 2004 Athens Games and then retired after a decade of dominance in the sport. *USA Wrestler* chronicled that career and her impact on women's wrestling, but coverage of Tricia Saunders and her colleagues remains slight, maintaining the ideology of wrestling as a male domain.

REFERENCES

Andrews, D. and S. Jackson. (2001). *Sport stars: The cultural politics of sporting* celebrity. New York: Routledge.

Birrell, S. and Cole, C. (1994). *Women, sport and culture.* Champaign, IL: Human Kinetics.

Birrell, S. and Theberge, N. (1994). Ideological control of women in sport. In Costa, D. M. and Guthrie, S. R. (Eds.) *Women and sport: Interdisciplinary perspectives*, 341–360. Champaign, IL: Human Kinetics.

Cahn, S. (1994). Coming on strong: Gender and sexuality in twentieth-century women's sport. Cambridge, MA: Harvard University Press.

Davis, L. (1997). The swimsuit issue and sport: Hegemonic masculinity in Sport's Illustrated. Albany, NY: State University of New York Press.

Dowling, C. (2000). The frailty myth: Redefining the physical potential of women and girls. New York: Random House.

Duncan, M. and Messner, M. (2000). *Gender in televised Sport: 1989, 1993, 1999.* Los Angeles, CA: Amateur Athletic Foundation of Los Angeles.

Fabos, B. (1999). From rags to riches: The story of class advancement in women's figure skating coverage. In Meyers, M. (Ed.), *Mediated women: Representations in popular culture*, 133–149. Cresskill, NJ: Hampton.

Fields, S. (2000). Female gladiators: Gender, law, and contact sport in America. Unpublished doctoral dissertation, University of Iowa.

Griffin, P. (1998). *Strong women, deep closets.* Champaign, IL: Human Kinetics.

Hall, M. A. (1996). *Feminism and sporting bodies: Essays on theory and practice.* Champaign, IL: Human Kinetics.

Little, L. (1992). The Saunders: Making wrestling a family sport. *Amateur Wrestling News* (March 18): 12.

Little, L. (1994). If you can't beat 'em, join 'em. *Amateur Wrestling News* (March 7): 10–11.

Little, L. (1998). USA wrestling wrap-up. *Amateur Wrestling News* (November 9): 38.

Mihoces, G. (1999). Women fight for respect in a combat sport; Wrestlers pin hopes on entering 2004 games. *USA Today* (May 6): 6E.

Saunders named 1997 USA Wrestling Woman of the Year. (1998). *USA Wrestler* (July/August): 17.

Saunders wins Sunkist Kids International Women's Open. (1993). *USA Wrestler* (February): 34.

Saunders wins Women's World title; USA places third. (1996). *USA Wrestler* (October 15): 15.

Schalles, W. (1994). Selling ones strengths! *Amateur Wrestling News* (September 12): 17.

Tricia Saunders wins Women's World gold. (1992). *Amateur Wrestling News* (November 23): 8.

Tuchman, G. (1978). Introduction: The symbolic annihilation of women by the mass Media. In Tuchman, G., Daniels, A. K., and Benet, J. (Eds.), *Hearth and home: Images of women in the mass media*, 3–38. New York: Oxford University Press.

USA Wrestling's women's program receives $35,000 USOC grant. (1993). *USA Wrestler* (November): 15.

Walton, T. (2005). Pinned by gender construction?: Media representations of girls' wrestling. *Women in Sport and Physical Activity Journal*, 14 (2): 52–68.

Walton, T. and Helstein, M. (2008). Triumph of backlash: Title IX, wrestling, and the failure of communities of identification. *Sociology of Sport Journal*, 25 (3): 369–386.
White, C. (1991). Women form own wrestling organization. *USA Today* (June 5): C2.
Witulski, T. (ND). Women in wrestling, a talk with Tricia Saunders. TheMat.com. Available: (http://www.themat.com/newusaw/database/showquestion.asp?faq=7&fldAuto=129).

About THE Contributors

Michael Atkinson (Ph.D., University of Calgary) is senior lecturer in the School of Sport and Exercise Sciences at Loughborough University, UK. His current research efforts are physical cultural studies (PCS) investigations of bioethical and bio-pedagogical issues in health and popular culture using a blend of cultural studies, post-structural and existential theories, which he has presented at conferences in North America, Europe, Australia and Asia. He is author of *Tattooed: The Sociogenesis of a Body Art* (2003); *Battleground Sport* (2008); *Deviance and Social Control in Sport* (2008), *Beyond the Masculinity Crisis* (OUP), *Key Concepts in Sport, Exercise and Health* (Sage), and coeditor, with Kevin Young, of *Tribal Play: Subcultural Journeys Through Sport* (2008).

Jochen G. Bocksnick is associate professor in the Department of Kinesiology at the University of Lethbridge. While his primary research is in the motivation and volition of older adults to be active, he has also recently completed an investigation of youth sport involvement as part of a four-year soccer-camp project.

Megan Chawansky (Ph.D., The Ohio State University) does research examining the interplay of sport, gender, and sexuality. She is currently a Program Director for PeacePlayers International-Cyprus and was an all-conference performer as a member of the Northwestern University women's basketball team.

Gina Daddario (Ph.D., University of Massachusetts-Amherst), a Lin Rong San Professor of Communication at Shenandoah University, teaches courses in mass communication and women's studies. She has a research interest in gender, sport, and media; her most recent publications include articles in *Journal of Sport Management* and *Journal of Sport Media.*

John Mark Dempsey (Ph.D., Texas A&M University), an associate professor of radio-television at Texas A&M University-Commerce, is the author/editor of four books: *The Jack Ruby Trial revisited: The Diary of Jury Foreman Max Causey*; *The Light Crust Doughboys Are on the Air!*; *Eddie Barker's Notebook: Stories That Made the News (and some better ones that didn't)*; and *Sports-talk Radio in America: Its Context and Culture.*

John P. Elia (Ph.D., University of California/Davis) is professor and associate chair of health education at San Francisco State University. He serves as editor for the *Journal of Homosexuality*, an internationally renowned peer-review journal, and is on the editorial boards of the *Journal of Gay and Lesbian Issues in Education* and *The Educational Forum.* His recent scholarship has focused on democracy and sexuality education in the public schools.

Linda K. Fuller (Ph.D., University of Massachusetts), a professor of Communications at Worcester State College and now a Senor Fellow at Northeastern University, is the author/coeditor of more than 20 books and 250+ professional publications and conference reports, including *Sport, Rhetoric, and Gender: Historical Perspectives and Media Representations* (Palgrave Macmillan, 2006) and *Sportscasting: Principles and Practices* (Routledge, 2008). Awarded Fulbrights to teach in Singapore and do HIV/AIDS research in Senegal, she maintains a website: www.LKFullerSport.com.

Shura Alexandra Gat (B.A., Wellesley; M.A., University of Iowa) writes and teaches self-defense and hatha yoga in Ithaca, NY. The author of *Fighting Women, Fighting Culture* (London: Women's Press, forthcoming), about women fighters in the U.S. and the U.K., is herself an aspiring boxer who will next write about the philosophies and techniques of self-defense.

Margery Holman (Ph.D., Michigan State University) is associate professor in the Faculty of Human Kinetics at the University of Windsor where, in addition to teaching, she has served as director of the women's sport program, swim coach and synchronized swim coach, and as women's volleyball coach. Serving with Ontario's Provincial Girls Team for the Canada Games, coaching regional and community teams, officiating at the World Student Games in England and Japan, and founding WECVA (Windsor Essex County Volleyball Association), Holman has held numerous roles within the OWIAA (Ontario Women's Interuniversity

Athletic Association), including being president, and the University of Windsor's first employment equity coordinator and sexual harassment advisor. She has an academic interest in the areas of sexual harassment in higher education (and sport) and sport and the law.

Joy Crissey Honea (Ph.D., Colorado State University) completed her dissertation project researching the effects of commercialization on professional athletes in alternative sports such as skateboarding, snowboarding, and bicycle motocross (BMX). She teaches in the Department of Sociology, Political Science and Native American Studies, Montana State University-Billings in the areas of social theory, gender, and the sociology of sport.

Jessica Hudson, educated at Cambridge University with a master's in Social and Developmental Psychology, has been captain of the Cambridge University Women's Rugby Football Club, winning the Varsity match again Oxford in 2001 and now involved in coaching the women's England Under 15's. She was the first female to box for Cambridge University and now works at the National Audit Office.

C. Richard King, an associate professor of comparative ethnic studies at Washington State University, has written extensively on the changing contours of race in post-Civil Rights America, the colonial legacies, and postcolonial predicaments of American culture, and struggles over "Indianness" in public culture. His work has appeared in a variety of journals, such as *American Indian Culture and Research Journal*, *Journal of Sport and Social Issues*, *Public Historian*, and *Qualitative Inquiry*. He is also the author/editor of several books, including *Team Spirits: The Native American Mascot Controversy* (a CHOICE 2001 Outstanding Academic Title) and *Postcolonial America*. He has recently completed *Native American Athletes in Sport and Society* and *The Encyclopedia of Native Americans and Sport*.

Jon B. Martin is a Ph.D. candidate at the Hugh Downs School of Human Communication at Arizona State University. Centered on the areas of critical theory, queer theory, and cultural studies, his research examines communication and identity at the intersections of race, gender, and sexuality. Jon is a "heavy consumer" of popular culture and a semi-closeted sports fan.

Debra Merskin (Ph.D., Syracuse University) is an associate professor and head of the Communication Studies sequence at the School of Journalism & Communication at the University of Oregon. Her research addresses issues of representational ethics in visual and verbal discourse in mass media texts. Her publications appear in a number of journals and in books such as *Growing Up Girls*; *Commodity Racism; Mediated Women; Sexual Rhetoric; and Dressing in*

Feathers. Completing a book about the social, psychological, and cultural context for stereotyping in American mass media, she is a dancer, writer, and yogini and has pursued extensive postgraduate studies in Jungian psychology.

Richard Moriarty (Ph.D., Ohio State University) is a retired professor from the Faculty of Human Kinetics, University of Windsor. Having served as the first director of athletics and director of men's sport, he founded and served as director of SIR/CAR (Sports Institute for Research/Change Agent Research), and in 1985 he was awarded the J. P. Loosemore Award for contribution to interuniversity sport in Ontario and Canada and the R. Tait MacKenzie Honours Award from the Canadian Association or Health, Physical Education and Recreation (CAHPER). Moriarty has had many publications and presentations throughout his career in the areas of sport law, eating disorders and physical activity, and violence and conflict in sport, and he remains particularly active with sport and the law through the University of Windsor and SSLASPA (Society for the Study of Legal Aspects of Sport and Physical Activity).

Victoria Paraschak (Ph.D., University of Alberta) is an associate professor in the Department of Kinesiology at the University of Windsor. Employed as a policy and programs officer for the Government of the North West Territories' Division of Sport and Recreation, she continues her work in cultural studies as historian, policy consultant, and researcher. Paraschak is also very active with the North American Society for the Sociology of Sport, and her passion for a fair and equitable society is demonstrated particularly through her continued work with indigenous peoples in sport.

Anne E. Price (M.A., Calgary), who teaches Communication Studies at Red Deer College in Alberta, Canada, is the author of *Writing Skills for the Fine Arts* (Thomson Nelson, 2006). She is interested in the ways in which cultural products provide insights into social and political disparities and has written about royalty as celebrity, female punk rockers, and British kitchen sink films of the 1960s.

Erin Reilly (Ph.D. University of Kansas) is an associate professor in the Physical Education and Exercise Science Department at Auburn University at Montgomery. Her doctoral dissertation is titled "Gender and Sociability in a Players Pool League," and she coauthored the article "Symbolic Interactions among Amateur 8-Ball Pool Players" in *Refashioning Sociology: Responses to a New World Order* (Queensland University of Technology, 1998).

Michael A. Robidoux is an associate professor of Human Kinetics at the University of Ottawa. His research focuses primarily on hockey and culture in Canada and most recently involves ethnographic research on hockey played by Canada's indigenous peoples.

Robert Sirabian (Ph.D., Purdue University), who teaches writing and literature in the Department of English at the University of Wisconsin-Stevens Point, is author of *Charles Dickens: Life, Work, and Criticism* (York Press, 2002) and has written articles about British literature. In addition to teaching sports literature, his research interests include play theory and nineteenth-century British literature as well as Victorian Anglo-Saxonism.

Maureen Margaret Smith is a professor of Kinesiology and Health Science at California State University, Sacramento. She received a B.S. and M.S. in Physical Education from Ithaca College, then an M.A. in Black Studies and Ph.D. in Cultural Studies of Sport at the Ohio State University. While she enjoys watching and participating in many sports and considers herself a sports fan, she is not a "fanatic."

Ellen J. Staurowsky (Ed.D., Temple University), a professor in the Department of Sport Management and Media at Ithaca College, is a coauthor (with Allen L. Sack) of *College Athletes for Hire: The Evolution and Legacy of the NCAA Amateur Myth*. Her primary research interests include gender issues, college sport reform, Title IX, Native Americans in Sport, and related social justice issues.

David "Turbo" Thompson (Ph.D., University of Texas at Austin) is an associate professor in the Department of First-Year Programs at Kennesaw State University where he teaches a NASCAR-themed first-year seminar course. Thompson is the coauthor of *Darlington International Raceway: 1950–1967* (Motorbooks International, 1999). "Turbo" has raced stock cars in Texas, South Carolina, and Iowa.

Theresa A. Walton, Ph.D., serves as an assistant professor in the School of Exercise, Leisure and Sport at Kent State University. Drawing on critical cultural studies, her scholarship focuses on investigations of power relationships and the ways those relationships are both resisted and maintained within mediated sport narratives. In particular, she has examined media discourse of Title IX and sport, women's amateur wrestling, and elite distance running.

Patricia Weir (Ph.D., University of Waterloo) is an associate professor in the Department of Kinesiology, University of Windsor, Canada. With particular expertise in motor control and research applications with the elderly, Weir has taught extensively in the area of research design and statistics. Her strengths in these domains, along with her feminist interests, provided a major contribution here.

Gust A. Yep (Ph.D., University of Southern California) is a professor of Speech and Communication Studies and Human Sexuality Studies at San Francisco State University. His research has been published in numerous interdisciplinary journals and anthologies, including Linda K. Fuller's *Communicating about Communicable Diseases* (HRD Press) and *Media-Mediated AIDS* (Hampton Press). Most recently, he has guest-edited a special issue of the *Journal of Homosexuality*, which will be released as a book, *Queer Theory and Communication: From Disciplining Queers to Queering the Discipline* (Haworth Press).

Index